HANNAH MORGAN

Nowhere to Hide

HARPER element

HarperElement
An imprint of HarperCollins*Publishers*
1 London Bridge Street
London SE1 9GF

www.harpercollins.co.uk

HarperCollins*Publishers*
1st Floor, Watermarque Building, Ringsend Road
Dublin 4, Ireland

First published by HarperElement 2021

1 3 5 7 9 10 8 6 4 2

A catalogue record of this book is
available from the British Library

ISBN 978-0-00-841859-5

Printed and bound in Great Britain by
CPI Group (UK) Ltd, Croydon

For my beautiful sweet children,

Everything I did, I did for you. Every second we survived, we survived for you. And all that I am, I am because of you, my reason to live.

I did everything I could. I left when I could.

I've always loved you and always will.

Until we meet again, Mammy xxx

For my close friend, I'm so immensely proud of you, more than you'll ever know, and will always be here for you. You are far more of a stronger mum than I will ever be … I love you xxx

For my close friend with the matching shoes, we've come a long way and I'll never find another friend like you! Thank you for always being there – I'm always here too. All my love and strong faith xxx

For the victims still suffering, the survivors still struggling, and for those who couldn't escape alive …

Contents

PROLOGUE

Spring

What do I do?

The words swirled around and around in my head: *What do I do? What do I do? Stay? Go? I don't know …*

Sitting on the cold iron bench on the station platform, I looked down at the bin bag full of my belongings at my feet. I hadn't taken everything – just a handful of clothes, shoes, underwear and toiletries, enough to get by for a few days. I'd left in a hurry. No time to think straight – I'd just raced around grabbing everything I could see then stormed out the house, never intending to go back. I hadn't gone far – just 20 minutes' walk up the road to the train station. But I'd been sitting here on this bench on the station platform for two hours now and still I couldn't decide what to do. My eyes slid over the black bin liner full of clothes, across the railway tracks in front of me and to the other side of the station. All it would take would be a short walk over the footbridge to the other side and from there I could get to my mum's house. Or I could stay on this side and walk back home to my fiancé Matt's house.

What do I do? Stay on this side or cross the bridge? I couldn't decide …

It had happened earlier that evening. Matt, his mother and I had been invited to their friend Sammy's retirement do but Matt hadn't woken up in the best of moods. To be fair, he'd been under a lot of strain recently and it made him snappy and irritable. Then, this morning he'd noticed a text on my phone from my old friend and immediately jumped to the wrong conclusion.

'I don't know what your problem is,' I'd said, sighing after he made several snide remarks about my 'secret relationship'. I'd always had male friends but that was all they were – friends – and I didn't see anything wrong with that. Matt knew that. I had been open and honest with him from the start, but now he was convinced I was seeing someone else behind his back.

'Matt, there's *nothing* going on between us,' I insisted for what felt like the twentieth time that morning. 'He's an old friend, that's all. You *know* that. I've talked about him, I've told you about him. I've known him for years, since I was at school. He's an old mate.'

But nothing I said soothed him and Matt and I arrived at the party, him still in a stinking mood. I decided to try to put the row behind us so we got a couple of drinks and went to sit in the garden at a table with other party guests nearby.

It was a lovely warm spring evening and I was enjoying a cool glass of Stella Artois in the sunset, meeting Matt and his mum's friends, completely forgetting about Matt's bad temper from earlier. But *he* hadn't forgotten. He just wouldn't stop going on about the text and the more I tried to change the subject, the worse it got. Then suddenly he flung his arm out and swiped my glass off the table. I could see it happening in slow motion but there was nothing I could do to stop it. The glass smashed on the floor and everyone fell silent as they turned to look at us. I was so embarrassed I felt my cheeks flush with shame. How could he do that in front of everyone? A handful of people looked startled but Matt pretended that the glass was knocked off the table accidentally. Seething, I stood up and left without another word, walking out of the cricket club and through the loud music the DJ was playing.

Matt followed me.

'Where are you going?' he panted as he chased behind me.

'I'm going home,' I fumed.

'I'm sorry. Please don't go, please don't leave,' he begged as I strode on ahead of him up the street.

'No. That was so embarrassing, Matt. I can't believe you did that.'

'I know. I know. I'm sorry. I didn't mean to … please, please … it was an accident. I didn't mean it. Please, come back to the party.'

'No, forget it.'

It was upsetting to be humiliated like that in front of so many people. Sure, Matt had been under pressure recently but it wasn't fair to take it out on me.

'Please, Hannah. Please, sweetheart … I know I upset you. I'm sorry. Please don't leave …' he was begging now, pleading in a pitiful way. He seemed genuinely sorry so I stopped walking for a second and turned round to look at him.

'Matt, I don't like the way you're behaving …'

In that split second he seemed to change.

'Me?' he exploded, his face full of fury. 'ME? *You* know what this is about. It's about *you* and this other bloke. Texting behind my back, making a fucking fool out of me ...'

'Oh for fuck's sake! You've got it all wrong ...'

I was about to say more but the next thing I felt his hand on my right shoulder, shoving me hard. I toppled backwards over a low hedge on the side of the footpath, banging my head on a tree stump as I came down, and cutting my right foot on something sharp on the ground. At first I was too shocked to even move. *What the hell just happened?* I'd gone from standing in the street to sitting in a bush. And now I was struggling to climb out and get back on my feet again. I was too shocked and upset to say another word. My foot hurt, my head throbbed. That was it! How dare he push me! So much for all his apologies. He obviously didn't mean a single word and I set off down the street again, determined that that would be the very last Matt saw of me.

By the time I got back to our house, I was still shaking with anger. I went upstairs to the bathroom to get a look at myself in the mirror. *Bloody hell – look what he's done to me!* I tried smoothing my chestnut-brown hair down so that the shocking pink bits underneath weren't all sticking out but it was all tangled up with leaves, twigs and bits of shrubbery. Plus my right foot was bleeding so I wiped it clean. *He can't get away with this ... I don't care that we're due to be married in three months, he's gone too far.* In my rage, I grabbed a black bin liner and stuffed it full of my belongings, then I left the house, determined never to go back. I figured I'd go round to my mum's place as she only lived half an hour's walk away.

But just as I was closing the front door behind me, Matt's mum Lindsey appeared on the footpath down from the front drive. She had followed me out of the party and walked the fifteen minutes it took to get home.

'Are you okay, Hannah?' she asked, with what I thought at first was genuine concern.

'No, I'm not okay,' I shot back. 'I'm going.'

'Why did you do it, Hannah?' she asked sadly. I looked at her in confusion and then it hit me ... Matt had told his mum his side of the story and she must have bought it without question.

'Fucking hell, I haven't done anything!' I exploded. 'I HAVEN'T DONE ANYTHING!'

And with that I left.

Carrying the heavy black bin liner over my shoulder, I trudged for 20 minutes along the road up to the station. By the time I got here I was sweating and out of breath so I sat down on the station platform for a breather before crossing the bridge over to the other side. From there it was just another 10 minutes to Mum's house. But as I was sitting there, getting my breath back, the surge of anger that had propelled me to this point began to fall away and the doubts started to creep in. Matt hadn't been himself for a couple of weeks now – I knew it was because he was having a tough time with the separation from his ex and it was putting him under a lot of pressure, he told me, and I suppose that after several of his ex's had cheated on him, it was only natural that he would have a tough time trusting other women. Was I being too hasty? It was just a push, after all ...

Until now, Matt had been the perfect partner. Even though I was just 17 and he was 34 by this time, we'd been together for a year and three months and he treated me better than anyone I'd ever known. From the word go, he had showered me with lovely gifts and was always there for me when I needed him. Matt had been the only person who had ever made me feel loved. During the first few months we were together we had talked for hours and hours about our lives, our pasts, our hopes and our dreams. There was never an awkward moment between us, nothing we couldn't say to one another. We shared everything and before we had even kissed, we were best friends. I'd never known anyone like Matt before – until this moment I had assumed that the only thing men wanted was to get into your knickers. But Matt was different, Matt treated me with respect and kindness. He seemed more interested in me and who I was than in my body and that made me feel so loved and wanted.

Matt had confided about how hurt he'd been by betrayal in his past relationships and said that all he had ever wanted was a happy, devoted wife. Meanwhile, I hadn't had the easiest of upbringings. I told Matt all about how my dad had left home when I was six and how I'd struggled to get on with my mum ever since. My relationship with my dad had not been easy either and by the time we met I had left home and was living with my sister in a shared flat. And yet, ever since I was a child, all I had ever wanted was to become a wife and a mother. It was my dream – nothing fancy, nothing grand. I just wanted a nice home, no matter how big or small, with a loving devoted husband, and together we would give our children the life that I never had. In my dreams, my husband was the breadwinner while I looked after our home and children and cooked wholesome homemade dinners each night. Matt offered me all that and more.

He had a house and earned a good living from his amusement arcade business – in the first few months of our relationship he showered me with gifts and took me out for nice meals. Then, after we'd been together six months, he took me to a very grand country hotel by the seaside for a birthday meal. It was a special occasion; Matt dressed up in his smart three-piece suit, complete with waistcoat, pocket watch and tie, and I wore a silver shimmery halter-neck dress which tied into a bow at the back, pulling my waist in, with silver, glittery high-pointed court heels and a matching bag. He treated me to an amazing three-course dinner with champagne and wine in the most sumptuous, beautiful surroundings. I felt like a princess! Afterwards, we went into the lobby where we sat in a couple of grand armchairs in front of a real log fire. It was so special. We were just chatting normally but I had butterflies in my stomach – I knew something was about to happen. Matt seemed nervous and excited all at once … Then he took my hand in his and said solemnly: 'Hannah, you do know that I haven't got years left of my life to be wasting. If we're going to marry, you need to make sure this is what you want.'

I nodded. I knew what he meant: Matt had one failed marriage behind him, so he didn't want to waste his time on another relationship that wasn't going anywhere. But I knew – Matt was *the one*. I knew it in my heart, in my soul, in my very bones. Marriage and a happy home life was all I had ever wanted and I wanted it with him.

'Yes, I'm sure,' I replied. 'I've always been sure.'

That's when he got down on one knee, opened up the dark-green leather square Ernest Jones box, lifted the lid up and asked: 'Will you marry me?' My eyes were locked on his and before I'd even looked at the contents of the box I smiled and said: 'Yes, yes I will.'

Then I looked down and there, nestled in the white leather lining, was a yellow-gold band with a princess-cut square solitaire diamond encased in white gold. An engagement ring – a promise of marriage. It was everything I had ever wanted.

I moved into his three-bedroom terraced house a month later and, to my delight, I saw he'd blown up a gorgeous picture of the two of us taken a few weeks earlier, our arms encircling each other. He'd framed it and put it on the wall above the fire as our official 'engagement' picture. It made me so happy to see it there. For the first time, it felt like my life was finally going in the right direction. I was so pleased to be with Matt and he treated me well. I'd never felt so stable and happy in all my life. Now I looked down at my hands and twirled the engagement ring round on my finger … Was I really going to throw all of that away because of one little push? Was I really going to break my promise? I thought about how Mum would react if I turned up on her doorstep, bag of clothes in hand, begging to be allowed to stay. The humiliation of admitting I'd made a mistake and that he wasn't 'the one' after all. I wondered how I would tell all my friends about why I wasn't going to marry my Prince Charming after all. Just the thought of having to tell them made me flush with shame. After all that boasting! I'd shown off all his gifts with pride, the beautiful necklace he'd bought me as a Christmas present when we first got together, the clothes he'd bought for me, my engagement ring …

What do I do?
What do I do?
What do I do?

Eventually, after three hours seated on the cold, hard platform bench, I'd lost all feeling in my bum and my earlier resolve to leave Matt had also ebbed away. I didn't really *want* to leave him. I loved him! This was just a normal couple's row, I told myself. I wasn't going to leave him over one silly disagreement. We'll get over this and then, once we're married, everything will be fine. It was pitch black now and the cold spring air stung my cheeks and crept under my thin jacket, making me shiver. I couldn't sit here forever. I sighed, pulled up the big black sack and in that moment I knew I wasn't going to cross the bridge. Instead I walked back up the road and back to Matt. He was waiting, full of apologies. He always apologised in the beginning …

Looking back today, I know that should have been the moment I left. I know that if I had got up and crossed over the footbridge, my life would have been completely different. It was the first time he had laid his hands on me, the first time his anger had hurt me, and it should have been the moment the bubble burst. I should have left him forever and never gone back. But I didn't. I didn't leave that first time – for all sorts of reasons I didn't leave. But mainly because I thought that it was a one-off, that this wasn't *him*, that it was out of character. It never crossed my mind for a second, for a single solitary second, that it would happen again. Or that it would get worse.

But what I know now is that it does happen again. Again and again and again … and it gets worse every time. And no matter how many excuses you make for him, no matter how many times he says sorry, the truth is that it will never get any better. And you just get used to life like that. You adapt, you change, your life becomes something different and after a while the decision to leave is no longer yours anymore. You don't have a choice. You can't leave. You're trapped. And you realise that there is probably only one way out – death. Maybe his, but most likely yours. Leave or die. It's that simple. Many women like me have gone through the same situations, faced similar dilemmas, and they are no longer here to tell their story. I'm here to speak for them because I know that I am lucky to be alive today.

If only I could go back in time to that moment on the bench, I would have taken that girl by the hand and walked her over the bridge, to the safety of her mother's house. Away from the pain, the torture, the heartbreak and the misery to come … I would tell her not to believe his apologies, not to make excuses for him and to abandon the dream of making a happy life together because it is all lies, and that her life is in danger. I would show her where that very first 'push' leads …

But I can't. I can't do any of that. I can't change what has happened. I'm just very fortunate that eventually I did manage to escape with my life. Now I tell my story to show the journey that I travelled and how it is possible to go from one little push to a near fatal stabbing through the chest. From independence to total domination, from a life of happiness to living in constant fear and misery … I share my journey in the hope that I can help others see more clearly than I did when I was a young teenager. None of us can know our own futures. but I hope that in telling my story I can help others to decide theirs. And to realise, while you still have breath in your body, that it's never too late to leave.

1

My Hero

I was born and bred in a small town. We were a working-class family and though both my mum and my dad worked, we weren't very well-off. Me and my older sister Mandy got used to going without compared to some of the other kids. My mum Denise was the breadwinner, working for a mobile-phone company. She got up at 6am every day to go to work and didn't return home till late so our dad Alan dropped us off at school in the mornings, then he would go to work as a chef between 10am and 2pm, finishing in time to pick us up at 3pm. We didn't see Mum much during the week and I would say that in my early childhood she was a little absent, working most of the time, only back in time for *Coronation Street* at half seven each night.

You would think with all those long hours we'd be comfortable enough to afford the basics but there wasn't a lot of money to spare – we couldn't afford school trips and our packed lunches were always the same: sandwiches, yoghurt and a pack of crisps. I didn't mind but it bothered Mandy, who was four years older than me. She wanted to fit in at school and when all the other kids got the latest Kickers shoes or trainers, it upset her that we couldn't afford the same.

Looking back, I don't really remember a time when my mum and dad got on well. One Christmas Day we took a picture of them together with my sister's Kodak camera, which Mum and Dad must have saved hard to buy, and I remember thinking how unusual it was to see them like this – cuddling, smiling, showing affection. Most of the time they were snappy and irritable with one another, arguing a lot about money. Mum gave Dad an allowance for the food shopping and school necessities but Dad liked to treat himself – to the latest MiniDisc player or a new program for his computer – instead of buying what we needed as a family. Late at night, Mandy and I would creep out of bed and sit on the landing upstairs next to each other, listening to them row.

'There's two kids up there who need food and clothes,' I'd hear Mum shout. 'You're so selfish!'

Mandy and I didn't think too much about it – it was just them bickering as usual – we didn't know any different. We certainly didn't think it would lead to anything serious.

But when I was six, Dad came to collect me and Mandy from my best friend Liz's house after a sleepover. Liz's mum Jen had two kids including a younger daughter so she didn't mind having us both over together. But this wasn't a normal pick-up – before he took us home Dad said he wanted a word with us first. He led us out of the back gate of Jen's house and sat us in his red Vauxhall Cavalier, me in the back and Mandy in the front. Then he looked at us with tears in his eyes and said: 'Your mother and I are going to split up.

We've both been seeing other people. Your mum has been seeing her boss. And I've been seeing somebody else as well. It's Jen.'

It was like my world ended. I don't think I have cried so much in my life. We were sat in that car for what felt like hours; maybe it was only about half an hour, but it felt like ages, and during that time I cried my eyes out. It was such a massive shock. Until then, all I'd ever known was a two-parent family. I couldn't imagine Daddy leaving us. And for Jen? Liz's mum? The whole thing was mad, it didn't make any sense. Dad did his best to comfort us.

'We still love you,' he said. 'It's nothing you've done.' But the news had shattered my otherwise safe little world and nothing could change that. We walked back into Jen's house, our eyes red and swollen from the tears, and Dad looked at Jen and said with a heavy sigh: 'I've told them.'

Jen's face crumpled with sadness. She swept me up in a massive hug and said: 'I'm sorry. I'm so sorry, Hannah. We're always going to be there for you, we want you to be happy. And we're sorry that this has happened but we love you.'

I didn't feel angry towards her – I couldn't. She was kind and loving and I accepted things as they were. She was lovely to me that day – she always was – hugging me so tight I felt like I couldn't breathe. *Is she ever going to let go?* I wondered as the hug went on and on. But I needed it, I needed it so badly and so did my sister. We were heartbroken. To this day I've never had a hug like that.

When we finally arrived home later that morning, at the start of our two-week Easter holiday, I looked at Mum and told her: 'It's okay. We know.' I was a sad little girl trying to put on a brave face but she must have known how upset I was. But I don't think my mum knew how to react. Perhaps she was shocked Dad had told us this way, without her. Perhaps she was so full of emotion herself she couldn't trust herself not to cry but she didn't throw her arms around me the way Jen had done. She just nodded briskly, said 'okay' and gave me a reassuring pat on my shoulder. We went to our rooms and from there on it just felt like a normal holiday. The split didn't seem real. Daddy was still at home during that time and even though I saw him packing his books and belongings into boxes, I couldn't imagine that he would ever actually leave. After all, I was Daddy's little girl, his favourite, his youngest. I couldn't imagine life without him. So when it did finally happen two weeks later, the shock was unbearable.

It was our first day back at school after the Easter holidays. Mum had got me and Mandy up, washed, dressed and breakfasted, all ready for the off, when we went to say our usual goodbyes to Daddy in his bedroom. He was ready for us, sat on the edge of the bed, and reached out his arms for a big hug and a kiss.

'Have a good day back at school. Love you,' he said. His breath smelled of fresh coffee and nicotine. What he didn't say was, *I'll see you later*, but I didn't notice at the time. Later, of course, I would replay that last scene over and over again in my mind, looking for the clues I had missed the first time. Then my sister and I went out of our front gate and walked down the road with Mum, off to the childminder Debbie's house. Dad told me later on that he had stood at the bedroom window watching us until we were out of sight: our matching black Puffa jackets disappearing down the road and my little blonde ponytail bouncing with every footstep.

But I knew nothing. None of us did. We went to school as normal and Mum picked us up from Debbie's later that day. Arriving back at the house, we saw that Dad's car was gone. This was nothing unusual – he often went out. But then Mum opened the front door and we walked into the living room. It looked like we'd been burgled. Everything was gone apart from the sofas, sideboard, coffee table and dining table. It was such a shock. Dad's desk and his computer were gone, all his boxes, his ornaments from the shelves ... everything! The pale outline of his desk and computer against the brown, nicotine-stained wallpaper was the only sign he had once lived there. That and a Post-It note on the landline phone with the curly wire, scrawled with his handwriting. We all cried. We just sat down and wept. Even my mum. The next day she scribbled a note to hand to my class teacher, Miss Bindell. I read it on my way to school: '*Please comfort Hannah as her dad left us yesterday.*'

Dad had gone to live with Jen and her children a few streets away. As for my mum, I don't think the fling with her boss had ever been serious. I certainly never heard her mention him much and in any case, she had to leave her job straight away to look after us. Life was hard after the split. Dad had been our main carer and I missed him desperately. We were close, me and Dad. He had been the parent I'd spent most of my time with until this moment and now I had lost him. Worst of all, he was now looking after some-one else's children just a short walk away. It was incomprehensible.

Up until that day, my childhood had been okay. I didn't know any different. I was content. Even though we were poor, I didn't mind. But the split left me angry and confused. I shouted at my mum a lot and my sister too – meanwhile, they were furious with my father. I just couldn't feel that way about him, even though the situation was so upsetting. It wasn't like he had disappeared – he was living at my friend's house and we had to get used to seeing him some days at the school gates with Liz and her younger sibling. *Liz had our dad!* While it confused me, it made Mandy angry as hell.

That first Christmas after he left we went round to spend time with him at Jen's house. He sat me on his lap and asked: 'What would you like for Christmas this year?'

'I want you to come home,' I replied.

'You know I can't do that,' he said kindly with a sigh. It had only been eight months since he left and I was still lost and confused. Fortunately, there were no problems with access. From the beginning Mum and Dad worked out an amicable arrangement where we would spend every other weekend with Dad and also one evening during the week after school. I looked forward to this time with Dad but not Mandy; she was still too angry and fairly quickly she decided to stop seeing him. So then it was just me. At first Mum and Dad were civil to each other but as the years passed their relationship deteriorated to the point where Mum wouldn't even let Dad come in the front door to collect me. I thought she was being unreasonable but Mum complained he was still putting his needs first. I wouldn't hear anything against him – it was too much to hear her and my sister bad-mouth him constantly.

As I got older, my anger and confusion grew. At home, I rowed with my mum and sister, especially over Dad. They were so down on him and I was the only one who ever fought his corner. I just couldn't hate my dad. He had always been so kind to me, I loved him and I was desperate for him to love me back. At 12 years old, following my older sister, I started experimenting with make-up, straightening my hair, wearing skimpy outfits and high heels like most other girls my age back then. Meanwhile, Dad encouraged my interest in boys.

'Don't be one of these women that goes off sex like your mother did because that's what broke our marriage down and I had to go elsewhere,' he said to me. Dad spoke to me like I was a grown-up; he didn't treat me like a little kid and I appreciated that. He would give me and my friends lifts so we could hang out at the park to flirt with the local lads and even bought us bottles of Lambrini, cans of beer and fags.

'If you are going to be drinking, I'd rather buy it for you so I know exactly what you're drinking and how much of it,' he'd say in a kind, protective way. He also insisted on picking me up at the end of most evenings, to make sure I was safe. To me, he seemed like the model of a concerned parent, though he said we had to keep the booze and fags a secret from Mum as she wouldn't approve.

Dad gave me tips on how to flirt with boys and his advice helped me to get my first ever boyfriend, Ricky, at 13. He was the same age as me and we were both quite sweet and innocent except that Dad suggested that I go all the way in order to keep him happy. I think my boyfriend was as surprised as anyone! Looking back, it seems wrong to me that Dad encouraged me to be so sexual considering how young I was. But I was so keen to please him, I listened and followed his suggestions because I wanted to be loved, by him but also by other males. I didn't want to be abandoned the way my mother had been. I didn't want to be on my own. Dad made me believe that the only way to keep a man was to keep him happy sexually.

By the time I was 14 I had dumped my first boyfriend and was seeing a lot of other guys. Then I fell for a guy who was much older than me – he was 24 and I really thought we were in love but he dumped me just after Valentine's Day. I was heartbroken. After that, I started failing at school, getting cocky with the teachers and giving them lip. Gone was the angelic girl who had soared through all her exams in first and middle school – now I stopped taking lessons seriously, I swore at the teachers, ignored my homework and went out to get pissed most school nights. I sold my free lunch tickets, forged parents' letters and signatures on PE notes to earn a few quid and even sold packets of fags that another boyfriend of mine had nicked from the local newsagent's he worked in. One way or another I managed to earn enough money to buy fags and booze most nights. And when I didn't have the cash, Dad would buy them for me.

Dad didn't approve of me getting tied down to just one bloke, saying that I should have lots of different experiences, so I started seeing lots of lads, putting it about. I'm not sure I enjoyed it – I was simply notching up numbers. Dad told me to go out on the pull, to be a predator, so that's what I did and I ended up getting a bit of a name for myself. I didn't care. I didn't care about much back then. I got mainly Cs in my GCSEs, then at 16 I left school and moved in with my sister, who by now was living in a flat with our dad as he and Jen had split up. By this time my mum had had my baby brother Owen. She had met someone through a friend, though sadly it was a short relationship and it didn't last. Though I loved my little brother dearly, I couldn't live with Mum anymore. I was too out of control. So when Mandy patched it up with Dad and they moved into a flat together owned by his sister it suited me to move in with them too. I worked part-time in Tesco and the rest of the time I knocked about with my mates in the park, getting pissed and sleeping around.

The first time I noticed Matt it was at the Co-op on the high street. I went in to buy something and as the automatic door slid to the right I noticed a man in the queue wearing a burgundy shirt, trainers and light-blue jeans, holding something in his hand. He looked at me, I looked at him and, bam, straight away, I thought: *There's something about that person.* I couldn't put my finger on what it was – it wasn't physical attraction – it was just something unusual. Back then Matt had a shaved head, was clean shaven, had a crooked nose and was shorter than average height. I thought he looked to be in his mid-twenties. In that split second we caught each other's eye I smiled, as I would to anyone, then I walked up the aisle and moved on. The next time I saw him it was when we were introduced through my friend Rebecca. She went into his arcade to ask if she could use his loo. Matt was really friendly – he invited us to the back to have a drink in the office with him, offering us each a glass of Captain Morgan's spiced rum. It seemed this guy was good for free booze!

We popped into the arcade a couple more times after that and then, about a month later, Rebecca and I enjoyed an unplanned night out with Matt. He was really friendly – and very generous with his rum, pouring us both large measures with just a splash of Coke for Rebecca. By the time he drove us into town a few hours later to get a kebab I'd had so much rum I was completely pissed. Earlier that day Mandy, who was now working full-time at Pizza Express, had given me some money for clothes and I'd bought a short white coat with fur on the collar from New Look. Matt had his arm around me, supporting me on a small wall at the edge of a car park as I ate the kebab. Then he said: 'I'm just going to move my arm away. Mind you don't fall backwards.' His arm moved and I toppled backwards. Somehow Rebecca and Matt got me home to the flat, just one road from Matt's house, and Mandy came to the door, appalled to find me in such a state with my lovely new white coat all black up the back from where I'd fallen.

'I ain't giving you money to spend on alcohol!' she raged. 'Look at the coat I bought you!' The next day I saw Rebecca and asked her what the hell happened last night – she laughed and filled me in on the details. So a couple of days later I went back to the arcade.

'I'm really sorry I got so pissed the other night,' I said sheepishly to Matt.

'It's fine,' he said, smiling. 'I like a drink as well.'

We saw each other a couple more times after that and each time Matt was kind and lovely. He even rescued me from a car once after a guy I'd been giving directions to refused to let me out. In strode Matt like a knight in shining armour, hauling me out of the car, telling this guy to sling his hook. Then he took me into the arcade, made me a cup of tea and made sure I was okay. He was my hero that night;

he was there for me and the more I got to know him, the more I liked him. It felt like I could trust him. We swapped numbers and started texting back and forth. Not long afterwards I had a row with a friend. I ended up at the park on my own late at night, sad and upset.

I was sitting on the swings, slowly rocking back and forth, when Matt texted: *R U Ok?*

Not really.

I'll come and meet u.

It was dark and late when I saw Matt's silhouette emerge through the blackness of the park. Just his presence instantly made me feel better. I stood up and fell into his arms. He smiled and wiped away my tears. *I feel safe, Matt is here for me, no matter what.* He liked me, I knew that. It was like something out of a film. As we cuddled, he turned his face to mine and our lips locked together. It was the first time we had kissed and it was magical – not like anything else I'd experienced before. There was real emotion there. It felt like it meant something. Matt was always there when I needed him and I knew that there was something strong between us. We hugged again and then Matt looked at me: 'Come on, I'll drive you home.'

For the first time in my life, someone cared about me, someone wanted to look after me. He didn't for a moment try anything on. Matt wasn't like that. He wasn't one of those blokes that only thought about getting what he wanted. Over the next few months our friendship grew. Matt and I talked for hours in the back office of his arcade or, after he drove me home, outside my flat in his car. He was 17 years older than me but that didn't bother me – he treated me well and that's what mattered. I loved the time we spent together, talking, sharing secrets and making each other laugh. Conversation flowed easily between us as we sat in his car, which smelled of Febreze and cold leather, well into the early hours. My feelings for him grew every day but at the same time I knew that he was struggling to get out of his bad marriage so I doubted we would get together properly.

At the time I was dating a man called Stuart, but my heart wasn't in it. I lied to him and told him I was at the flat when really I went to see Matt at the arcade. Stuart followed me there so he knew I had fibbed to him. 'Do you want me to get rid of him?' Matt offered. There was no need – Stuart left of his own accord, after asking for all his Christmas presents back! I walked back into the arcade a free woman and me and Matt enjoyed a kiss and a cuddle. Then Matt disappeared for a moment out the back and reappeared holding a long box, wrapped up with Christmas wrapping paper and a gold bow.

'Here, this is for you,' he said, smiling shyly. 'I got you a Christmas present but I didn't know when I was going to be able to give it you.'

I unwrapped the paper – inside was a red leather jewellery box from H. Samuel. My heart started to thump and my hands shook – *jewellery? We aren't even going out. I can't believe he's bought me jewellery.* I flipped open the lid and there, lying on the white cushion, was the most beautiful gold-and-diamond necklace I'd ever seen. It was stunning.

'Oh my God,' I gasped and my hand flew to my mouth. No man had ever bought me anything so pretty before.

'I can't have this!' I exclaimed.

'No, you can. It's for you,' he insisted.

'No, I can't accept this.'

'I want you to have it.'

I smiled: 'Okay, well, if I put it on, would you do it up for me?'

He did it up around my neck and from that moment I never took it off. I was so proud and so happy to wear it. Matt and I were serious – we were in love. Eventually we slept together but there was no rush. I knew Matt loved me for who I was and not for what I could give him. Five months later he proposed and a month after that I moved into his house.

2

Let the Bells Ring Out

I breathed in the cold early-morning air and watched as it came out again in billowy clouds. I was standing at my front door, still wearing my pyjamas but I didn't care. I was too excited to care. As soon as Emma pulled up at 6am on the dot I jumped in the passenger seat for the short drive to ASDA. There was already a giant white ribbon over the bonnet of Emma's black Citroën which she had put on the night before. It looked brilliant – a big car bow! Just for me. I hugged myself with delight. I just couldn't believe it was finally the big day. The streets were almost completely deserted on the drive to the shop except for one elderly man who was walking a small white dog on a tartan lead. I couldn't help myself. I wound down the window and shouted out: 'I'M GETTING MARRIED TODAY!'

The man looked up, startled for a second, then he gave me an encouraging thumbs up as we sped past.

'Oi! What are you doing, you maniac!' Emma laughed. 'You'll wake the whole bloody street.'

'I don't care. They can all come if they want!'

It was our wedding day, the day I had dreamed of ever since I was a little girl. Matt and I had been engaged for over a year already and though we had some elements of our wedding planned well in advance, some arrangements had been left to the last minute. We had booked the church months before but our reception venue was only organised two days before the wedding. And while I had bought my dress the previous autumn we had actually assembled the wedding cake ourselves using three plain cakes covered in white fondant icing that we piled in a tower using white columns and then decorated with sugared flowers and a big purple bow. The night before the Big Day I had planned a fun evening with my two bridesmaids but Matt, who was meant to be spending the night at his friend's, just wouldn't leave and he hung around in the kitchen until 10pm. When he finally got up to go, we said our goodbyes on the doorstep.

He kissed me.

'I'll see you in the morning. I love you,' he said.

'Okay, bye!' I waved him off. *Finally!* Now I could have some time alone with my childhood friends Beth and Leah.

Matt and I had agreed to have no further contact now until we saw each other in church the next day, not even texting, just like a traditional wedding. Matt favoured the old traditions and I agreed it would make the day more special. But that night, because Matt had spent so long at home, my plans were set back and in the end I was so busy messing around with the flowers I didn't get to bed until 3am. Then I was up again at 5.30am for the trip to ASDA. But I didn't feel tired, not in the least. I was filled with excitement and nervous energy.

Emma and I raced around the supermarket, gathering the colourful mixed bouquets of roses, gerberas and carnations that we would be giving out later that day, then we came home, with plenty of time to get ready. The service was at midday so I planned to take it nice and slow. I had a long, relaxing bath, and then my bridesmaid Anna arranged my wavy brown hair in tiny loops, all pinned back on my head, leaving a few dangly bits at the back and front to frame my face. Then she placed my veil on top and sprayed my hair with glitter. Leah did my make-up and I touched it up, and then it was time to put on my dress. This was the best bit! I loved my dress so much – I'd actually bought it nine months earlier for the knock-down price of £200, even though it was worth a lot more. (Back of a van, don't ask!)

'How do I look?' I asked Emma, Beth, Anna and Leah, as I gave them a twirl in my bedroom.

'Gorgeous!'

'Amazing!'

'Wow!'

'Honestly, you look amazing, Han!'

'Are you sure?' I replied nervously, fiddling with my nose stud. My nails were so long and my fingers shaking so much I couldn't get it in.

'God, this damn thing …'

'Here, let me do that,' Emma offered. 'What you need is a drink. Let's crack open that second bottle of bubbly in the fridge.' We had already downed the first bottle of bubbly over breakfast, still in our pyjamas, laughing and posing for pictures in the front garden, Beth with her hair half done. So now we all grabbed our glasses and I popped open the champagne, managing to down a glass before there was a knock at the door.

'Must be the photographer again,' I said to the others as I went to open the front door. But instead of the photographer, standing on the doorstep was a kid from a couple of houses down.

'Oh, alright Josh?' I said. 'What's up?'

'Hannah, I got a present for you. It's from Matt,' Josh said as he handed me a wrapped box. 'Matt says – can you open it before you leave?'

I smiled – *how sweet! Typical Matt – giving me a surprise gift on our wedding day*. I ripped off the wrapping paper and opened the lid of the box. Inside were two little 'Me to You' ornament teddy bears. So thoughtful – Matt knew I collected the grey Tattie Teddies with the blue noses. And this pair were getting married under a flowered arch, one wearing a top hat and tails and the other dressed in a white wedding dress. My heart swelled. Matt knew me so well.

By 11am, it was nearly time to leave for the church so Emma took the bridesmaids over first in her car while I waited nervously with Amy, my maid of honour. Amy and I had been best mates since we met at secondary school when we were 12. She had been so helpful and supportive, even arranging my hen night when we got the VIP lounge in the local nightclub after a pub crawl.

'Are you alright?' she asked as I lit up another fag using my Audrey Hepburn-like cigarette holder. I felt like I'd already smoked half a packet that morning.

'I'll be alright,' I said, but she could tell from my shaky voice that I was a bundle of nerves. Emma soon returned to pick up her daughter Betsy, aged three, who was a bridesmaid, and Amy – then my dad arrived. Dad helped me safely onto the back seat of the hired Mercedes for our short trip to the church with my train half folded into the footwell and half on my lap – there was so much dress! Then he came round the other side and got in beside me. I could barely speak the whole way there. Then, as we turned off the high street and towards the church, I caught sight of all the cars parked on the gravelled grounds, spilling our wedding guests onto the road. They were all just milling around, chatting and smoking – nobody seemed in any rush to get inside the church. I felt a wave of panic crash over me …

'Dad! Dad, they've all got to go in. They can't see me before the wedding …'

'Alright, alright, Hannah … don't worry. We'll make sure they get inside.'

So I called over my friend Nick and instructed him to start herding the guests inside. Dad and I waited silently together in the car as the minutes ticked slowly by. I watched the big clock on the church tower. Still only 11.45am – too early to go in – but with every second that passed, I felt sicker and sicker with nerves. By now my arms were weak and floppy and my heart was banging so hard I felt like it would pop out of my chest.

Dad looked at me: 'Are you sure you want to do this, Hannah?'

'Yeah, course I am,' I replied.

He nodded slowly, then said: 'Forever is a long time to be unhappy.'

It was an odd thing to say to me, here on my wedding day, but I didn't think too hard about it. Dad could be a bit odd at times. I was 18 years old and I knew exactly what I wanted: I wanted a good home, a good man and children of my own. *Oh God, this waiting is killing me …*

'Dad, I can't sit here any longer,' I blurted out. 'Let's go. Let's get out.'

The big brass clock on the church read 11.53am when we emerged from the car and I had another quick cigarette from the pack in my white satin dolly bag with silk roses on my wrist to calm my nerves. Just then the vicar came out to greet us.

'Hello, Hannah!' he said, grinning. 'How are you feeling?'

'Nervous. Sick,' I replied. 'But I'm sure I'll be alright.'

I could see my three bridesmaids huddled in the doorway of the church entrance, all ready for the off. There was no point hanging around any longer.

'Well, if everyone's here and we're ready to go let's just do this,' I said to the vicar and he nodded briskly before turning around and going back inside the church as our group arranged ourselves in the right order. Dad seemed nervous as he turned to me, grabbed my veil and pulled it over my face. Then I heard the organ start up and my heart thudded wildly. *Oh my God, this is it!*

Out in front I heard the vicar say: 'Please stand.'

I quickly looked behind me at my bridesmaids, their eyes dancing with excitement:

'Okay … you good? You ready?' I asked. All of them nodded excitedly. Dad took my arm and together we started walking in time to the music …

We processed slowly up the aisle together as a sea of faces smiled back at us from the pews – on the left side my family and friends filled every aisle while on the right side, Matt's side, the pews were about a third full. I suppose that was to be expected for his second marriage. There was my mum, Dad's fiancée, my sister and on the other side, Matt's father and his missus, Matt's mum Lindsey, his half-sisters, nephews and cousin Sherie who was already like a sister to me – my future in-laws. I was so happy, I felt like I would burst.

Matt said it wasn't traditional for the groom to see the bride before she arrived at his side but I had told him I wanted him to see me walking down the aisle. And there he was now – in his grey morning suit, cream waistcoat, top hat and lilac crushed-velvet cravat, grinning away as he watched me walk towards him. Everything about this moment felt right. In my heart I knew I was doing the right thing. The photographer's camera flashed away. I arrived by Matt's side, Dad lifted my veil off my face, then he looked at his future son-in-law and the pair shook hands. I handed my artificial bouquet of wild meadow flowers to my maid of honour and then Matt and I embraced in a lovely warm hug. It was just what I needed to calm my nerves.

'Sorry I'm early,' I whispered in his ear. 'I was going to keep you waiting but ...'

I tailed off as I saw that he didn't care one bit, he was brimming with pride and happiness, and now we both turned to face the vicar to exchange our wedding vows.

A few weeks earlier the vicar had come round to our house to have a chat about the wedding and what we wanted. We had made all the various different choices about the day – whether we wanted organ music, bells, all that sort of stuff – and then the vicar had asked us about the vows.

'We want the traditional ones,' Matt had said adamantly. 'Love, honour and obey … we're traditional. That's what we like.'

The vicar shifted uncomfortably in his seat.

'I understand,' he said, coughing. 'But personally, I would advise you to go for the more up-to-date version. The traditional vows are very old-fashioned. We don't really recommend them for couples in today's modern world.'

'Well, that's what we want. Isn't that right, sweetheart?' Matt turned to me.

'Yeah, definitely,' I confirmed. 'That's what Matt wants so we'll have them.'

The vicar tried once more to dissuade us but it was no use, Matt was firm in his resolve and he wasn't backing down. And so, on our special day, the vicar gave us the traditional ceremony and I nervously repeated the words in front of all my friends and family, vowing to 'love, honour and obey' my husband, confident that he would never ask me to do anything that was against my own wishes.

'… and forsaking all others,' I concluded, '… be faithful only to him as long as we both shall live.'

Then we exchanged our matching yellow-gold wedding bands and the vicar turned to our assembled guests.

'Everybody, I think they deserve a round of applause,' he announced and the audience erupted into wild clapping and enthusiastic cheers. Elation swept through me …

Carried away by the excitement, I grabbed Matt and we shared a passionate kiss. I saw the flashes of the camera in our faces. The nerves had disappeared and all I felt now was a deep sense of joy. Together, we went up to the table to sign the register, alongside our witnesses, while the photographer danced around us, snapping away. Then, as we came out of the church, the wedding bells pealed overhead for a good ten minutes as our guests threw pastel-coloured confetti over us. It was perfect – just perfect!

We were still posing for photos in front of the church when the bells stopped ringing – I asked the vicar why they had stopped.

'That's the end of the round,' he said.

'Well, get them to ring them again!' I insisted. And so they did.

From there Matt and I jumped in the Mercedes and the driver whizzed us round to the reception venue, a social club just out of town. The DJ was there to meet us with none of the songs we had requested on our 'favourites' list.

'What a fucking joke!' Matt seethed. 'He's taking the piss.'

'I swear, mate, I left all them records at home by accident ...' the DJ said.

'Look, there's not much we can do about it now,' I reasoned. 'Come on, Matt, let's just pay him and let him play.'

'It's not like we've got much choice now, is it?' Matt was still fuming but he went ahead and gave the DJ the £200 we'd agreed, just as the last of our guests started arriving. It was an amazing afternoon – we had 100 friends and family for our wedding breakfast of curry and shepherd's pie and I loved watching everyone tucking into the lovely food. Then Matt got up to say a few words.

'Firstly, I'd like to thank you all for coming today. It means so much to both of us that you're here to share this special day with us.' I nodded as I looked out at the tables crammed full of our friends and family.

'Secondly,' Matt went on, 'I'd like to thank Hannah's mum and dad for creating her so that I could marry her. She makes me so happy and this is the best day of my life.'

I giggled with embarrassment as I felt a warm blush spread across my cheeks.

'Seriously,' Matt now looked down at me and I met his gaze, 'Hannah, you are a beautiful woman and I can't wait to spend my life with you.'

I thought I might cry but I managed to hold it together because next it was my turn to say something. I would have liked it if my dad had said a few words but that really wasn't on the cards. He hated public occasions and was appalled by the idea of getting up and talking to a roomful of people. It had been hard enough to persuade him to walk me down the aisle. So I said a few words instead.

'Thank you all for coming,' I started. 'You all look amazing so thank you for making the effort and for being here today. There's a wedding guest book going round so please do write in it. Hope you've all enjoyed yourselves. There's more food so go back for seconds … and if you've had seconds already, go back for thirds. I want you all full-up. Make use of the free drinks (courtesy of Matt's parents) and later we'll all have a boogie on the dance floor. Before that, I'd just like to thank my bridesmaids and my maid of honour for doing an amazing job today. Matt and I have some little gifts here for them all …'

Then I handed out the bouquets Emma and I had bought at 6am from ASDA to my mum Denise, sister Mandy, auntie Jane, Matt's dad's missus, his mum Lindsey and one of course to Emma herself. It never even crossed my mind to say anything about Matt!

The rest of the afternoon and evening sped by in a blur of drinking, dancing and chatting to all my guests. I didn't get drunk – I wanted to remember every single second of my special day so I only had four drinks during the whole day, including the champagne in the morning. We had a fantastic evening and by midnight, after the last of the drunken guests had staggered out, Matt and I went to a hotel where we had booked the bridal suite for the night. We were both buzzing from the excitement of the day so we ordered up some sandwiches to the room, and, still wearing our wedding clothes, we opened some of our wedding cards and read the messages to each other.

'You two are a beautiful couple, clearly devoted to each other, and I wish you a lifetime of happiness and hugs …' Matt read out loud and I felt a lump at the back of my throat. It had been such a big day, so emotional, and now, at three in the morning, I finally felt it all creeping up on me. Matt undid the satin bow at the back of my dress. I carefully placed it on a chair, then I crawled, exhausted, under the covers.

'Happy?' Matt asked as my eyes started to close.

'Really happy,' I said with a sigh, then fell into a deep and dreamless sleep.

We were woken by the sound of banging on the door. It was the hotel housekeeper trying to get into our room to clean it for the next guests.

'But I thought we were here for three nights …' I said groggily. A quick phone call to reception confirmed the hotel had double booked the room. Matt was furious but I told him it wasn't worth the aggravation.

'Let's save the money and just go home,' I suggested. 'We're married now anyway. The important bit is over.'

So we gathered up our things and drove home. Matt insisted on doing things right – even though we'd been living together for a year by then, he carried me over the threshold, to start our new lives together as man and wife in the proper way. I couldn't have been happier.

If only things had stayed that way. If only Matt hadn't changed. But he did. He changed completely and the married life I'd dreamed of since I was a little girl disappeared in a puff of smoke. The joy I'd felt on my wedding day, surrounded by family and friends, soon became a very distant memory …

It happened almost straight away. Just a couple of weeks after the wedding, Matt stopped treating me as the beautiful trophy wife he adored and instead started to talk down to me, criticising me for everything I did. It was as though he didn't have the same respect for me as before and though at first I would stand my ground and argue back, I soon realised that there wasn't much point. There was really only one way of doing things and that was Matt's way. We were still having sex regularly but the kissing and cuddling disappeared fairly quickly. I blamed it on the stress of trying to conceive. Even before we were married Matt and I had been trying for a baby. It was all I had ever wanted – to be a mum. I was very maternal. My mum's youngest sister had four kids and I was there for each of them, to change their nappies and help take care of them as babies, even though I was still only a child myself. Matt and I had discussed this very early on and agreed we would start a family straight away. I don't know where this desire came from – maybe it was just an instinct in me, maybe it was something to do with the fact that I'd had a difficult childhood and I yearned to give my own children something better.

However, by the time of the wedding there was no sign that I might be pregnant. It was disappointing. Being a mum was so important to me. By now I had given up my job and had started working with Matt at the arcade. Together, we redecorated the business and he even changed the name to 'Hannah Morgan's Arcade'. But now, since the wedding, Matt was more critical of me, telling me off for all sorts of things I did wrong and insisting that I perform my 'wifely duties' of serving him cups of tea, washing the clothes and keeping the house clean.

'You're the woman!' he instructed. 'It's you that's supposed to serve me with cups of tea, not the other way round. You don't get a dog and bark yourself.'

I should expect this, I told myself. *Matt is a very traditional man, and he expects his home life to be traditional too.* So I accepted the changes and tried my best to keep him happy. All I wanted was to start a family together. All I wanted was a happy home life.

So when nothing happened we spoke to our GP who referred us to the hospital. By now not only had the affectionate hugs and kisses stopped between us, but the sex we were still having most nights felt mechanical, as if there was no love in it. *It must be the stress of trying to get pregnant*, I told myself. *It's only natural that some of the emotion goes out of it when we're trying to have sex on certain days and times.* When we went to our appointment at the fertility clinic, they found the problem was with me, so I was given medication to help me release more eggs and that very same month I fell pregnant! I could hardly believe it when I saw the test result, I was so happy. This was everything I had ever wanted: I was married to my soulmate, we had a good business and now we were expecting our first child. Everything was great. The next night we went out to celebrate my sister's birthday. I thought everything was falling into place and that from this point my happiness, like the little baby inside me, would just continue to grow. How wrong I was.

3

Changing Circumstances

Even before we went out that night, I was tired. I knew it must be the pregnancy but even so, it was a surprise to feel so exhausted. This wasn't like me. I usually had bags of energy but now I felt utterly drained. We joined my whole family for a meal at the Frankie & Benny's restaurant in town and I tried my best to put on a happy face – after all, it was my sister's birthday and I wanted her to have a good time. Still, it was a relief when we called it a night at 11pm. *At last – now I can get myself to bed!* But Matt had other ideas. I drove us back – Matt had had a couple of drinks and I wasn't drinking or smoking because of the pregnancy – but as we turned down towards the high street, Matt said: 'Let's swing past the arcade and see how business has been this evening.'

I let out a sigh: 'Oh, please, Matt, let's not. I'm so tired. Can't we just go home?'

'No, come on. We'll stop by the arcade. Have a chat to Keith.'

Keith was Matt's friend and though he was a nice man and had a full-time job, he was an alcoholic and had ended up homeless. Matt let him sleep at the arcade, which worked out well for Matt because Keith could keep an eye on the place for us at night. Matt knew I was tired and he also knew I was pregnant, but that didn't seem to make a difference. Once we arrived at the arcade, he put the kettle on, put his feet up on the counter and appeared to settle in for a long chat with Keith. The minutes ticked slowly by. I yawned and tried not to fall asleep right there in the office. *All I want is my bed!* It got to midnight, then 1am and finally, when the clock hit 2am, I begged Matt to let me take the car and drive myself home.

'Please, just let me go to bed, Matt, and you can walk home. It's only five minutes from here.'

'No, no, I'll be there in a minute,' he insisted. 'Just be patient.'

Finally, I got so frustrated, I went out and sat in the car, waiting for Matt to come and join me. I couldn't believe how long they were chatting for. It was too cold in the car to sleep. At around 3am he came out and we drove home. Once we were back I headed upstairs to change and get ready for bed but Matt was still messing about downstairs. *Urgh, I can't wait any longer.* It was 4am and I needed to sleep. Finally, Matt came upstairs. I lay down next to him, closed my eyes and surrendered myself to sleep until … BANG, BANG, BANG!

I sat bolt upright, my eyes wide open. *Jesus – who the hell is banging on our door at four in the morning?* I turned to look at Matt, feeling scared. Then we heard a voice, somebody calling through the letterbox.

'Matt! It's Sherie!' Sherie was Matt's cousin. She lived with Matt's mum Lindsey in the house across the main road.

'Go and answer it,' Matt mumbled.

So I hastily pulled on my dressing gown and slippers and crept downstairs. I could tell from the moment I opened the door that something was desperately wrong. Sherie was white as a sheet. My mind raced … *Was it Matt's mum? Had she had a fall?*

'There's been a fire at the arcade,' she blurted out.

'What?'

'It's on fire … come on! You better come quick.'

I turned around to shout up the stairs for Matt but he was already running down the staircase behind me, buttoning up his jeans as he ran. I didn't even think to change.

'Right, let's go,' I said, still in my slippers, dressing gown and pyjamas.

I smelled it before I saw it. The smoke drifted all the way down the high street, a choking toxic fog of burning metal, wood and plastic. It was awful. Police had blocked off the road so we parked at the bus stop opposite and ran across the road. By the time we arrived at the arcade most of the flames were out but the building was still smouldering, surrounded by three fire engines and a dozen firefighters. Matt ran up to the first one he saw.

'What's happening? What's going on?' he yelled.

'Massive fire in the arcade,' the man responded.

'It's my business. That's my business,' Matt shouted back.

'What about Keith?' I asked. I was petrified the fire had claimed the life of Matt's friend who had been sleeping in the back room at the time.

'It's alright,' Matt patted me on the shoulder. 'He's there, look!'

Keith was stood by a fire engine, looking dazed and shocked, rolling himself a fag, but obviously still alive.

He wandered towards us.

'It's gone, Matt. The whole lot, it's gone,' he muttered.

The four of us just stood there, staring helplessly at the smoking embers of our former business. *How in the world had this happened?* I wondered. *And how are we going to provide for our child now?*

From the moment the business was gone, Matt was at home 24/7 and now things seemed to get increasingly difficult between us. I fretted about how we were going to provide for the baby but Matt seemed unconcerned.

'We've got good customers, loyal customers,' he said. 'We can set up somewhere else, we can run the business from home even. We'll just buy some new arcade machines. It'll be even better than before.'

The problem was the insurance company didn't pay out. I didn't quite understand the full ins and outs because Matt was quite vague and by now I had learnt not to question him closely but, from what I could work out, an investigation had discovered the fire was started deliberately. A Coke bottle filled with petrol had been dropped down the flume of the chimney and then when the boiler clicked on at a certain time in the night, it melted the plastic, releasing the petrol and starting the blaze. Matt insisted it must have been some local teenagers, pranking him, but clearly the police didn't believe him because he was arrested and bailed a couple of times pending a criminal investigation. Frankly, I didn't really know what was going on at the time because Matt refused to discuss it with me. He said the arrest had nothing to do with the fire and I believed him. I believed everything he told me at this point.

In the end there were no charges brought against Matt but the insurance company still refused to pay out. Now we were under financial pressure and we failed to keep up our repayments on our £4,500 wedding loan, which Matt insisted was taken out in my name. I called the bank to tell them about the fire but they refused to stop the repayments and started calling up to ten times a day, demanding their money back. It was really stressful so Matt took matters into his hands and the next time they called he insisted I hand over the phone to him: 'My wife is pregnant and you are hounding her,' he roared down the line. 'Have you any idea the stress you are putting her through? If you cause my wife to lose the baby, I'm going to fucking kill you.' I never heard anything more from them after that.

By now the morning sickness had kicked in and it was far worse than anything I was prepared for. I was throwing up almost constantly, up to 30 times a day. Anything and everything made me sick: baked beans, crisps, toast, tea. You name it, it made me hurl. It was so bad at times that I'd be stood there talking to someone and I'd have to throw up in my mouth and swallow it back down because I had nowhere to be sick into. I couldn't keep anything down at all so in the early stages of the pregnancy I lost a lot of weight very quickly. I thought Matt might have some sympathy for what I was going through but, far from being kind and understanding, the longer the pregnancy went on, the more emotionally distant he became.

It was early winter and we had dropped off our washing at my sister's house earlier in the day. Our washing machine had broken down and so she had generously offered to put our laundry in her machine, and on our way back from the shops that night, we stopped off at hers to collect the towels we had dropped off earlier. She didn't have a dryer so we planned to hang them up at ours to dry once we were home. But Matt was brooding over something I had said earlier that day about needing to get some money coming in soon because of the baby. He was still angry when we got to Mandy's. She came to the front door and before I had even had a chance to say hello he was having a go at me. Then he stormed off, leaving me standing there on the doorstep, upset and humiliated in front of my sister.

There was a moment's silence, then Mandy asked gently: 'Is everything alright, Hannah?'

'Yeah, it's fine,' I said, sighing. 'He's just had a bad day, that's all.'

I was too embarrassed to say no. After all, I had only been married for five months – it felt ridiculous to start complaining about my new husband so soon after the wedding. So I made an excuse, shrugging off his outburst as 'no big deal'. Mandy nodded and disappeared inside to get the bag of towels.

'Right, well, here you go,' she said as she handed me the sack. God, it was heavy! Sopping-wet towels weigh a tonne and now, because he'd left me here on my own, I had to carry them all the way home. I struggled back with the bag and to my annoyance I found that he wasn't even home when I arrived! Worse, he had the key so I couldn't get in either. I just sat there, on the bench in the front garden, shivering in the cold night, waiting for him to come home, a two-month-old foetus inside me and a heavy bag of wet towels at my feet.

I hoped that soon after the business burned down Matt might get back on his feet and get another job – after all, we were going to need an income to look after us – but he didn't seem in any rush. So to keep some money coming in I got a part-time job in the New Year, covering the lunch hour at a private nursery three days a week. By now I had assumed my full responsibilities as the housewife – cleaning, washing, ironing and generally making sure the house ran smoothly. But the morning sickness was so bad that some days I was on the sofa, unable to move, so on those days Matt did help out, sticking on a load or hanging up the washing, cooking or clearing up. It was hard because there were times I just couldn't even look at a cup of tea without being sick and Matt took that personally.

'I've made you that – why aren't you fucking drinking it?' he'd yell as I lay prone on the sofa.

'I'm sorry, Matt. I really can't. It'll just make me sick.'

One time Matt made a batch of homemade soup in an effort to get some healthy food into me as he thought that I wasn't getting enough nutrients for the baby. It was a combination of lots of different root vegetables but by the time he called me down to eat it, I already had my head in the toilet bowl upstairs. Just the smell of all those simmering vegetables wafting up the stairs – the carrots, swedes and parsnips – was enough to make me vomit. But Matt's insistent voice called me from the kitchen and I knew he was only trying his best, so, slowly and delicately, I made my way downstairs. But the closer I got to the kitchen, the more my gut churned. My stomach muscles ached now from being sick all the time. I sat down heavily on a chair and Matt handed me a flask.

'Here you are. Get that down your neck. You haven't eaten today.'

I looked at the thick gloopy yellow-orange soup – he had blended all the vegetables together – but just the thought of trying to swallow a mouthful made my stomach heave.

'I don't think I can, Matt, honestly …'

'You don't have to eat it,' he snapped. 'It's soup. Just drink it.'

'I don't think I can,' I repeated. By now my stomach was heaving and I felt the saliva pooling in the base of my mouth. I was going to gag. A heavy silence fell between us now as Matt fixed me with a dark look.

'I fucking stood there to make this soup to feed our child,' he growled menacingly. 'That's *my* baby you've got growing inside you. I have a say in the matter as well.'

It was true – it was his baby too – I felt so bad. Obviously, I wasn't refusing his food to harm the baby … I just physically couldn't eat it because everything made me so violently ill. Nevertheless, I had to try at least, for his sake. Matt stood there and watched me until I took a swig, which I made look like a big one but literally only just touched my lips. Later, he left the room and I poured the rest down the sink.

We started claiming benefits to support ourselves. The Jobseeker's Allowance money went into my account but Matt decided how this was spent and by the time we'd bought all the food shopping and paid the bills, it was all gone. Now Matt said we had to watch every penny. So the next time I asked Matt if I could put a tenner on my SIM card to top up my pay-as-you-go phone, he refused.

'We've lost the business. Don't you get it?' he yelled. 'We don't have spare tenners knocking about. No, you don't need to top up your phone.'

'Well, what if I need to call you for anything?'

'It won't happen. I'll always be with you. Or you'll always be with somebody with a phone.'

I supposed Matt was right because the only time we weren't together now was when I went to work in the nursery and that was just a ten-minute drive away.

'But what about speaking to Mum?'

'You can use the landline or my phone. Look, we can't afford to throw away money on luxuries we can't afford. You know that.'

He was right but, still, it was strange not being able to call people. I stopped speaking to a lot of my friends because if they didn't call me I had no way of contacting them. If I wanted to communicate I relied on my Facebook account on Matt's computer. Although that was never easy. It seemed the moment Matt knew I wanted to use the computer to make contact with the world he would take hours doing what he wanted to do on it.

One night I had been waiting several hours to go on Facebook and it was late in the evening when Matt eventually got up, indicating that I was now allowed to use the computer.

'Why are you so keen to get on Facebook anyway?' he sneered as I hastily tapped in my password. 'So you can chat to one of your *boyfriends*?'

'Oh Matt, for goodness' sake!' I said with a sigh, and shook my head.

In a flash, he picked up a pint glass with some Coca-Cola in it and threw it in my face. I was so shocked at first I didn't move. Then he leaned forwards and said very quietly: 'Better not. You watch – I'll kill your little brother and I'll cut your eyelids off and make you watch. Then I'll kill your mum.'

A big lump formed in my throat and I struggled to hold back the tears as I wiped Coke off my face. Matt knew the bond I had with my little brother. He knew how much I adored him. His words cut me to the bone. Now he could see I was trying not to cry in front of him and I think there was something about my reaction that pleased him. Still, I tried to focus on my Facebook account. There were several messages from friends I hadn't had a chance to read. I tried to concentrate but Matt started throwing Shake n' Vac on the carpet around me. He was standing over my shoulder, watching my every move. *Bloody hell, what's he going to do? Throw another glass of Coke?* I was too scared to do much except read my messages but the words refused to go in. My mind was in turmoil.

Then, as soon as he had finished powdering the carpet, Matt turned off the living-room lights.

'Come on,' he said. 'Let's go to bed.'

By this point I'd been on the computer for about ten minutes.

'I'll be up in a minute,' I replied.

'NO, YOU WILL COME TO BED NOW!'

Matt always insisted I go to bed at the same time as him. He had some very set ideas about married life. He liked to tell me how a woman should be up before the man to bake the bread and scrub the front doorstep. We never made bread from scratch, or scrubbed the doorstep for that matter, but I had to accept what he said because in my wedding vows, I had agreed to obey him. So now I switched off the computer and followed him up to bed. It was getting harder and harder to stay in touch with my friends and family.

By the time I was seven months pregnant I had a neat little bump out in front of me and I loved it! Matt, however, wasn't so keen on my pregnant body; he said I was a 'fucking fat bitch' and an 'ugly cow'. I tried not to let his insults bother me – I knew that the changes to my body were natural and I tried to enjoy this special time. In fact, I wasn't fat at all because of the morning sickness and I really loved my swelling bump. I cradled it, hugged it, sang to it … and I adored the little kicks I felt at night when I was lying down. There were times the baby even got the hiccups inside my belly and that was funny – watching the little bump jump up and down. This was *my baby*. It made me smile whenever I felt it moving around. Despite the sickness, the swollen ankles, the tiredness and everything else, I loved pregnancy! It was such a wonderful experience and I'd waited so long to feel this way …

Matt was less enthusiastic.

'Jesus, why the fuck do you look like this? You didn't look like that when we were first together, you were a size six!' he complained when he caught sight of me first thing in the morning. 'You better lose some of that fucking weight after you've had this kid. Why do your fucking eyes look so close together? They're like piss holes in the snow! And look at all this flab on the backs of your arms.'

One afternoon I returned from working at the nursery and went straight upstairs to lie down. Now in my third trimester, I was really beginning to feel the strain. I was constantly tired and had fat, swollen ankles. I'd been on my feet from the moment I had got up at 9.45am and had carried my seven-month bump all around the playground. Now I was tired, everything hurt, including my head, and I needed a quick lie-down and a ten-minute power nap. I hadn't been on the bed long when Matt called up to me from the bottom of the stairs.

'I've done you some food – a bacon sandwich and a cup of tea.'

'Can I come down in a minute?' I called back. I knew Matt had offered to help our friend Nick this afternoon by driving some fence panels round to his nan's house and he was keen for us to set off. But I just needed a little rest.

'I got this ready for you for when you got home from work.' Matt sounded impatient. 'It's ready, it's getting cold ...'

Oh God, do I have to? I was so very tired ... My eyes closed shut but even as I felt myself drifting off I heard Matt's thumping footsteps as he climbed the stairs and stormed into the bedroom.

'OI, YOU! I'VE STOOD THERE AND COOKED YOU A FUCKING BACON SANDWICH!' he yelled. 'I'VE COOKED AND I DON'T HAVE TO DO THAT. YOU'RE THE WOMAN!'

Then he pulled his trousers down and pointed to his penis.

'I'VE GOT ONE OF THESE. I'M THE FUCKING MAN. I MADE YOU A CUP OF TEA AS WELL. I DIDN'T HAVE TO DO THAT. IT'S NOT MY JOB. IT'S NOT MY DUTY.'

Then he grabbed me by the hair and dragged me off the bed. *Bang*. I hit the floor. Overhead I heard something rattle on top of the chest of drawers from the impact.

Owwww … my scalp seared with pain as he dragged me by the hair out onto the landing. I tried to hold onto my hair and protect my bump at the same time. He yanked me head first to the top of the stairs. *Oh Jesus … I hope I'm not going down there.* And just at the point when I thought he was going to hurl me down the stairs, he let go. Then he walked downstairs calmly in silence. I was too stunned to move at first. It had all happened so quickly. But lying there, panting, as my head throbbed, it suddenly occurred to me: *I'd better get downstairs and eat that sandwich* and I scrambled to my feet. *I'd better do as I'm told because I don't want to find out what happens if I don't.* So I hurried down the stairs, sat down on the sofa and ate my bacon sandwich in silence. Afterwards, I said: 'Thank you, Matt. That was lovely.'

Ten minutes later, we went out and helped Nick with the fence panels. We never talked about the incident, though it played on my mind a lot. He was so quick to anger – I resolved to double my efforts to keep him happy.

4

The Birth of a Very Longed-for Baby

'Sweetheart, we've got a problem.'

Those were his exact words, the words that let me know there was something seriously wrong. I was 35 weeks pregnant and literally glowing with happiness. The morning sickness had stopped, my baby was growing well and all I felt was excitement at the thought that in just a few weeks' time I would meet our daughter. By now we knew from the scans that she was a girl and we had agreed to call her Poppie, a name we had settled on in the very early weeks of our relationship. I dreamt of Poppie at night and fantasised about what she would look like during the day. With every passing hour I grew closer and more bonded to the little life growing inside me. Then those five little words brought everything to a screeching halt: 'Sweetheart, we've got a problem.'

Matt had been up early that morning, getting dressed and washed while I pottered around, folding the laundry and clearing up from breakfast with *GMTV* on in the background. It was unusual that Matt was up at this time – he usually liked to lie in – but I didn't think too much about it.

At around 9am he announced he was popping out. I knew better than to ask him where he was going. He never reacted well to my innocent curiosity.

'Don't fucking question me,' he'd reply angrily. 'It's nothing to do with you. Do you think my dad's wife would have said that to him? Do you think my mum said that to my dad? I'm the man, I do as I like.'

So I just accepted that he was going out and offered to make him a packed lunch.

'No, it's fine,' he replied as he put on his jacket. 'I'll be back in a couple of hours. Just going to see a solicitor. It's about the arcade.'

'Okay,' I said, smiling, and then he left. I had planned to spend the morning painting the baby's room so I didn't mind having a few hours to myself.

A couple of hours later, Matt was back. I made him a cup of tea as usual and as I put it down on the table in front of him, he patted the arm of the chair he was sitting on.

'Come here a minute, sweetheart,' he said.

So I went to sit down on the arm of the chair next to him: 'Yeah?'

He looked at me with a serious expression and said: 'Sweetheart, we've got a problem.'

Then he took out a letter from the inside pocket of his jacket and handed it to me. It was addressed to both of us – Mr and Mrs Gower – but I'd never seen it before as Matt always took the post before I had a chance to look at it. The letter was from our local authority. They had been in consultation with our social services provider and our healthcare provider as well as the police, and after serious deliberation they had decided to put Baby Gower on a child protection plan. They had concerns about our unborn child's welfare. The words swam in front of my eyes … *Concerns about our baby's welfare? Why? What is wrong?* I couldn't take it in. *What does this mean? Am I going to lose the baby?* I looked at the date on the letter and saw that Matt had had this letter for over a month already.

'Why didn't you tell me?' I gasped.

'I didn't want to worry you.'

'But it says here I need a solicitor …'

'Yeah, well, that's why I went to speak to my solicitor today. He says you do need one too. Don't worry, we'll straighten this out. We'll appeal and we'll get it all sorted. Those bastards don't have a leg to stand on.'

Until this moment I'd had no idea that there was anything wrong. No clue that Matt's behaviour had put him on social services' radar. But reading the documents that they supplied with the letter to support their decision, it all began to fall into place. The first time we came to their attention was at our first midwife appointment when I was eight weeks pregnant. How could I forget! That appointment had been a total disaster.

Matt had initially accompanied me to the GP's surgery, as he did for everything these days – I rarely left the house alone! According to him, I couldn't be trusted with the simplest of tasks like getting the shopping right, listening properly to the doctors or asking the right questions, so it was better if he was with me. It was draining, having him constantly at my side, like a leech, sucking the life out of me. It was also horribly degrading – I knew I could do the shopping or talk to doctors without screwing up. I wasn't an idiot, but I didn't have the energy to fight him on this.

Our GP confirmed the pregnancy and two weeks later we were invited to attend our first midwife appointment. We waited silently in the crowded reception area until the midwife called out: 'Hannah Gower?'

We both stood up to follow the midwife into the consultation room but, as we did so, she smiled politely at Matt: 'Can we speak to Hannah on her own for a moment, please? This is standard procedure, we do it for all our midwife appointments. Just a few moments, then you can come in.'

I scanned Matt's face for a response … *Is this okay or should I insist he come in too?* By now I had learned to read Matt's expressions for clues about what he wanted me to do.

Matt said quickly: 'We're married, it's our child.'

But the midwife stood her ground: 'Yes, but we like to speak to mothers on their own first. It's just for a minute, sir.'

'No, it's fine,' I jumped in. 'He can come in. I don't mind.'

'No, I'm sorry, it's our policy,' the midwife wasn't budging. 'Even if you consent, we must speak to you on your own first.'

There was nothing we could do so Matt had to sit and wait outside as I went in on my own first. The midwife asked me a couple of questions about whether I'd been pregnant before and a few other things, but after just a couple of minutes Matt opened the door.

He was fuming and he started to rant.

'You've made me sit outside all this time but that's my child as well,' he pointed at my belly. 'Why have I been excluded? And you, Mrs Midwife, why did you talk to me the way you did in front of all them people out there?'

The midwife answered calmly: 'Some women may have had previous pregnancies their current partners don't know about. It is their right to be able to talk to us in confidence and they are afforded privacy in this regard.'

But Matt didn't like it, he didn't like it one bit.

'My wife even said she didn't mind me being here,' his voice rose. 'You prevented us from sharing this together. This should be a special moment for us, this is our first child and you've ruined it. You've shut me out and spoke down to me ...'

Just then, there was a knock on the door. A female doctor appeared in the doorway: 'I'm so sorry to disturb you. I just need to borrow your midwife for a moment. I have a patient in with me and need a second opinion ...'

Our midwife got up with a nod, apologised for the short delay and left with the doctor.

The moment she shut the door behind her I knew that the excuse was bullshit. I knew why the doctor had knocked on the door – she'd heard Matt shouting and come to ask the midwife if she was alright. It was obvious, except I didn't say anything to Matt at the time – he was angry enough already and would have hit the roof if he suspected they were talking about him. But I knew. I knew they had gone out to discuss us. Only I thought that it hadn't gone any further because nobody had said anything to us since. Now I read the notes that accompanied the local authority letter – the surgery had been straight on the phone to social services that day. Matt was 'very volatile', they wrote, and appeared 'controlling towards his wife'. They had safeguarding concerns. Of course, we didn't know this at the time.

I had more midwife appointments as the pregnancy progressed and Matt came to every single one. They kept an eye on us, recording our behaviour, and then, to be sure, social services checked Matt against the police records. That's when everything began to unravel – they found out that Matt had attacked a man delivering flyers that very same month. At the time, I had put his violent outbursts down to the stress of losing his business, but social services claimed there was a 'pattern of volatile behaviour'. One winter afternoon we had been expecting some flyers to be delivered and the bloke who printed them came round at 4pm. I went to answer the bell, then closed the door behind me. At that point Matt appeared at the top of the stairs, dishevelled, still wearing just his boxers, his face distorted into an ugly mask of rage. He had slept in all day and despite the fact that it was now late in the afternoon, he was outraged to be woken up. He clattered down the stairs, stormed out the front door and strode up the path after the figure disappearing up our front drive.

'Oi,' he shouted out after him. 'OI! YOU!' The man span around.

'WHAT FUCKING TIME DO YOU CALL THIS?' Matt bellowed.

'I'm really sorry,' the man started apologetically, 'we're really busy and I've had tonnes of orders in. I wouldn't normally be here so late in the day but …'

He didn't get a chance to finish – Matt grabbed him by the collar and threw him into the hedge. I stood in the front doorway, mouth gaping open in horror, as Matt walked back up the garden path, came in and slammed the door shut behind him.

The man ended up in hospital with a broken thumb and early in the New Year Matt was arrested for assault. He tried to brazen it out. 'You saw what happened,' he said. 'It's our word against his – two against one. It won't stand up if we both say it was someone else.'

I didn't have any choice in the matter – by now I knew I wasn't allowed to disagree with Matt so if he told me to go into the witness box and say it was someone else, that's what I had to do. I was his wife, as he constantly reminded me, and I had solemnly sworn to obey him. So I did obey him. I couldn't do anything else, knowing that if I refused, I risked a beating. And then I'd have to do it anyway. So, two months before my due date, I stood up in the magistrates' court and repeated the lie Matt had prepared for me.

'You've got to tell them it was Nick Baines who hit him,' he drilled into me. 'You say Nick was there cos you two are secretly having an affair and it was actually Nick who beat the bloke up. That makes it believable, you see, admitting you did something naughty. Then they'll believe you. The affair, it makes it sound more real.'

So I did as I was told, hoping of course that Matt would be happy I had defended him in court. Instead, his reaction shocked me.

'Yes …' he cackled when he saw me afterwards, rubbing his hands with glee. 'So now you've admitted to having an affair under oath. That will go in my favour just in case I want to divorce you at some point.'

Bloody hell – he'd walked me straight into a trap. I felt hurt and confused – I'd just lied for him in court, I'd done him a massive favour, but he had set me up. I pretended it didn't bother me but when I saw the headline in our local paper,

'MY LOVER WAS THE CULPRIT, SAYS MARRIED HOUSEWIFE', it bothered me a lot. My family would see that headline. My friends too. What would they think of me? I had no opportunity to speak to them to tell them it was all a lie. The worst part was that it didn't matter in the end anyway, because Matt was found guilty and sentenced to community service. He appealed against the conviction but he lost that too.

Now the local authority said that our baby was at risk from Matt's violent and unpredictable behaviour. They were also concerned that I appeared to be isolated, with no family around. It wasn't strictly true, although Matt had made it harder and harder for my family to get in touch and see me. They could only call me on the landline and if Mum wanted to come by, she had to make an appointment first. Matt had banned her from just 'dropping in' as she used to so now I saw her around once a month. He insisted I call her to ask her to attend the child protection conference with us. His own mum Lindsey would come too, and his dad.

'We have to show them we're one big happy family,' he explained. 'They think if there is family around then nothing bad will happen.'

Losing my baby? It was my worst nightmare … I fretted and worried every day that the local authority would take my child. This baby I had fought so hard for, the one I had dreamed of for so long, the one I had put myself through horrendous illness for, I wanted her so badly. I couldn't believe they were threatening to take her away. In the run-up to the conference, letters flew back and forth between our solicitors in which the local authority also threatened to put me and my daughter in a mother-and-baby unit away from Matt. Of course, it wasn't a threat from their point of view, it was an offer – an offer of help. But I didn't need help. I really didn't. Okay, so Matt was a bit unpredictable at times but I knew he would be a kind and loving father to our daughter. And once our business was up and running again our family life would settle down and everything would be okay.

The child protection conference took place two days before my due date. My mum came, as did Lindsey and Matt's dad – we presented a united family front, insisting I had a strong network of family supporting me and our baby. They all thought everything was fine between us – nobody suspected Matt of being anything less than the model husband and Matt had been on his best behaviour since that first letter. He was hitting me less and in front of the social workers he was the 'perfect husband'. Now, with the help of our solicitors, we managed to get the local authority to give us a chance to prove ourselves. They agreed not to take our baby away as long as she was placed on the child protection register and we engaged regularly with the health and social service professionals. Once I was at home with our child a social worker would visit every ten days for an assessment. It was the best we could hope for, our solicitors advised, so we accepted the offer and when I got home that night I cried with relief, and prayed my thanks to God. *Thank you, God! Thank you – they're not taking our baby!*

But Matt was smarting all night long.

'Fucking scumbags!' he fumed. 'They think they can interfere with our family and do what the fuck they like. What gives them the fucking right? I'd like to know …'

I agreed with him out loud but inside I just prayed that in time he would calm down and try to work with the professionals. After all, if we were nice and pleasant, it could go well for us.

The next day was Saturday and we worked hard all day and night, wallpapering in the house, finishing off tidying up the garden and adding summer plants along the borders. I didn't start my bedtime routine until 3.40am Sunday morning. Dozily, I sat on the toilet, did a wee, then wiped myself – to my surprise I saw blood on the toilet paper. Was this a *show*? I wondered. A show was the early sign of labour. I had read about this in my pregnancy book – a show happened when the mucus plug on the cervix came away. Thirty seconds later, I was doubled up in pain. Matt was up the stairs, not far behind me.

'Matt!' I called him into the toilet and showed him the blood.

'This is a show, isn't it?' he said, slowly clapping his right hand to his mouth and rubbing his chin.

'Yeah, I think so ...'

But from what I'd read there was still a long time to go before I'd be ready to give birth. So I brushed my teeth, put on my pyjamas and tried to get comfy in bed, thinking I would be like this for hours. I didn't get a wink of sleep over the next three hours; the pain was excruciating. And since Matt had said it was pointless attending antenatal classes I didn't know what to do when the contractions came so I just held my breath until they passed. By 7am the contractions were coming every 20 minutes so we rang the hospital for advice. They recommended taking paracetamol, having a bath and managing at home for now because they thought I still had some way to go.

But I didn't cope well at home. For one thing, I didn't take the drugs because I wanted to experience childbirth in its entirety, pain and everything. And after an hour the contractions were coming every 15 minutes so Matt suggested we go to the hospital. We left the house at 8am for the 45-minute drive but, in the car, the pressure down below was so bad I couldn't even sit down properly. I wrapped my arms around the headrest behind my head and pulled myself up off the seat.

'Urrrnngggg …' I bore down hard against the agony of another contraction. 'Please, please hurry up!' I screamed at Matt, now petrified the baby was going to arrive before we got to the hospital.

But when we finally got there I was examined by the midwife who said I was still only two centimetres dilated. They showed us to a room on the labour ward and there I got in the bath, which gave me some relief from the contractions. Every few minutes, I'd ask Matt to alternate running the hot and cold taps, which also seemed to help, and I stayed this way for the next two hours, during which time my waters broke. I felt a popping sensation and I knew that the waters had gone. *Wow* – I turned to Matt with tears in my eyes. This was such a powerful, beautiful experience; I know a lot of women hate going through labour but not me. I embraced it all: the pain, the pleasure, the discomfort, it was all extraordinary and I couldn't believe how lucky I was to go through it all.

At 1pm, I got out of the bath and my lovely midwife Jill measured me again: 'Okay – ten centimetres, we're ready to go. I can see the head. When you're ready, you can start pushing.'

'Really? Can I really push? It's not too soon?'

'It's fine. Just breathe, listen to your body and when you're ready and you feel like pushing, push.'

I was sat completely naked, propped up on the bed, a towel over me for modesty with Matt on my left, Jill at the foot of the bed, ready to deliver our daughter. Then, as another powerful contraction took hold, I gave a huge push.

'Nearly … the head's nearly out,' Jill sang out. 'Let's do a second push, Hannah!'

I pushed again.

'Yes, she's here. Her head is out, Hannah,' she said excitedly. I looked at Matt's face; his eyes shone with tears. 'Now just one more push …'

On the third big push she was out. Three pushes and that was it!

Then the midwife calmly asked Matt to push the button on the wall next to him. For a second I wondered why she did that but there was no time to think because the next moment the room was filled with people and by the time I realised they had come in to perform resuscitation, Poppie had started to breathe on her own. Then I heard her cry. *Oh thank God!* Jill wrapped her in a blanket and put her straight onto my chest for skin-to-skin contact. *My baby!* I looked at her for the first time and I was surprised to see that she looked exactly like the baby from my dreams. It was like looking into the face of a child I had known all my life. She was new but at the same time totally familiar. I thought my heart would burst with happiness. 'Oh, Poppie,' I whispered to her, my voice choked with emotion. 'Hello, Poppie. So good to meet you at last.'

We had been blessed with a perfect, healthy little girl and I felt like the luckiest woman alive.

I took to motherhood like a duck to water – Poppie latched onto my breast straight away and I felt no anxiety or fear about her at all. It was like this was meant to be. Everything about being with Poppie felt right – I knew that I was born to do this and at first, in the security of the labour ward, Poppie and I were in a happy little world of our own. Her name suited her perfectly. I had to stay in hospital for four days in total as the midwives found that I was group B strep (GBS) positive, which meant I needed intravenous antibiotics for a minimum of four hours during labour, but seeing as everything happened so quickly there wasn't time, so for several days after the birth we had to stay in so Poppie could have antibiotics every 12 hours. GBS is an infection in the vagina that only becomes active during pregnancy, which can be dangerous if left untreated. And I must admit, those first four days were lovely – I didn't have to worry about doing any washing or cleaning. I could just lie in bed and bond with my baby and breastfeed her. The hospital food was nice, the midwives were lovely and the nurses kind and helpful. Matt came and saw us every day, as did his mum and my mum too. Matt even took the washing home and washed it without fuss, even though, as was amply demonstrated, I was the woman!

Then, once we were home, Matt's mum Lindsey visited for the first few weeks to help with the housework. Matt left me to do most of the work usually but he was gentler with me after Poppie arrived. He told me to sleep if the baby was sleeping, did the ironing occasionally and once or twice he bathed Poppie. He would smile when he was with her and I saw that change in him. And because I saw a softer side to Matt I had renewed hope things would get better. All I wanted at this point was to spend time with Poppie. I was completely wrapped up in her and couldn't bear to be apart from her, even for a second. I didn't mind showing her off to family and friends but I didn't want anyone to hold her for too long. She was *my* baby, after all, and my arms ached to hold her when she was being cuddled by someone else. The midwife came round every morning to check on us until she was 10 days old and she admired my natural parenting skills and our joint efforts to make Poppie's room nice for her. We had decorated from floor to ceiling in Winnie-the-Pooh branded items. From the changing mat, to the wallpaper, uplighter and cot mobile, everything was Winnie-the-Pooh. Everything was laid out beautifully, all the cupboards organised perfectly with her nappies, clothes and towels. Every single item of clothing had been washed in fairy powder, ironed and hung on baby hangers before her arrival. It was lovely, perfect, just as I had always dreamed it would be … And in the quiet of the early morning, when the sun was just peeking through the curtains and the room was filling with warm sunlight, I'd sit on the sofa with her in my arms, feeding her and enjoying our special time together. It was perfect, just perfect … If only it could have stayed that way.

5

Auntie Mandy

I tried, I tried so hard, but nothing I did was ever right. Every day I had new lessons to learn and yet those lessons could change from one day to the next. If I made Matt a cup of tea one day there would be too much milk in it so the next time I made it with less milk and of course now it wasn't milky enough. It wouldn't have enough sugar or there was too much sugar – now it was too cold, too hot, not strong enough ... too strong. Oh, the possibilities of how I could fuck things up were endless and forever changing! If I made him a cup of tea in the exact same way that he liked and had praised the day before it would be wrong by the next day. *It is exactly the same!* I wanted to shout, but I couldn't. If I dared to stand up for myself I'd get a slap across the face. I soon found out that no matter what I did or how hard I tried, whatever I put down in front of him was wrong.

'Fucking stupid, stupid bitch!' he'd erupt. 'Do you want to be wearing this fucking tea over your head? You will – unless you make me another one properly. It's hot, do you not realise that?'

I would come home from working at the nursery and he would tell me he needed his feet rubbed and a cup of tea. That immediately set me up with a dilemma. *What do I do first – make the tea or rub his feet?* In the end I worked out that no matter what choice I made, it would always be the wrong one.

'I fucking said I need my feet rubbed, why aren't you rubbing my feet?' he'd yell if I presented the tea first.

Or: 'I just said I need a fucking cup of tea. Why didn't you do that first, then it could be cooling down while you rub my feet?'

I was trapped. Nothing I could do was right. Nothing.

Matt had very particular ideas about how he wanted food cooked and served to him and if I didn't meet these very strict standards, the plates or pans would end up tossed into the garden. Steak had to be timed to the exact second or it was overcooked or undercooked and even when I set a timer to ensure that the steak was not cooked a millisecond over his preferred time, it could still end up in the garden. Bacon had to be crisp, but not burnt, tea strong and milky at the same time, pork chops must be seasoned well with salt and pepper but not over-seasoned. I was required to pour cream into his coffee by running it off the back of a spoon instead of straight into the cup. Matt even preferred his toast cut a certain way: triangles. And this would have been fine if it had stayed that way but later his preference changed to triangles in the morning and rectangles in the afternoon. I had to get that right – if I served him rectangles in the morning and triangles in the afternoon, I'd be in a world of trouble. And the food, of course, would end up in the garden or thrown at me and up the wall, which I would later have to clean up.

Despite my obvious failings as a wife, I felt much happier and more confident in my role as a mother. I adored my daughter and took endless photos of every moment of her life. I wanted to record everything, capture every little detail of her childhood: from her cheeky smile, to her gurgly laugh, the way she splashed excitedly in the bath, even the soft noises she made when she slept. She filled my world with happiness. So despite the frequency of Matt's complaints and angry outbursts, I managed to push them from my mind when I was with Poppie. She was the apple of my eye and every social services and health visitor report noted our bond and the fact that our daughter appeared to be 'thriving'.

They visited us every ten days in the first year of Poppie's life and, during that time, Matt was on his best behaviour. He was actually quite sweet with Poppie when he wanted to be, and it was lovely when he showed affection to his little girl. But it was always on his terms. Matt ignored Poppie's cries for the most part, because as the mother it was my job to look after her. So I timed my baths to coincide with the baby's nap time so Matt would never be disturbed by her. And he would only watch Poppie on the condition it was for something he approved of. And in this instance it was always Matt doing me a favour. It wasn't expected that he should have to look after his own daughter. Meanwhile, I marvelled at every new milestone my little girl reached – from her first bite of a strawberry to the first time she was let loose with a crayon, to the first dead fly she had on her bedroom windowsill! And it wasn't just me – our whole family and neighbours adored her too.

About a week before Poppie's first birthday Matt and I agreed that my sister Mandy could have Poppie for the whole day. This was a big deal for us both. I was super-protective of my daughter, especially since I was still breastfeeding her, and none of the other family members had had her on their own before now. Even Matt's mum, who was the most frequent visitor to our house, wasn't allowed to have Poppie on her own. So I talked Mandy through Poppie's routine and I gave her a couple of bottles of milk I had expressed, her change bag, spare clothes and food. Then, just before she left, Mandy asked if it was okay to take her niece round to her friend Lisa's house before bringing her back home. I said that would be fine as I'd known Lisa for years but I decided not to tell Matt as I thought this might throw a spanner in the works and I knew how much my sister wanted to spend time with Poppie. As it turned out, not telling Matt about Lisa was a big mistake.

It so happened later on that same day Mandy took Poppie, we ended up driving behind her car when we were on our way to B&Q. But instead of turning down the road to go to my mum's she drove on to Lisa's house. Matt decided to follow her as he was curious about where she was going. She parked up, we parked up behind her, and when she got out of the car, we saw Poppie wasn't with her *Uh oh.*

'Where's Poppie?' said Matt sharply. 'Where's my daughter?'

'She's in the house with Lisa. She was asleep so I just nipped out to get a loaf of bread. She's fine. I've only been gone a few minutes.'

'Matt … Matt … it's okay,' I started to say but I knew it was already too late.

'You left my daughter alone in that house with a stranger? Poppie doesn't know her,' Matt yelled at Mandy.

Mandy tried to get a word in but he was fuming.

'I DON'T GIVE A SHIT. I don't want any of your bullshit excuses. I didn't give you permission to take care of my daughter just for you to palm her off on someone else. I trusted you. I trusted her in your care. And you just left her!'

I wanted to say that it was okay, that I knew Lisa and trusted her, but I didn't get a chance. Matt was so angry and I felt bad that I hadn't told him that Mandy would be taking her to Lisa's. It was all over before I got a chance to speak. Matt told Mandy to get Poppie because we were taking her home right then and there and Mandy's special 'auntie day' was over before it had even begun.

Later that night, Mandy came round to try and sort everything out. I felt sorry for her; she apologised over and over again, but Matt was immovable in his anger. I was sat on the sofa at this point, listening to my sister as she pleaded with my husband for another chance. My heart went out to her – I knew she was desperate to be close to my daughter – but at the same time I knew better than to speak up for her. God knows what he would do to me if I took her side over his! So when she asked me to confirm to Matt that I'd said it was okay for her to visit Lisa's I pretended I hadn't heard her properly at the time. I thought she was talking about something else. I felt terrible for lying but I was frightened of what he might do to me if I confirmed it was true – and luckily they both believed me. Now I let them argue it out between them, sticking up for Matt when prompted to. All the while Matt became more and more irate, and he started banging his fist on the dining table in front of her. Then Matt stood up in a fury and I saw him squaring up to my sister. At this point I leapt from my seat and planted myself between them. I didn't know if he would actually have put his hands on her but I couldn't risk it. I stood between them because I didn't want him to hurt my sister. Could she tell? Did she know there was the threat of violence in the air? I didn't know. I had never confided in her about Matt's outbursts so maybe she didn't have a clue. Even if Matt had hit my sister, I would have had to pretend that that was the first outburst of physical violence I had ever witnessed from him. He was already in control of me by now.

At this point Matt changed tack.

'You did a stupid thing today, you admit it,' he said slowly and deliberately. 'But then how can I trust you not to do *another* stupid thing? How do I know it won't happen again? You're ignorant and stupid about some of the most basic things. I mean, when did the First World War start? Hmmm? Answer me that.'

My sister was completely thrown by the question.

'I don't fucking know! History at school never interested me.'

'Of course you don't know. You're stupid. I don't like that – I don't like the fact that you're stupid so I don't know if I can trust you anymore. I don't like your ignorance, your stupidity, I don't even like the way you dress ... You're common. Why don't you just fuck off, Mandy? The damage is done now. You can't fucking change it.'

A few days later we had a tea party to celebrate Poppie's first birthday. We had invited my family as well as Matt's mum, a few friends and neighbours. It was a lovely afternoon and Poppie even took her very first steps during the party, clinging onto the sofa and the table as her little legs wobbled beneath her. Everything had been fine but Matt was still seething with Mandy and when he was in the kitchen, Mandy overheard him muttering to himself.

'Matt, if you've got something to say, just say it to my face,' she said loudly, in front of several people. He shot daggers at her but he didn't say a word and the rest of the afternoon went off okay. But after everyone had left Matt said to me: 'She ain't coming back in this house again.' I knew he meant my sister. So that was it. My relationship with Mandy was effectively over.

I couldn't speak to Mandy behind Matt's back because Matt had stopped me making calls on my mobile and he had even taken control of my Facebook account. A few weeks earlier I had gone to log in to my Facebook account and the page came up: 'Password incorrect'. Matt had gone into my account, changed my password and refused to let me back in. Then, after our falling out with Mandy, he claimed that she was posting nasty stuff about me on Facebook. Of course I couldn't go on to verify it myself so I had to just take his word for it. He seemed to find this quite amusing and would frequently report on the awful things she was saying about me on Facebook. I had my doubts – Mandy wasn't normally the kind to air her dirty laundry in public, and despite everything that had happened, I felt she would still be loyal to me. So I challenged him.

'Show me!' I replied one day after he taunted me once again by claiming my sister had posted some sick claims about me online.

'You don't believe me? You're not allowed to question me. How dare you! I've got one of these.' He pointed at his penis, then slapped me round the face.

I stopped challenging him after that because I really couldn't win. Whatever I said, it always ended with me getting hurt in some way – either emotionally or physically. So that was how I lost my sister. I lost everyone eventually.

One autumn day I went to give blood and came home afterwards to find Matt in one of his stinking moods. The cause was a mystery to me. I knew I must have done something wrong but he wouldn't tell me what it was. This happened quite frequently – I would break some unknown and unknowable rule and then he would act as if I knew exactly what I had done wrong. It could be anything from leaving a crease in his shirt to failing to put an ornament back in its exact spot – to the millimetre – after doing the polishing. On this particular day I had come home and started hoovering the lounge while Poppie sat in her bouncy chair in front of the telly watching CBeebies and Matt lay horizontal on the sofa with his feet up.

Matt eyed me angrily, then he said quietly: 'Come and sit down for a minute.' So I did as I was told. I turned the hoover off, leaving it plugged in, plonked the pole down on the floor and sat on the armchair.

'You know what you did, don't you?' he started in a quiet, controlled voice. He fixed me with an intimidating glare and I could see the smirk playing on his features. 'I'm not going to spell it out to you. You know what you did and that's why you've come home and started hoovering. Cos you don't want to talk about it.'

Talk about what? My heart sank. It was one of *those* days. I didn't have a clue what he was going on about but still, I wasn't allowed to argue back. I had to sit there and 'explain myself' in a nice, calm, quiet voice.

'I'm not really sure …' I started quietly.

'DON'T FUCKING PRETEND!' he exploded. 'WHY HAVE YOU GOT TO ALWAYS FUCKING WIND ME UP LIKE THIS? YOU KNOW WHAT YOU'VE DONE AND YOU'VE ALWAYS GOT A FUCKING ANSWER FOR EVERYTHING.'

Then he picked up Poppie's cup and threw it at my face.

The yellow plastic beaker hit me hard on my right eyebrow and split my eye open. It had been a present from our neighbour Rona and had two little yellow handles either side, a red lid and the words 'Best Girl' written on the side. For some reason I had looked at it just a moment before it left the table and a little voice in my head said, *That's coming for you in a second*, but I had no more time to think about it because the next thing I knew it had hit me. It was heavy, full of juice, and it smashed hard across my face. Then Matt jumped up, grabbed the metal hoover pole, ripping it away from the black tubing where it attached to the vacuum, and started to beat me with it. I was in the armchair and now I brought my knees and arms up instinctively to protect my head. My hands covered my face and I had my eyes closed, scrunched up against the blows.

For a second I opened my eyes and I saw I was covered in blood. I screamed and Matt stopped whacking me. I had had a pair of scissors in my hand, and where he had smacked me with the pole my cheek was sliced open and now I was bleeding heavily. Matt put the hoover pole down on the floor and straight away I jumped up and grabbed hold of the back of Poppie's bouncy chair. *We have to get away*, I thought. So I pulled Poppie's chair behind me as I headed for the front door. *We have to escape.* But the front door was locked so I turned and ran upstairs to the bathroom, fearful that he would attack me again. I turned round to lock the door behind me but in that split second, Matt was right behind me, the anger on his face now replaced with concern.

'Come on, sweetheart. Come on … let's have a look,' he said. 'What's happened to you? What have you done?'

What's happened to *you*? What have *you* done? As if it had nothing to do with him! I was shaking and my whole head seemed to be pouring with blood. There was nothing else I could do in that moment so I stood there as he examined me.

'Hmmmm …' He held my face in his hands and he turned my cheek from side to side to get a better look. I could see dark blood stains all over my New Look navy maternity top.

'That cut …' he murmured. 'That's quite a big cut. We'll get you cleaned up in a minute. I'll just check on Poppie.'

He went back downstairs to move Poppie back in front of the telly, then he came back upstairs with a wet flannel and started wiping the blood off me. It was everywhere – I had blood on my crucifix necklace, all down my cleavage, my hands, arms, face, hair and all over my clothes. As he mopped me up, he looked me square in the eyes.

'It's quite bad actually,' he said quietly. I turned then to look in the mirror and he jerked my head back towards him.

'Why are you fucking moving your head away from me?' he snapped. 'I'm trying to help you.'

'I just want to look in the mirror. You said it was quite bad ...'

'Just let me fucking finish cleaning you up first.'

Once he was done, Matt urged me to sit on the sofa downstairs while he 'looked after' me, making me a cup of tea loaded with sugar and feeding me some orange Mr Kipling Halloween Fiendish Fancies. But no matter how much pressure I put on the wound it wouldn't stop bleeding. An hour later it was still seeping through the flannel and Matt said that considering I'd already given a pint of blood earlier in the day, I might need to be seen professionally.

He phoned his mum up: 'Hannah's had an accident. Can you come over and watch Poppie for a bit while we go to hospital?'

Half an hour later Lindsey arrived and asked what had happened. I looked at Matt.

'Hannah was out with Poppie in the pushchair, posting a letter, and somebody tried to mug her,' he said without missing a beat. 'Somebody tried to grab her handbag off her.'

'Oh, that's terrible,' she replied, though I could tell Lindsey didn't believe a word of it. She knew what Matt was like and was always too scared of him to say anything.

We were seen pretty quickly at A&E and the nurses glued my cheek back together. Now that I knew what I was supposed to say, I repeated Matt's lie to the nurse in the hospital.

'Somebody attacked me,' I said. 'I didn't see who it was.'

Matt called the police and repeated the lie that I had been attacked on the street by a stranger. The next day a policewoman came round to the house to take my statement. By this time Matt had created an elaborate back story, putting my ex-boyfriend in the frame by saying that the attacker had deliberately targeted me, shouting 'Stop telling lies about Dave' during the attempted mugging. It was a weird claim – nevertheless, I did exactly as I was told. It didn't cross my mind to tell the truth, not for a single second. I lied because I had been taught to lie. I knew that if I didn't I would be hurt, either physically or in some other way. Funnily enough, social services had taken us off the child protection plan only the month before, satisfied from all their observations that our daughter was no longer at risk. The regular visits from the social worker stopped, and pretty quickly Matt's behaviour changed.

The policewoman took photos of my face, promising to investigate thoroughly, though to my knowledge the case was put on file and nothing ever came of it. In a way I was glad there was no investigation. It would have been a waste of police time and resources. Matt did it. He knew it, I knew it, his mum knew it and quite possibly the policewoman knew it too. It was all an elaborate charade to cover up the horrible truth that my husband had beat me up, something I dared not even admit to myself, let alone anyone else.

Matt and I never spoke about that incident with the cup – it was all just forgotten, brushed under the carpet, like every other unpleasant outburst. I wanted to put it behind me and look to the future. Yes, I knew what he had done was wrong, and of course it crossed my mind to leave him, but I couldn't. I didn't want my daughter to grow up without a father. I never wanted to be a single mother like my own mum had been. I was convinced he would never harm our child – he loved Poppie – and by now we were trying for another baby. I say 'we' – Matt had decided we should have another child and I wasn't allowed to say *no* to sex. The first time he suggested it I felt like a tonne of bricks had just fallen down on my head.

'I don't know, Matt. I don't think it's the right time yet,' I stammered. 'I want to enjoy my time with Poppie for a while.'

'It'll be great. She'll need a brother or sister anyway. Don't you want my babies?'

'Yeah, course I do. You know I do.'

'You love babies anyway.'

'Yeah.'

'Well, that's decided then …'

I did love babies, it was true. And I desperately wanted another one, but I couldn't shake the feeling that I wasn't ready yet, that we weren't in the best of places. But Matt put his foot down. We were trying and that was that. *I suppose a lot can change in nine months …* I reasoned. *Things are bound to improve. He'll get better when he's back on his feet. He'll be happier once the business is up and running again, when we have our second child. I'll put up with this. It's fine. It's because he's depressed. Once he's working again he'll be happier. Everything will be better.*

That's what I told myself over and over again. I had hope. At times, it was all I had. I never thought for a moment that things would get worse.

6

An Unbroken Promise

Why didn't I tell someone?

That's the question I have been asked over and over – it's the question that I think most people struggle to understand when it comes to abusive relationships. Why the silence? After all, in the beginning I had my family and friends around, people who loved and cared about me. If I had told someone what was happening, shared my private suffering, then surely they could have helped. What stopped me from confiding in those closest to me? It's hard to explain – at first you don't tell anyone because you're ashamed. You have put all your love and trust in a person who it turns out has a nasty streak. It's shameful to admit that you made a mistake, you misjudged them. And, in the beginning, they manage to convince you that this is a one-off, that it won't happen again, that this is not 'them', this particular occurrence has happened because of a particular set of circumstances – the day, the time, the stress they're under. Only, it starts to happen more frequently.

By the time you realise it's not a one-off they have chipped away at your confidence and self-esteem so much that they have convinced you the reason for all the violence is *you*. Since I was so perpetually in the wrong Matt's behaviour towards me was always justified. Of course I deserved that smack – I had served him his tea wrong, I had spoken back to him, I had failed to iron a crease from his shirt, I hadn't washed up properly, I was slow to bring him his dinner … oh, the list was endless. And, after a while, the constant digging, niggling and nagging gets to you. Your confidence shattered, you start to believe that you deserve it too. You think that the only person to blame for their violence is you. And therefore only you can sort it out.

Once we had our daughter I could no longer see a way out. Matt had convinced me that if I let slip any clue as to his real behaviour behind closed doors, the authorities would step in and take away my child. He even threatened to make accusations against me.

'You fucking tell them anything, you do that and I'll fucking call social myself,' he'd snarl. 'I'll tell them you're a shit mum. I'll say that you abuse the kid and I'll make sure I get her taken off yer. You'll never see her again.'

So now I had to protect Matt in order to protect my child. I had to lie or I risked losing my little girl. By the time I fell pregnant naturally again, I still had hope that my life would improve, that Matt's unpleasant behaviour towards me would get better, and my faith in God gave me strength. If He was testing me, there was a reason, even if I didn't know what that reason was. I put my trust in Him because He knew where my path lay. So I said my prayers every night, reaching out to the Higher Power who could exercise any control over my life. And by now I had been so thoroughly isolated and cut off from friends and family that the idea of reaching out to them for help was beyond my thinking. Matt had stopped me getting credit on my phone, prevented me from using social media and wouldn't let my family visit unless by appointment. My relationships with my friends and bridesmaids had broken down. To them, I hadn't called, texted or stayed in touch so, in their eyes, I hadn't bothered. If I did contact them out of the blue, would they even believe me? Matt convinced me they wouldn't.

After the arcade burned down Keith had moved into our spare room, though we didn't actually see him that much. He was up and out of the house by 8am during the week, as he had a job in a plastics factory. In the evenings he'd park his van near the house, walk across to the bus stop and go to the local working men's club. And at the weekends he would sleep in until mid-morning, then go to the pub again. He paid us rent and sometimes late in the evening we would see him. He witnessed lots of Matt's outbursts against me but I knew he couldn't help me either. He was far too scared of Matt to do anything about it.

Perhaps his mother's reaction to our good news should have warned me of what was to come. It was Lindsey's birthday and we were throwing Lindsey a birthday tea at our house. Earlier that day we had been to the supermarket to buy some pavlova and tiramisu for the tea and while we were there Matt suggested we pick up a pregnancy test. When it came out positive, I had mixed feelings. While I felt blessed to be having another child, I was aware that my

situation was far from ideal. *Is it really the right time for a second child?* I loved the idea of having more children – I would have had a whole football team if I could – but I did worry that Matt was not himself yet, that he needed to get the business up and running so that things would go back to normal. The problem was that I wasn't in control of the timing – it was all out of my hands and when I even suggested using contraception, it was met with fury.

'I was brought up a Roman Catholic,' he'd erupt. 'My nan didn't believe in contraception and neither do I. You just don't want to have my baby, do you? Is that it? Do you not think that Poppie should have a baby brother or sister?'

So here we were!

We hadn't planned to tell anyone that day – after all, it was still very early on in the pregnancy – but when Lindsey offered me a slice of tiramisu Matt blurted it out: 'She can't eat that – she's pregnant.'

Lindsey threw me a quizzical look, as if to say, 'Are you joking?'

I grinned shyly and said: 'It's true. We're pregnant again!'

What was I expecting? Happiness, perhaps? Squeals of delight and warm hugs? After all, this would be another grandchild for Lindsey ... At the very least a heartfelt 'Congratulations!' But Lindsey couldn't hide her displeasure. She gave me a weak smile and nodded: 'Well, that's nice for you.' Then she turned away – couldn't bear to look me in the eye. It was an odd reaction and I looked at Matt, confused, but he just shrugged. He didn't care what his mother thought. But it bothered me. Later that night, I replayed the scene in my head. *Why? Why hadn't she been pleased for us? What was she really thinking?* A small, unwelcome answer swirled in the back of my mind, one that I really didn't want to face: *she doesn't want him to have any more children. His own mother! No, that can't possibly be true. It must be because of the timing – too soon after the last one and we are broke. Just bad timing. That must be it.*

But Matt's behaviour towards me seemed to worsen with every passing day. I was always up early with Poppie, giving her breakfast and playing with her in the mornings while Matt slept. Now I began to dread the signs that Matt was awake – the sound of the taps running in the bathroom upstairs, the gurgling of the water through the pipes, the slamming of the chest of drawers as he pulled out his underwear. My stomach would churn with dread the moment I heard his angry stomps across the floorboards overhead. And if he didn't have a freshly ironed pair of boxers, vest and shirt in his drawer that morning, I'd have to quickly nip up the stairs and put them in his drawer to avoid a beating. He wouldn't walk down the stairs to the pile of ironed clothes and get them himself! Then, once he was downstairs, it was my duty to hand him the perfect cup of tea. For that I wouldn't expect a hug or a kiss good morning, not even a smile. The best I could hope for was not to get a slap in the face or a sharp kick up the bum. And that was just the *start* of the day …

On the three days a week I worked Matt would be up by 11.30am to look after Poppie while I went to nursery. And on those mornings, he would make me a cup of tea. It wasn't out of kindness, it was another trap. I'd be racing round the house, getting my coat and bag together to leave and he'd saunter into the lounge with a wicked glint in his eye and two mugs of tea in his hands.

'Tea?' he'd enquire innocently. My eyes would flick up to the clock on the wall – 11.36am. I had to leave at 11.40am to be at nursery on time. He *knew* that. He *knew* I had to go!

'I can't, Matt …'

'I've just made you a cup of tea,' he'd growl menacingly. 'Are you not going to sit down and drink it with me?'

'I'm going to be late for work, Matt. You know I've got to leave to go to work.'

Then I'd dash out of the house, knowing that I'd left him in a foul mood. And for the rest of the day, instead of concentrating on my job, my mind would be turning over with anxiety about what I was going to come home to later that afternoon. Some mornings I couldn't face the worry so I'd down the boiling hot drink to shut him up and the rest of the week I'd have a sore throat from throwing scalding hot tea down it.

There was no intimacy between us anymore, certainly no love. Matt's view was that it was my wifely duty to satisfy him sexually, and that meant he could take sex any time he wanted. Whatever I was doing, whether I wanted to or not. I could be stood at the sink, doing the washing-up or walking up the stairs and he'd come up behind me, pull my trousers and knickers down and ram himself inside me. Then, when he was done, he'd zip himself back up and leave me there, with my trousers still crumpled around my ankles. This happened quite frequently. Of course, it usually meant I had to go to the toilet afterwards but one time I nipped up to the loo after he'd left me in the kitchen and he told me off for taking my eye off the food on the cooker. His semen was literally dripping out of me but I wasn't allowed go upstairs to wipe myself!

By Poppie's second birthday I was used to a daily diet of physical assault and verbal abuse. It was constant, though Matt was careful not to leave his mark on me. Occasionally he would give me a black eye but more often than not the attacks came to the parts of my body that were hidden – my head, arms and legs. One Sunday, at the end of the month, I was doing some ironing when Matt came in from the garden. I could tell, just from the way he moved, that he was unhappy.

'That shirt's still got creases in it!' he snapped, nodding at a blue polo shirt hanging up.

'It's fine ...' I started.

'It's not fine, it's a fucking mess!' And he grabbed the iron and lifted it above me. I froze, bracing myself ... *something's coming, I can feel it.*

Matt came right up beside me and, very slowly and deliberately, he pushed the scalding iron into the side of my arm. I could hear it sizzle as it started to burn my flesh but I didn't react. I didn't scream or push him away. By now I'd learned that the safest thing to do was just take it. Had I moved, he might have thrown the iron at me and what if our daughter came toddling into the room just as he did that? I couldn't risk Poppie getting hurt. So I just let him hold that red-hot iron against me as it burned through my skin. He didn't say a word. He just stood there, silently, and after he was done he threw the iron down and walked back out into the garden.

As soon as he was gone, I breathed out hard as the pain raged around my body. Later that day, after I'd made lunch, I put some burn gel on the wound. I didn't go to hospital – I didn't want to attract unwelcome questions. And anyway

Matt would never have let me. I just tried to clean the wound and treat the burn at home. My main concern was getting an infection because I was carrying a baby. Two days later I was about to leave the house to go to my job when Matt insisted I put a cardigan on.

'Why? It's hot,' I replied. The summer heat was unbearable at this time of year and it never crossed my mind to put on a jumper over my light summer top. But Matt wasn't thinking about my comfort – he had something else on his mind.

'You're not going to put a cardigan on?' he repeated.

'It's hot,' I replied, confused. By now I was carrying a seven-month bump and, with the increase in my circulation, I felt hotter than most people.

'YOU WILL PUT A FUCKING CARDIGAN ON.' And with that he threw my dark salmon cardigan at me. I shrugged it on and, as I left, he slapped the back of my arm at the exact spot where he'd burned me. *Fuck!* It stung like hell. *Ah, now I understand – Matt's covering his tracks as well as my arms.*

Matt was generally quite effective at concealing his violence towards me – the only thing he hadn't reckoned on were the next-door neighbours. They were a young Danish couple who ran a tutoring service. We didn't have much to do with them because they kept themselves to themselves. However, one evening before my second child was born, one of the mums who used their service came to pick up her daughter. She pulled up on the drive next to our car but instead of getting out and ringing the doorbell as most of the other parents did, the woman beeped her horn. This riled Matt – he jumped off the sofa and stormed outside.

'Oi! Madam! You're beeping your horn after 7pm at night …' he yelled. I hovered in the hallway behind him, thinking I needed to be on standby in case he was going to do something. He saw me there.

''Ere, sweetheart, come out here.' He motioned to me. I waddled out onto the driveway, now nearly eight months pregnant, and he put a protective arm around my shoulder.

'My wife here is pregnant,' he said. 'She needs her rest and there you are, beeping your bloody horn, disturbing her, putting her nerves on edge. It's a bloody disgrace. Tell them! Tell them, sweetheart, you're tired, you're pregnant.'

I knew the drill. Straight away, I repeated every word that he'd just said. By now the wife next door was out on her doorstep too and Matt was working himself up to a real lather, haranguing her, giving her a good piece of his mind.

The wife scoffed: 'You moan about us making noise? Every day we hear you beating your wife. Every day!'

Oh my God, they know! They know! My cheeks flushed. A million things ran through my mind at once. *Thank God someone knows.* And – *fuck! I hope they don't do anything about it. What if they do? Will they help?*

'WHAT? What is she talking about? How dare she make ridiculous insinuations!' Matt blustered.

At that moment Matt nudged me in the ribs.

'I don't know what you're talking about.' I picked up my cue.

'Do I beat you?' Matt asked me.

'No!' I scoffed.

'How dare you make up outrageous lies about us!' he shouted back. 'How dare you! You can make up lies all you like but nothing will excuse your appalling, thoughtless behaviour today.'

And with that he ushered me inside and slammed the door behind us.

My life had become a constant lie. Matt didn't even need to feed me the lines, I lied automatically to cover for him because I knew what would happen if I didn't. So now we knew that our neighbours knew, though Matt didn't seem too concerned. After all, if they'd known all this time and hadn't done anything, why would they suddenly go to the authorities now? I thought that he was probably right, but still, I held out a little bit of hope. I could never tell the truth about Matt myself so the only possible way of escaping the marriage would be if someone else gave evidence to the authorities against Matt. Not me, never me. He had made it clear that if I ever dared speak out against him, I risked losing everything, including my life. Matt went on as usual, unconcerned, but from that point onwards, whenever he physically assaulted me, he told me not to shout out his name. Just in case they were listening.

A few weeks later I was stood at the sink again and about to serve up a steak I had just cooked, when Matt walked into the kitchen, took one look at the steak I was just about to serve him and spat at me: 'What the fuck do you call this?'

Before I had a chance to reply, he threw the pan into the sink, then he reached over and grabbed a screwdriver and a small sharp knife from the windowsill. Leaning down, he jabbed the screwdriver into the back of my knees – *jab jab jab jab jab jab*. The screwdriver pierced the soft flesh in the back of my legs but I didn't react. I just held myself perfectly still. After he'd finished with the screwdriver, he threw it onto the kitchen counter, *clunk*, like the sound of a conker hitting the work surface. Then with the knife he did the same thing. *Stab stab stab stab stab* … once again I just stood there, holding myself still. All the while he swore and muttered behind me about what a fucking stupid waste of space I was. I didn't move, I didn't say a word – I knew that if I did anything at all it would just inflame him further and I would probably end up with worse injuries.

Come on, hurry up and get this over and done with … you're hurting me. What a waste of a good steak … again! You didn't even bother to try it. The steak was perfect but, no, you have to throw it away just to make a point … now hurry up because the baby's wriggling from all the shouting. And hurry up cos now I know I need to do you another dinner, which you're going to moan about all over again. Please just hurry up, get this over with and stop shouting at me … Eventually he stopped and left the room. I didn't even bother to look at the damage until later that evening when I saw dozens of tiny blue bruises dotted across the backs of my knees, and several blood stains where the skin had been broken. It hadn't gone in deep, just enough to pierce the skin, and anyway, no one would ever see these as long as I wore trousers or my leggings.

That night I went through the motions of feeding Poppie, giving her a bath and putting her to bed. But after I'd read her a story and tucked her in, I crept through to the bedroom and quietly shut the door behind me. Matt was downstairs on the sofa with his feet up, half watching the telly, half playing on his laptop. Now I sat down on the edge of my bed. Alone with my thoughts for the first time that day, I let the emotions wash over me. My head bowed, I stared forlornly at the floor. *What has my life come to? What have I done to deserve this? God, please tell me what I've done to deserve all this pain …* Now all those tears I had held back came welling up from deep inside me and I started to weep. I cried silently, my whole body and my large bump shaking with emotion. Then I lifted my head up and stared at the chest of drawers straight ahead of me. *Hannah, you've got to stop all this crying. It's no good. It's not going to help you. Can't you see? It won't make any difference … It's the only thing you have left so don't you dare let him see you cry.*

From that point forward I made a pact with myself that I would never let him see me cry again. It might wind him up but it was the one way I could protect myself. I just wouldn't let him get to me anymore. I had a baby living off my blood supply and that little life inside me could feel it when I was upset. My daughter could see it too. So I wouldn't let it in anymore. I wouldn't let myself feel unhappy or cry. *I refuse to pass that misery on to my children.* From now on all I had to focus on was getting through the day – whatever he did to me, I would be strong. He would never see my pain.

7

A Quick Blessing … Katie and the Potatoes

'Here's another mouthful!' I lifted up the blue plastic spoon topped with blended broccoli and mashed potato in front of Poppie and 'zoomed' it into her open mouth, as if flying a little aeroplane. At that moment a horrible pain engulfed me. *Oh my God!* It was a contraction but not like I remembered from the first time. This was far worse than anything I'd ever felt before. The pain was so bad I thought I was going to vomit right then and there. My hand instinctively flew to my belly. *Breathe, Hannah, just breathe.*

It was 8.30pm and the day before my second daughter's due date – we knew she was going to be a girl and I was thrilled to be having two daughters. Until this moment I had been happily spoon-feeding Poppie at her chair and table. She was now two years and two months old and had taken to puréed food like a duck to water, eagerly hoovering up all the new foods I was introducing to her diet. At this age she was such a lovely, caring little girl, full of cuddles and kisses for me. She would sit on my lap and talk to my bump. Her words and numbers were advanced and she loved Mickey Mouse and Handy Manny. Her favourite colour was yellow and she had tonnes of energy, shooting around the block on her Handy Manny bike for hours at a time. She was as happy in her own company at home, reading books or playing with her tool box all day long.

Funnily enough, I'd only stopped breastfeeding her a couple of weeks earlier on the advice of the midwife. She had said that in order for the new baby to get the early milk – the colostrum – I had to stop feeding Poppie first. It had been a bit of a wrench. I loved breastfeeding my little girl. It made me feel so close to her and even though I was now weaning her onto solid food, she still got lots of nutrients from my milk. Now *Top Gear* blared in the corner of the room and I closed my eyes and breathed hard against the pain. *Just keep going*, I thought to myself, *you've still got a long way to go so let's just keep going*. I finished spoon-feeding Poppie and, 20 minutes after that initial pain passed, I had my second contraction.

Now I cleared up the dinner plates, wiped the high chair and took her upstairs for her bedtime routine. First I gave her a bath and washed her curly blonde hair, then I got her out, dried her off and gave her her Johnson's Baby Cream. All the while I was still smiling and singing to my little girl but every 15 minutes or so I had to stop, stand up and sway my hips to relieve the pain. *God, this was far worse than before*. I pulled on her pyjamas, gave her her water in a beaker, tucked her up into bed, read her a story and kissed her goodnight. By the time I tiptoed out of her room, the contractions were coming every 10 minutes. Matt was in our bedroom, sorting out the Moses basket and putting the sheets on the mattress. I hadn't said anything to him yet. I was too frightened.

I stood on the landing, my hands on my hips, swaying from side to side. Matt suddenly appeared in the doorway and instinctively I stopped swaying. I couldn't tell him. I just couldn't. I was too frightened of his reaction. If I gave away any sign that I was in pain, I knew he would have a go at me, telling me off for 'making a fuss', so I didn't say anything. I just bore it in silence. I felt the need to pee so I went to the toilet and shut the door. It was a relief to be able to give in to the pain on my own so I sat on the toilet for some time. Maybe I was there a long time or maybe he heard me breathing hard because after a little while I heard Matt on the other side of the door: 'Are you alright in there?'

'Yeah.'

Silence.

'Are you sure?'

Another contraction. 'Urgh ... no.'

'Are you in labour?'

'Yeah, I think so.'

Eventually I waddled out of the toilet, grimacing and holding my sides in agony. It was getting late now and I guessed it was probably time to go to hospital.

'You need to call Mum and ask her to come over,' Matt said. He didn't mean *my* mum, he meant *his* mum. I knew there was no way in hell he would let my mum come over to watch our daughter – he always had issues with her and it would have created an argument. Besides, my mum still had my little brother at home with her.

'She won't hear it from me,' he said. 'You need to call her.'

I sighed. Lindsey hadn't been round our house in three weeks and for very good reason – the last time we had seen her, Matt had pushed her over and broken her arm. I'd seen it with my own eyes. It was a warm day in early autumn and I'd been out in the garden at our house, playing with Poppie. She and Matt had been arguing about something and she wanted it to end but Matt, still haranguing her, shoved her to the kitchen floor. She came down with a solid thud onto her right arm. I heard a gentle crack, almost like a twig breaking. She scrambled to get up, holding her limp arm with the other hand, then hobbled out of the back door. Matt's cousin Sherie and her friend drove Lindsey to the hospital after we went home. We hadn't heard from Lindsey since.

The contractions were coming every five minutes now so I knew there was no time to waste. I phoned Lindsey from the bedroom and begged her to come to watch Poppie for us. With one hand leaning heavily against the chest of drawers and the other pushing the phone tight against my face, I begged and begged.

'Please … please, Lindsey. For me …' I stopped as I felt another contraction overwhelm me.

'Umm … Ahh … I don't know …' She was frightened. I could tell she was frightened of him but I didn't have any choice, I kept begging, reminding her that Matt wouldn't be at home as he would be with me. And eventually she relented: 'Yeah, okay, I'll come over. For you. I can hear the contractions are pretty close together. Just give me 10 minutes to get my bag together and put my shoes on …'

'Oh thank you. Thank you so much, Lindsey.'

By the time she arrived I'd managed to ease myself down the stairs and now I gave her instructions on what to do if Poppie woke up.

'And if we're not back in the morning … phew … she'll have porridge and sultanas for breakfast.' Lindsey nodded and at that point Matt trotted down the stairs behind me, pulled on his trainers and marched out of the front door, shouting: 'Come on then! Let's go!'

I looked at my flip-flops down on the floor and I was in so much pain I realised there was no way I could even bend down to put them on.

'Can someone help me get my shoes on?' I asked in a small voice.

Lindsey bent down and moved the shoes in front of me so I could slip my feet into them. Then it was a mammoth task just to get out of the front door and to the car door. It can't have been more than 12 feet but even in that short distance I had to stop twice for the contractions. Then I clung heavily to the top of the car door as I tried to lower myself gently into the passenger seat.

'Come on …' Matt sighed. 'Just get in there.'

'Hang on, I've got another one coming!'

Finally, I was safely inside the car and off we sped for the longest drive of my life. We left the house just after midnight for the 40-minute journey to the same hospital where I had had Poppie. But I was in so much pain I had to lift myself off the seat again, the same as last time, by wrapping both arms up on the headrest behind me and pulling myself up. It felt like the baby's head was coming out.

'Oh please! Hurry … HURRY!' I screamed. *Was he driving at 10 miles an hour? We'll never make it on time at this rate!*

'I can't go any faster!' he shouted.

Then, ten minutes before we arrived, I knew I couldn't hold on any longer. We were about to go round a roundabout when I asked Matt to stop.

'You're going to have to pull over,' I puffed. 'This baby's coming ...'

'NO, you can't fucking do that. Hold on!'

'I'm trying. I'M TRYING!'

Somehow I clung on and we pulled up at the front of the hospital but now it was so late at night the whole place was dark. Matt dropped me off at the main doors, instructing me to go in while he parked the car, but when I got to the front doors, they refused to open. Inside, I could see the lights were on but the doors remained stubbornly shut. *Oh my God, what do I do now?* I kept walking towards the sliding doors, hoping they would automatically spring to life but nothing happened. Out of the darkness, a nurse on a fag break stepped forward.

'You alright, love?'

'I'm in labour ...' I managed to gasp.

'You're in the wrong place. You need to go to A&E. It's down there on the left ...' and she pointed into the darkness. *Where was Matt? Jesus! I can't walk off into the darkness on my own.*

'Here, I'll walk you round,' she said, sensing my distress. And as she stubbed out her cigarette on the ground she took my arm and we started to walk together. I've never felt so grateful for the touch of another human being in all my life.

'Thank you ... Thank you ...' I whispered.

We walked slowly because now, every ten seconds, I had to stop for another contraction. Matt had parked the car and caught up with us so now I had one on either side.

'Jesus,' the nurse exclaimed, 'you should have been here hours ago.'

We made it to the front doors of A&E and the nurse said: 'You'll be alright from here. I need to get back to my shift.'

We thanked her and Matt approached the receptionist for a wheelchair. I could barely take another step.

'Just walk a bit further and we'll grab you a wheelchair and take you up,' said the lady in her fifties. At this point I'd just gone over the threshold of the automatic doors of A&E and I was flooded with relief: *You're safe now, you're in the grounds of a hospital, you can relax.* At that moment I had another contraction and my waters broke.

Matt was up ahead with the receptionist, grabbing a wheelchair, when I felt the warm gush of my waters spreading down my light-blue jeans and onto the floor. He span around and saw my waters had gone, then he grabbed the wheelchair and headed back to pick me up. I tried to ease myself down onto the seat but the head was coming out so I put my hands on the handlebars to hold myself up.

'Down the end of the corridor, turn right, there's a lift. Take it up to the third floor …' instructed the receptionist, then she returned to her desk.

We headed down the empty, half-lit corridor and eventually, after a couple of wrong turns, we found the lift. He pressed the button and the doors immediately pinged open but as he was dragging me backwards into the lift and the doors were just about to close behind us I felt the head coming out.

'OH, HELP! HELP!' I screamed.

'Be quiet!' Matt snapped.

'Don't go in the lift. PLEASE! PLEASE DON'T GO IN THE LIFT, MATT. I MEAN IT – DO NOT GO IN THE LIFT!'

And for once, Matt listened to me. It was so close, only my feet were hanging out as the lift doors nearly shut on me. Now Matt pushed me forwards, back into the corridor, just as a smart Asian doctor in glasses and a white shirt came past.

'The head's coming out!' I yelled and the doctor ran towards us.

'Okay, let's get her on the floor,' the doctor said to Matt and they each took a leg and started pulling me, but as they did that the wheelchair rolled too. They were just pulling me along the corridor. If it hadn't been so serious it would have been comic.

'Can you please just take my fucking arms as well?' I exploded. So they took an arm and leg each and got me on the floor. Now I looked up at the doctor: 'Can I push?'

'Yes.'

And that was it – one push and her head came out into my trousers. I stared up at the ceiling tiles, which now seemed very far away from where I was lying on the floor.

'Can you get my trousers off me!' I yelled up at them both and the doctor ripped off my amniotic-fluid-soaked trousers and my great big granny knickers. I turned my head to one side. Curiously, one of my shoes had ended up halfway down the corridor while the other was by my elbow. As soon as my clothes were off, I said to the doctor: 'Can I push the rest of her out now?'

'Yes.'

So I gave one more push and she was there! My second daughter was born outside lift no. 2 on the ground floor of the hospital.

It had been instant and effortless. I had barely pushed at all. She just slid out and the doctor immediately picked her up and, just like with her sister, she didn't cry at first. Matt was panicked – he was pacing up and down from left to right above my head, with his hands tucked into his jeans. But then the doctor gave my daughter a big whack on the back and she started to cry. Then he passed her to me. I lifted the frilly hem of my khaki top and shoved her under. Now I peeked down at my baby for the first time – and she was so cute, even though she was all slimy and covered in white greasy stuff. Thirty seconds later we heard what sounded like a heard of elephants coming down the stairs next to the lift: *boom boom boom boom boom*.

Around five midwives were galloping down the stairs towards us. One of them, her name was Stacey I later found out, exclaimed: 'Oh, we missed it! We tried to get here but you are super-duper quick.'

I lay there, in a complete mess, holding my daughter close to my chest, as they all started to move around me. Down the corridor I noticed an elderly pot-bellied janitor, ambling along, mop in his hand, pushing a little rubbish trolley. He looked just as surprised to see me there on the floor.

'Can we get some screens, please?' one of the midwives shouted at the receptionist.

By now it was around 1am, we didn't have an exact time of birth because no one was there to record it accurately. I lay there, in that puddle of blood, gunk and waters, as Matt cut the cord, right there outside the lift. Then somebody took the baby off me and wrapped her up while I was helped up and eased into a wheelchair. I thanked the Asian doctor who had stopped to deliver my daughter and then, finally, I did actually get in the lift, leaving the poor, shocked, elderly janitor to clear up the mess behind us. *Thank you, God! Thank you for letting me out of this lift ten minutes earlier or I would almost certainly have had my baby in there.*

Once again, I had to stay in hospital for four days as I needed intravenous antibiotics for the GBS but I enjoyed spending that special time bonding with and breastfeeding my baby. We named her Katie and she was just as perfect as our first daughter. I was besotted once more and I loved holding her in my arms as she fed and slept. It was only in the early-morning hours when the ward was quiet and peaceful that I allowed the small fears to creep into my head about what was going on at home: Would Matt get up in time to give Poppie her breakfast? Would he play with her? Would he shout and swear around her? I never thought Matt would hurt our little girl but Matt rarely thought about anyone's needs but his own and I worried that Poppie would miss me.

It was late afternoon and dark on the following Wednesday when Matt brought me home with our new baby. And since Katie had fallen asleep in the car, I decided I would take the opportunity to jump in the shower. So I took Katie upstairs, fast asleep in her car seat still, undressed and got in the shower. Matt had prepared a casserole earlier that day and once I was in the shower, he shouted up the stairs at me – something about potatoes … something about going out to the shop. But the shower was too loud and I couldn't hear him properly. *What was it he said?* The question went round and round in my head. *Was it a trap? What was I meant to do?* Now I panicked and my heart beat hard in my chest. It felt like I was about to have a heart attack. I got out of the shower, still covered in soap, grabbed a towel, blood running down my ankles, and rushed downstairs to the kitchen. By now Matt had left with Poppie. *Why? Perhaps he was going to the shop to buy potatoes?* In the kitchen I found there were potatoes in a saucepan. The hob was off so he couldn't have been asking me to turn it off. *Perhaps he was asking me to turn them on? Was I supposed to boil them again? Drain them? Put them with something?* My body felt ice-cold with fear, my heart nearly pounded out of my chest. If he returned any minute and I hadn't done what he'd said because I didn't hear him, what would he do? I touched the water in the saucepan – it was warm and the potatoes were cooked. Fuck, fuck, fuck … *What to do? What to do? What to do?*

I was dreading his return but I went upstairs and finished my shower, certain that I'd failed to carry out this unknown task about the potatoes. I was a wreck, a complete bundle of nerves, petrified of his reaction. But ten minutes later he swanned back in and carried on his business in the kitchen without another word. It took a good hour for me to calm down and realise there was nothing wrong. Everything seemed to be fine and gradually the panic subsided. To this day I don't know what he said about the bloody potatoes but I'll never forget the fear that engulfed me that afternoon …

8

Everything Hurts and Nothing Changes

I had become a 'Matt expert', watching his every move, every flick of the eye, every inflection in his voice to try to anticipate what he wanted and what his next move might be. I had to be constantly on my guard to try to please him and prevent another attack. It didn't always work. There were times I never saw it coming. When Katie was about ten days old I was sitting on the armchair, feeding her in my arms, supervising Poppie's breakfast, when Matt and I started discussing the merits of various different breakfast choices. Personally, I wasn't a big fan of porridge but Matt had always liked his porridge.

'It's got everything you need to start the day,' he'd explained. 'And you just add a few sultanas and it's nice and sweet.'

'Yeah, but porridge doesn't really fill you up, does it?' I returned, innocently enough, I thought. I was still in my pyjamas at this point – a little navy-and-white short set bought from a catalogue. Matt jumped up, enraged, grabbed the metal spoon off the table and dug the stainless steel handle down hard on my thighs, just above my knees. He did this a couple of times on each leg, so hard and quickly he broke the skin. I didn't react. I had our ten-day-old daughter in my arms so I couldn't afford to jump up. I just sat there, silent, as the pain in my legs spread throughout my body. Matt simply carried on talking normally afterwards, acting as if nothing had happened.

Two days later we were upstairs in the bedroom, Poppie playing in her room next door. I'd just finished putting Katie down after a feed, and I noticed that Matt was watching me closely. *What's he looking at?* I wondered, as his eyes darted down my body. Is he going to attack me? Is there a weapon he's going to use? I was wearing another pair of pyjama shorts and now I saw that he was eyeing the marks he had made a couple of days earlier on my thighs. By now the skin was bruised and the dead skin had wrinkled up on one side of each bruise and he had a lustful look in his eye. *He wants you, Hannah. He is going to have sex with you. Whatever happens, whatever you say or do, he's going to have sex with you so just go with it.* My stomach heaved. I felt sick.

I didn't want to have sex. I was still bleeding from the birth and sore down there. I felt protective about my body – it had just gone through a huge trauma and I was trying my best to care for our new-born baby, not even two weeks old at this point, and also look after our two-year-old at the same time. There was only so much I could take. But what Matt wanted, Matt got. Now he patted the duvet next to him and told me to come and sit down. I moved slowly towards him and placed myself tenderly on the duvet beside him. Even sitting down was painful. I kept my eyes down, just fixed on the sheets. We had bought these sheets with some wedding money and I loved them. The dark-purple silky bedcover had burgundy embroidered roses in each corner, matching pillow cases and a chocolate-brown bottom sheet underneath. I tried to focus on those pretty red roses now as Matt yanked down my shorts and rammed himself inside me. For a moment, I resisted. *Just go with it*, I told myself. *There's no point holding back*. I knew in my mind it was always easier if I let it happen, but instinctively my body recoiled. Every fibre of my being screamed out to push him off me and run out of the room. I had a big dry lump in the back of my throat and inside I cried until it was over. After he was finished, he left the room and I allowed myself a few tears. I was so fragile, so fresh from the birth, but Matt's needs came first. Always. There was another occasion on the bed when Matt sensed my resistance and whacked me hard across the face – hard enough to split my lip open. I gave up and turned my head to one side, letting my lip bleed onto the pillow while he satisfied himself. A few days later, when I went to change the covers I noticed the blood from my lip had soaked right through to the pillow underneath. And that dark-brown stain was there, as a constant reminder, every time I changed the sheets.

All I wanted was to care for my infant child, to look after her and feed her the way my body was meant to – but Matt made that hard for me. For one thing, he was constantly putting me down about my post-baby body.

'Why can't you be slim and skinny like all these other fucking horn bitches?' he'd say to me. 'Horn bitches' was his name for the women on porn sites. 'There's plenty of women I know that have had kids,' he went on. 'They're stomachs ain't fat like that. Where's your fucking abs?

Where's your six pack? Look at you! Why are your tits so saggy? Look, your nipples hang down to your belly button. Disgusting, fat bitch!'

I wanted to scream back at him – I'VE JUST HAD A BABY! Maybe he'd like to try carrying a child in his stomach for nine months and see if his skin snapped back immediately afterwards. In my head I could enjoy the last word in these two-way arguments but in reality I didn't talk back to Matt. There was no point defending myself, it only made things worse, so my comebacks stayed firmly in my head. *At least he has no power over my thoughts. He can throw whatever hurtful comments he likes my way but he can't control the insults I hurl back in my head.*

There were times I could withstand the verbal abuse, when I felt mentally strong enough to look him squarely in the eyes and tell him to 'Fuck off' inside my head. But not always. There were plenty of times he'd go on and on and on – and it ground me down. Yes, I was fat, yes, I was flabby in ways I'd never been before. How could I help it? I was a young mother. He knew how much I wanted children and how much I wanted to be a good mother. Was it jealousy? Did he rage against my baby body because it stopped him being the centre of my world? My body became yet another weapon, another way for him to degrade and humiliate me, a way to make me feel awful over my precious children, the two things I loved and wanted the most in the world.

A few weeks after Katie's birth, I was hoovering the downstairs hallway when the doorbell rang. Matt was still upstairs in bed. I saw the outline of the Hermes lady through the glass panels in the front door so I turned off the hoover, opened the front door and signed for the parcel delivery. It was a soft package from Debenhams. But within seconds of shutting the door, I heard his heavy footsteps pounding down the stairs and suddenly Matt appeared, wrapping his dressing gown around him. He looked angry.

'Who was that?' he snapped.

Uh oh … here we go …

'Parcel for you,' I replied and nodded at the soft plastic parcel now resting on the sofa in the living room.

'And how do you know it was for me?'

'Because it has your name on it.'

'So did you open the door then?'

'Yes.'

'Did you sign yourself for the parcel?'

'For the parcel …?'

'OI, FAT COW! Yes or no? Simple fucking answer.'

'Yes.'

'Why did you sign for that parcel, you fucking whore?'

'I … erm … well …'

'Hey! I'm talking to you – why did you sign for that parcel?'

'Because …'

'NO! WHY DID YOU SIGN FOR THAT FUCKING PARCEL?'

I didn't know what to say anymore. What was I meant to do? What was I meant to say? He stared at me, venomously, still waiting for an answer. I tried reasoning it through.

'The lady rang the doorbell. I was just here, in the hallway, hoovering. She must have seen me in the hallway. I wasn't going to pretend I wasn't here so I opened the door.'

'Exactly! That is exactly the point!' He was furious now. 'You were just here in the hallway. She must have seen you.

So if you hadn't answered, she would definitely have left the parcel on the doorstep ...'

'Yes ...' I was confused. *Where is he going with this?*

'Left it there, without getting a signature ... and then we could claim it never arrived and get our fucking money back.'

Oh, I understood now. It was a scam. He wanted the parcel AND a refund ... But I wasn't a bloody mind reader. The doorbell rang, and, as any sane, normal person would do, I opened the door.

'But how was I to know ...?' I started.

'YOU FUCKING MORON. NOW, THANKS TO YOUR STUPIDITY, I'M GOING TO HAVE TO FUCKING PAY FOR THEM ...'

Matt grabbed hold of my hair, at the very base by the scalp, and as he threw me across to the other side of the hallway, I heard the sound of my hair being ripped out at the roots. It was like the sound of a plant root being ripped out of the soil – right next to my ears. I fell back against the door of the hallway cupboard. He picked me up again by my clothes and the fat on the back of my arm and threw me back the other way. I landed with a hard thump but there was no time to catch my breath as he punched me hard in the head. Then he grabbed and threw me again. And again. And again. And again. He grabbed anything he could get his hands on – my stomach skin, my hair, clothes. He just dug his nails in and flung me around the hallway as if I was a rag doll.

He only stopped to hit me and the blows landed on the side of my head, my stomach and my face. All the while he was shouting and screaming at me but I couldn't hear the words. All I could hear was the smack of my own body as it hit the walls and my own screams and shouts. Then he grabbed me by the neck and squeezed both hands together hard so I couldn't breathe. I was just on the point of losing consciousness when he yanked me to one side and then he picked me up by my arm and hair and tossed me hard again against the cupboard under our stairs. I started to fall and now I didn't stop. I hit the door so hard, the bolt broke and I went straight through the door and into the cupboard.

Where am I? For a moment I couldn't get my bearings. I'd been hurled about so much I didn't even know which way was up and now I was in a strange, dark place. I was panting, breathing hard, trying to catch my breath ... Then I saw Keith's bed. *Bloody hell – I've gone through the cupboard.* When he first came to live with us, Keith had a room to himself but once we knew we had another baby on the way, Matt fitted out the cupboard under the stairs with a bed, wardrobe, bedside table and shelves, so now Keith slept here. As I lay there, half in and out of the cupboard, dazed and gasping for breath, Matt came up in front of me, the metal pole of the hoover in his arms and started to beat me with it. Automatically, I put my hands out to try and cushion the blows but they rained down over me again and again until I was beaten black and blue.

Maybe it lasted five minutes, maybe ten, I couldn't tell, but when he'd finally exhausted his anger and thrown away the pole, I crawled upstairs to the bedroom and collapsed on the bed. The kids were in the living room so they hadn't seen what he had done, thank God. But now I was so battered I could barely move. It took all my energy just to get through the day, looking after Poppie and caring for Katie. Everything hurt. *Everything.* My cheekbones had been struck so much it felt like they were going to burst out of my face. Weeks later, even after the bruises had faded, my cheekbones were still sore to the touch. This time, Matt hadn't held back. He hadn't been careful at all and both my eyes were black and swollen with bruising. The next day my mum called up. Could she come over to spend some time with me and the baby? My heart sank. I knew I couldn't see my mum now for at least a month. I asked her which day she was thinking of, stalling for time. Time enough to think up an excuse.

'Next Saturday, perhaps?'

'Oh sorry. I can't make it Saturday, Mum,' I said. 'We've got an arrangement.'

'Oh, that's a shame,' she said. 'Well, when can I come, then?'

'Urm ... it's tricky. We're a bit busy trying to sort out new premises over the next few weeks. Why don't I call you back when things are a bit less hectic here?'

'All right,' said Mum. 'But don't make it too long.'

I couldn't let my mum see me like this. My face was a mess. She had only seen me with a black eye once before and that had been a mistake on my part. I was usually careful to cover up any visible bruises with make-up, but on this occasion the bruise was old and fading, and because I'd been busy with Poppie all day, I had forgotten to put on my foundation.

'Oh, no,' she pointed at the bruise around my left eye. 'What happened to you?'

Damn! I forgot about that. My hand flew up to my eye, my mind racing.

'Oh that? Poppie threw a Lego brick across the room

and it hit me,' I told her with a smile. 'Wrong place, wrong time ...'

Mum had bought it – she wasn't a suspicious person by nature so the lie seemed totally believable. Now I used what felt like a legitimate excuse to put her off – the developments in our new business venture.

While I was still pregnant with Katie, Matt had found us new premises to restart the business. He had seen a warehouse unit at an industrial estate on the outskirts of town and the lease was both long and cheap.

'We'll start the arcade business up again from there,' he said. 'But this time, it'll be in your name. We'll soon be on our feet again.'

Matt had been declared bankrupt recently – I didn't have all the ins and outs of course but I assumed the bankruptcy wiped out his debts from the old business. The downside was that he wasn't allowed to sign a lease or take out any loans so it all had to be in my name. I didn't mind – I was just relieved that Matt was planning to restart the arcade business again. It was a positive step.

Shortly after Katie's birth, Matt took me along to our new business rental. It was just a ten-minute drive from our house and a big space – there was both an upstairs and a downstairs, plenty of room for the machines, with high ceilings and navy floor tiles. But first we needed to put down some money to pay for the initial lease. For this, Matt insisted we take out a loan in his mum's name, making me ring up the bank pretending to be her. He said that once the business was paying out we'd clear the loans and she would never even notice. Still, I didn't like it and I didn't want to put Lindsey in that position.

'No, Matt, I'm not doing that,' I said.

'Yes you fucking are … or else!'

I didn't want to know what the 'or else' was so I went ahead and made the calls to Halifax as Matt directed. It was all done on the phone, my answers scripted by Matt. There were two separate loans – one for £20,000 and another one a week later for £10,000. He recorded every conversation to make sure I said all the right things. And, as he explained later, for evidence that it was me who committed the fraud, should I ever consider leaving him or going to the police.

'Don't even think about it, sweetheart,' he said, laughing. 'You're in it up to your fucking eyeballs and I've got the evidence now to prove it. Ten years for fraud – that's the maximum prison sentence. Ten fucking years! You'll never see these kids growing up.' And there it was – another knot in the noose around my neck that kept me tied to Matt's side. He had the evidence to prove I had committed a serious crime. Who would even believe me if I told them he made me do it? Was that even a defence? I didn't know. I didn't want to find out.

Matt created a limited company, listed me as the managing director, and then marched me into Lloyds TSB to open a business account for the company. Three months after Katie was born, we signed the lease on the property, which meant we could now start redecorating. Previously, it had been the offices for a radio station so we started by ripping out all the soundproofing from downstairs, and clearing up the upstairs offices. Then we advertised to rent out some of the space while we got our business up and running. We rented one office upstairs to an arts foundation for £500 a month.

Meanwhile, the loans paid for five second-hand arcade machines. Matt insisted that I be the one to hand over the cash to the man and woman selling them. Then we hired a pallet forklift truck to move the machines into the downstairs of our new business premises. I imagined that more machines would soon follow, and then we would fit the place out properly to create a new arcade. After that we could start to advertise the business and recoup our investment. But the machines sat there for a few days and then a few more. Matt never talked about the next stage of the plan so two weeks after we bought the machines, I asked him: 'Matt, what's going on with the arcade? What are we doing?'

'I'll do things when I'm good and ready,' he snarled. 'Don't fucking question me.'

So I left it at that. But two weeks later the machines were still sitting there and no word was spoken about them so I asked him again what we were doing. Still no response. I was confused. We needed to start earning back some money or we would soon run out of cash again. If Matt had a plan for restarting the arcade business he certainly didn't seem in a hurry to put it into practice. Little did I know, Matt had a different plan for the business premises. And it had nothing to do with arcade machines …

9

A Life of Maybes

I stared into the face of my little girl as she fed contentedly from my left breast. Lying on the bed together, side by side, I watched as her squidgy baby cheeks puffed in and out. I listened as she swallowed rhythmically, small gulps at regular intervals, her tiny little eyes closed, shut tight in concentration. She was so close I could count every single one of the lashes on her lids. *Oh, she's so little, so vulnerable … she needs me. She needs her mother's milk. How can I stop doing this for her?* Now I picked up her little hand, balled into a tiny fist, and let it rest gently on my finger. *Keep this moment safe*, I told myself, *keep this feeling, this memory, locked away in your heart forever.* It was so peaceful. Together, here, lying side by side, Katie and I were in our own little world, a safe, innocent world away from everything and everybody. This was the last time I would breastfeed my daughter and yet I didn't want it to end.

It had happened two days earlier. Matt had wandered into the lounge where I was on the floor, changing Katie's nappy, and exclaimed: 'Look what I've got!'

He held up a small package that had come through the post. I was mildly curious – after all, he seemed very excited. Then he opened up the package and out fell several boxes filled with pills. They looked like medication of some sort.

'For you!' he said, smiling, and threw one of the boxes at me. I caught it and turned it round in my hand.

'T5 Fat Burners …' I read on the side. 'Tiromel – used for the treatment of underactive thyroids. You want me to take these?'

'You want to lose all that baby weight, don't you?' he replied. 'Look – this is a quick, guaranteed, easy way to get rid of all that fat. I've researched it, they're perfectly safe. The only thing is you can't take them while you're breastfeeding.'

'Oh, so I'll have to wait then …' I concluded. After all, I had breastfed my first child for two years. Katie was still only four months old and I planned to feed her for the same amount of time.

'No, you have to stop breastfeeding,' Matt corrected me. 'Come on! She's had the best bit and now you've got to start thinking of yourself, thinking of us too. Don't you think I might find you a bit more attractive if you lost weight? Hmmm?'

I turned the bottle round in my hand and thought about what he had said. *My daughter was my priority. Still, if I took these and lost weight like Matt said maybe he would find me more attractive and things might improve between us. Maybe he wouldn't get so angry with me. He hated the fact that I had put on so much weight. Maybe this was the answer …*

I mulled it over for the next couple of days and Matt kept dropping hints about how much he would love it if I lost weight until finally I agreed to take the pills he had ordered. They had come from Turkey and were designed to help people with an underactive thyroid but Matt convinced me they were the quick fix I needed to kick-start my weight loss. Now I lay next to Katie, cuddling her, allowing her a final feed on each breast, cherishing this last precious time I would feed her from my own body. I wasn't ready to stop, to let go of this bond. Not every woman could do it, not every mother is able to feed their child, produce their own milk. I was so lucky that it had come so easy for me. But I wanted my relationship with Matt to improve and I wasn't happy being this big – I was 14 stone and wearing size 22 clothes. If this helped … well, why not give it a go?

I started taking the pills the next day and almost immediately regretted it. The side effects were horrendous. I was running to the toilet constantly either to throw up or because it was exploding out of me the other end. On top of that I had terrible, blinding headaches from the moment I woke up to the moment I went to sleep. By day four, I felt like death warmed up. Even worse, I had stopped breastfeeding, which, considering I'd been feeding for almost three years continuously, was a real shock to the system. Without all those lovely hormones, my hair started to fall out and I felt really tired and washed out. Each morning I woke up to see great big bags under my eyes. At the same time, Matt put me on a strict diet – 'to give yourself the best chance possible of losing weight' – so I was starving hungry all the time. *Was this really worth it?* I wondered as I dragged myself round the house that first week, barely able to summon up enough energy to look after the kids, let alone hoover or wash the dishes. The answer came pretty swiftly

– yes! The weight dropped off me instantly. I may have looked and felt awful but getting on those scales every morning to find myself two or three pounds lighter was a real boost. Nothing on earth could make me feel beautiful anymore, not after so many years of insults from Matt, but I did feel slightly happier, knowing that I was actually losing weight.

It didn't take long for Matt to become super-strict about my diet. He said there was no point taking the pills, spending all that money, if I was just going to sabotage myself by eating crap all the time. So he put me on a punishing regime of just two SlimFast shakes a day and, in the evening, a tiny, child-size portion of fat-free food. I was literally starving but I lost 4 stone in just under seven weeks. Soon I was down to a size 10 and as much as it wasn't my choice, I did feel good about losing weight. Not so much for Matt but for myself. It was so satisfying to ditch the huge, oversized T-shirts and trousers that I'd squeezed myself into and return to some of my old clothes – jeans and blouses I hadn't worn in years. Standing on the scales and seeing the dial stop at 8½ stone just felt good. At my heaviest, when I'd been pregnant with Katie, I was 15½ stone so it was amazing to me that I'd actually managed to lose so much weight so quickly.

Some people thought it was a little too quick – my mum kept telling me to slow down. I told her I was on a health kick, trying to lose my baby weight, but she was worried I had become anorexic, starving myself into a state of thinness. I couldn't tell her that it was all down to diet pills bought by Matt. He told me not to tell anyone that I was taking them since they were from abroad and were probably illegal in this country. I couldn't tell her either that I felt like hell – tired all the time, unable to keep my eyes open. It was like a slow death. Even though Matt had been careful to buy me lots of vitamins and supplements to maintain my health – multivitamins, iron, zinc, vitamin C, selenium, cayenne pepper – the lack of basic nutrition left me undernourished, emaciated and in a state of near-total exhaustion.

By now I was back to the nursery where many of my colleagues noticed that I was rapidly losing weight. One colleague told me that a male assistant had made a comment to her about it.

'You must have lost a hell of a lot for a man to notice!' she said, grinning at me. And I did feel good about my weight loss, though I felt sad it had come at the expense of breast-feeding my daughter. By now I was training to become a nursery keyworker. I loved working at the nursery. It was my sanctuary, my quiet time, even though for the most part I was surrounded by a playground full of screaming children. Those few hours away from Matt were my only 'break' from the torment and I hated leaving at the end of the day. A few times I became tearful when it was time to sign out and go home. *Just five more minutes until the bell rings, just five more minutes* ... I didn't ever want that bell to ring.

Sadly, I didn't always get to go to nursery. There were times when the bruises were so bad I had to call in sick. Once, during my training, I had my keyworker assessment and the lady spotted more than I bargained for. She usually came in once a month to watch me in the classroom, then, afterwards, we would go through my performance together in a one-on-one session. On this occasion we were sitting in the back office, going through her feedback, and she said: 'Oh, you've got a black eye. How did you do that?'

The question was posed in an open, inquisitive way. She wasn't grilling me.

Quick as a flash, I replied, 'I do sparring,' though I was kicking myself inside for not putting on enough make-up to cover up the bruise. The 'sparring' excuse was one Matt had made up, should I ever be questioned about the multiple bruises on my body. It was a clever, catch-all answer and totally believable.

'Oh right ...' she replied. 'I do a bit of taekwondo myself.'

I was dreading her questioning me further – Where did I train? What style did I learn? Who did I box with? – because I knew absolutely nothing about the sport. But she didn't. Perhaps, because she thought we had a hobby in common, she didn't ask me anything more specific and, to my great relief, we just carried on the session. Later at home, I told Matt of course. I had to, in case she reported it, which she didn't.

I really didn't think Matt was going to allow me to train to become a nursery keyworker, objecting to the increase in hours away from him. It would be an extra 16 hours a week for a year. But to my surprise, he encouraged me.

'Yes, you do that,' he said. 'Sounds like a very good plan. And then if those bloody social services ever come sniffing around again, they're going to look pretty fucking stupid to find out you're a teaching assistant.'

Later he signed me up for a home-study course in social work with children and families and another in child psychology. He knew it looked good, that it all played well with the authorities. There's no question that Matt was an intelligent man. He was always scheming with an eye to the future. One of his favourite phrases was: 'Get your defence in before the battle commences.' And I honestly think that if he was an honest man he would have been successful in whatever field he chose to work because he certainly employed strategic thinking. He put a lot of effort into everything he did and always gave himself an insurance plan. At this stage I never thought for a second that Matt's plan to help me lose weight was anything other than what he said it was. He was so cunning.

'What about your hair?' Matt mused one day. 'Why don't we do something about it?'

I wondered what was wrong with my hair – by now I had gone to a light golden-brown colour, but Matt thought I should 'treat myself' to a colour. He loved the look of women with long, dark hair. I knew this because he showed me pictures of the women he considered 'horn bitches'. They were the dominatrices on BDSM websites who wore black rubber catsuits, thick make-up and brandished whips. They all seemed to have dark, slicked-back hair scraped into long straight ponytails.

'See! She's horny and slim,' he'd say as he showed me a selection of his favourite porn. 'You're nearly as slim as her now. Wouldn't it be good if you looked like her? I could have my own one of her at home.'

Matt suggested we go to the shop together to choose some hair dye. So the next time we were out he marched me into Superdrug and let me choose between his two selections: a Schwarzkopf black/purple dye or a Schwarzkopf black/red dye. It was my choice, he said, but only between those two black dyes. So I chose the black/red and, with Matt's help, we put it on that night. He loved it and insisted we dye it a few more times in the next few weeks to get it really dark. It was a shock at first to see myself with dark hair – catching sight of my reflection in the mirror made me jump because I thought it was someone else! But I soon got used to it.

One day I was preparing vegetables in the kitchen when Matt came up behind me and, for the first time in years, put his arms around me. It was so unexpected, so out of the blue, I nearly flinched.

'Now you're starting to lose weight I'm starting to find you more attractive,' he whispered in my left ear. It was what I had hoped for – the whole reason I had stopped breastfeeding my daughter. A change in his attitude towards me so that our lives together would be more peaceful. Happier. *I must keep on doing what I'm doing and maybe he'll stop being horrible and start to love me.* There were still times when he hit me, times when he threatened to rip my face off or beat me, but the attacks weren't quite as frequent as they had been. *Maybe if I keep the weight off and make myself more attractive to him then everything will be better. Maybe, maybe, maybe …* My whole life was built on maybes.

But it was hard. I was hungry all the time and I yearned for some proper food. Even though there was plenty of food in the house for him and the kids, I was forbidden from putting certain foods anywhere near my mouth. On the banned list were butter, full-fat milk, bacon, mince, rice, pasta, bread, chocolate and anything sweet. It was torture preparing his and the kids' food every day – smelling the bacon fat as it crisped up under the grill or watching the butter ooze into the jacket potatoes that I made for the girls. I was so hungry I felt faint at times but I didn't dare sneak anything into my mouth because Matt would have seen me.

And he was always careful to check the cupboards every night. He counted the biscuits, for God's sake! So I stuck to my rigid diet – two shakes a day and then, perhaps, a 'light supper' of mushrooms, cucumber and tuna sprinkled with chilli powder. No more than 500 calories a day; that was his rule. And since the shakes were approximately 200 calories each, that was 400 gone already. I had 100 calories to use on food. Lindsey realised that I was starving and she knew too that it all came from Matt, so when she came over, she'd wait until he left the room then sneak me a yoghurt bar or a Go Ahead! Fruit Bake. My eyes would nearly pop out of my head! I'd lean against the kitchen cabinets, wolfing down one bar after another, while Lindsey stood at the door, keeping a careful lookout. Once, when we were on lunch break at nursery, I went to the shops with a colleague and bought garlic cheese dips for £4 in small change that I'd found lying around the house. I sat on a wall hiding in case Matt drove past, munching it as fast as I could.

Hunger became my constant companion. It was there from the first stirrings in the morning to my prayers last thing at night … and even when I was asleep, it stalked my dreams too. At times I was so ravenous, I would open up the cupboard and scoop up the leftover powder that had fallen on the shelf from the tin of the slimming milkshake meal replacements. Or, if there was no milkshake powder, I would eat handfuls of Katie's milk powder instead. I was desperate, driven mad by the constant, gnawing, craving hunger in my belly that never, never, *never* went away. Occasionally, if I was feeling risky and Poppie asked for a biscuit from the tin, I'd get two digestives, break them both in half, then into quarters, and give her four pieces. Then

I'd give myself the other four quarters so if her daddy asked her how many biscuits she'd had that day she would say 'four'. So then I could eat my four quarters and two more biscuits from the packet. During the nights when the hunger kept me awake, when I could think of nothing else but food, I'd wait until Matt was asleep, then I'd sneak downstairs and binge on milkshake powder and the kids' sweets in a bag in the fridge, being careful to leave things exactly how I found them. Sometimes I'd eat raw carrots with the skin on, knowing that if I'd peeled it he would see the peelings in the bin. Then I would put my fingers down my throat and throw it all up again because Matt weighed me every two days and if I allowed myself to keep the food in my stomach, I wouldn't lose the required amount of weight. Matt wanted me to get down to 7½ stone and I was inching closer and closer. Now I was 8 stone.

One evening Matt was eyeing me from the armchair and he said: 'Your hair is nice and dark now. What if your eyelashes were a little darker? You haven't worn mascara for a good few years. How about we buy you a new one?'

I hardly knew what to say. Matt never offered to buy me anything. Was it a trap?

'Yeah, okay …' I replied. I couldn't say no.

'What's the latest good one?' he asked. 'Let's have a look online. Come on, come and look with me.' So we sat down together and searched all the latest make-up online. Eventually he bought me a new foundation, blusher, mascara, eye liner, eye shadows and lipstick. I could hardly believe he was treating me to such a lot of expensive stuff from good brands like Rimmel and Max Factor. But he was keen for me to try it all on and even helped me to work out how to put on foundation properly, using brushes, which I'd never done before.

One day, around 4pm, I was upstairs in the bathroom, putting the finishing touches to my make-up in the bathroom mirror. Matt said he liked me to wear make-up every day so now I put it on whenever I found the time. I examined my face in the mirror and saw someone completely different from the woman I'd known just three months earlier. Gone was the fat, mumsy, downtrodden, beaten-up face, the face of misery and defeat. With my cheekbones now visible and contoured under exotically made-up eyes, I felt glamorous and sophisticated for the first time in years. This was Hannah as I had not seen her for a long time and I felt my confidence and self-esteem grow.

Now Matt came to the bottom of the stairs and shouted up to me: ''Ere, sweetheart?'

'Yeah?' I called back.

'Sweetheart … come down here a minute.'

'Okay …' I placed the mascara wand back in the tube and walked downstairs, not realising I was being led down a dark and sinister new path. All of Matt's intricate plans were about to come to a head, all of his careful scheming was about to come together. I had no idea then but as I padded softly down the stairs, I was walking blindly into a whole new circle of hell …

10

Wife for Sale

I found Matt in the living room, sitting on the sofa, his eyes watching my every move.

'Yeah?' I asked.

'Sit down, Han.' So I sat on the sofa.

'The phone's going to ring in a minute,' he said slowly and carefully. 'A man's going to ring you up, he's going to arrange to have sex with you and he's going to pay us for it.'

Fucking hell – that is just a really lame joke. It's not even funny.

'No, seriously, Matt. What do you want?'

I didn't have time for this nonsense. My mascara was drying and I needed to separate the lashes.

'No, no, no …' he said, laughing. 'It's just like I said, the phone's going to ring. Make sure you answer it.'

'Okay, well, who's ringing me?'

'I told yer,' he replied, grinning. He had that smirk on his face, that one he wore when he was playing around with me, so I couldn't take him seriously. Matt had a really sick sense of humour and this was just the kind of joke that would tickle his funny bone.

'The phone's going to ring,' he repeated. 'Answer it. It'll be a man. Arrange a time with him and he's gonna meet you.'

'Ok-ay …' I still didn't believe him.

And then the phone started to ring.

He nodded at it – answer it – so I quickly said: 'Okay, what time should I say?'

'Six.'

I still didn't believe him. Even so, my hands were shaking as I picked up the mobile and clicked the 'answer' button.

'Hello?' I said nervously. Matt gave me an encouraging look and gestured with his hands – *Be happy, be chirpy, be confident.*

'Hello,' I repeated, now putting on my most cheerful voice. 'How are you?'

'Yeah … erm, so we've been messaging online. Thanks for your number. What's your availability?'

Fuck. This isn't a wind-up.

'Erm, about 6pm.'

'Yup. Lovely, can you text me the address?'

'Yeah, yeah, okay.'

'Alright, looking forward to it.'

'Yeah, thanks for calling. Bye!'

I put the phone down and just sat there on the sofa, my hands trembling. Matt stood up, towering over me. I looked up at him. *What the hell was going on?* My brain refused to believe what Matt was telling me. It couldn't be true. It just *couldn't.*

'So what are we meeting this person for?' I asked.

'I told yer. They're gonna pay yer, you're gonna have sex with him. Don't worry – you're only going to do it for 15 minutes. By the time you've got him hard it ain't gonna be for that long. It'll be over in a couple of minutes. He's going to give us 40 quid.'

What? NO! Not in a million fucking years.

'Uh-uh …' I shook my head. 'No. No way, Matt. I'm not fucking doing this. I don't want to do this.'

But I knew – I just knew I was going to do it, no matter what I said. I didn't even want to have sex with Matt, let alone with a stranger, somebody I'd never met … for money! But Matt was still smiling as he opened up the laptop and he showed me a website. Here was the profile he'd set up for me five days earlier, using naughty pictures he'd taken of me years earlier. He'd written out a whole description of what I was like, as well as my rates for what I did. *Fuck, fuck, fuck. This is real.*

'I think I'd better finish my make-up,' I said mechanically and walked back upstairs in a daze. Then I stood in the bathroom, staring at myself in the mirror. Just a few moments ago, it was a face I liked, it was the face of someone I knew, someone I recognised. Now it was a mask.

Matt followed me upstairs and started rummaging around in my drawers.

'What have you got to wear?' I heard him say.

'I don't know … I'm not sure.' I mumbled as I walked through to the bedroom, still in a daze.

'I know … you've got that little denim skirt and those stilettoes, the black ones … put them on. Oh yeah, and that sexy basque thing …'

So we dug out an old Mary-Kate and Ashley denim skirt from George at ASDA that I'd had since I was 15 and now fitted me again. It had big round silver buttons on the pockets and pink stitching up the sides. He matched this with a pair of black fake-leather almond-toe stiletto heels from Dorothy Perkins and a black-and-red basque I'd had since our first year together.

'Right, put that lot on.'

I did as he instructed, then I stood there as Matt appraised me – his perfect little whore.

'That will do.' I threw on a baggy jumper over the top and we left the house.

It turned out we were going to meet this man at our new office block. Matt texted him the address on the way as the kids sat quietly in the back of the car. The phone rang twice more while we were in the car – two more 'punters', according to Matt – and I was instructed to arrange to meet the other men in 20-minute intervals after the first. Matt discreetly told me what I should do with the men as we sped towards the office block. But my mind was a whirl – *What's going to happen? Is it really what he says or is he planning to get someone to beat me up once we're there? What's going on?* The top half of our premises was separated from the bottom half with its own entrance – now I took the kids into the downstairs warehouse while Matt opened up the boot. *I recognise that!* He pulled out an old blow-up sex couch Matt and I had had from our first year together. A black, inflatable couch, shaped like a wave, which had been in the shed for years. I waited downstairs while he set it up in the office upstairs, blinking back the tears as I played with Poppie. *What the hell has this relationship come to?*

Ten minutes later, Matt reappeared.

'Right, sofa's all blown up. Here's the phone – you've got a couple of minutes. He's probably going to ring to let you know he's here.'

'Are you sure you're not lying?' I said, still disbelieving.

'How dare you call me a liar!'

'Okay, is this a joke, Matt?'

'No – get up there!'

So I went towards the stairs, with the 'business' phone in my hand and Matt's words echoing in my ears: 'When they ring, fucking answer it!' I had fallen into an alternative reality. Was any of this real? I couldn't be sure. I pulled off the jumper, as instructed, and left the downstairs area, closing the metal fire shutter behind me. As the red shutter started to descend noisily, I stood there on the steps, watching numbly as it separated me from my children, from my life as a mother, from the world I had known until this moment. Then the shutter was closed and they were gone. If anyone came into the building now they would never know there was a little family hidden behind those red shutters.

Upstairs, in the first office, I found condoms and baby wipes on the windowsill and the now inflated sex couch in the middle of the office floor. It looked so weird and out-of-place, sat there in the middle of the office, set against the white office walls and the strip-paper light-blue blinds at the windows. *What is it doing here? What am I doing here?* I gripped the phone in my sweaty palm and tried taking deep breaths to keep the panic at bay. *Pinch yourself, Hannah! Punch yourself. WAKE UP!*

Then the phone sprang noisily to life. For a moment I

fantasised about not answering it, but the fantasy soon disappeared. I knew I would get a beating if I didn't.

'Hi – I'm here,' came the male voice on the line. 'What building is it?'

I gave him directions and told him to come straight up the stairs. Click, the phone rang off and now … *Bang, bang, bang.* My heart was beating so hard I thought it would explode out of my ribcage! *Make yourself look nice*, I said to myself. I tried smoothing my hair down – *what do I look like?* I felt like a mess, with my jet-black scraggly hair, thin from malnourishment, growing back in clumps from where it had been ripped out at the roots. I heard the door open downstairs and it swung shut, making the shutter rattle. I counted in my head – *one, two, three, four, five … and when you get to 20, he'll be at the top of the stairs*. I waited, counting silently … and then, he was there. Instantly, something in me changed. I had to be confident, friendly, warm, welcoming. So I switched, I put on the mask. I was no longer Hannah. I was 'Lydia'.

'Hello, darling,' I said, smiling warmly. He was an Asian man, around 5 feet 5 inches, slim, average build, called himself Rash. He had a nice smile and was polite and respectful. Now I invited him into the room.

In my head, I could hear Matt's voice: '*Get the money upfront. Strictly no kissing. Caress them, stroke them, if you're going to suck their dick make sure they've got a condom on. If they want to lick you they can. For penetrative sex, make sure they've got a condom on.*'

I had to do everything right – so, money first. Fortunately, Rash seemed to know the rules, producing two £20 notes straight away. I placed the folded notes in my top under my left breast as there was nowhere else to put them. The office was completely empty.

Now what? I was nervous as hell and out of my depth, so I told Rash I was still new to 'all this', without saying he was actually my first. He was nice enough not to make a big deal out of it and at first we just talked about general stuff: How's my day been? Isn't the weather nice? Blah, blah, blah ... *Oh, just fucking get it over and done with, Han. As much as it's nice to stand here and chat, you're just delaying the inevitable. Let's get this over and done with. But what do I do? Do I wait until he has got himself erect or is that my job? I don't know. Matt didn't tell me.* Luckily, Rash had no trouble getting it up. So I grabbed a condom from the windowsill, took it out of the packet and went to put it on him – but my hands were shaking so much he had to help.

'Okay, how would you like me, baby?' I asked in a flirty way.

'Shall we start off with a bit of doggy?'

Phew! At least I wouldn't have to look at him. I had my heels on but no knickers, as Matt instructed, so now I just bent over the arched part of the inflatable, hitched my skirt up a little but left the bottom half of my bum cheeks hanging out so he could see my bits. He had his hand on himself and he was touching me. He held his penis and he was feeling around for my hole and once he found it he worked his way in.

What did I want most at that moment? I wanted someone to come along with a gun and shoot me in the head. I didn't want to be there. I didn't want to be doing this. I didn't want to be me. I didn't want to exist anymore. Rash banged me from behind for about two or three minutes and all I could think about were my ankles. Every time he thrust himself inside me it felt like my ankles were going to break apart sideways. I was in agony. *Do I make a noise? Am I meant to be enjoying this?* I thought about making some 'ooh aah' sounds but it was over before I got a chance. Rash was mercifully quick.

'That was nice, babe,' he said as he pulled himself out. 'Sorry if that's a bit too quick for you.'

'Oh no. That's freshened me up a bit …' I replied in a silly, giggly voice. *What?* I didn't even know what words were coming out of my mouth. All I knew was that I needed to get rid of him before the next guy arrived so I offered him a baby wipe and we chatted as he cleaned himself up.

'Okay, well it's been nice to see you, babes.' I guided him to the door. 'Take care.' Quick peck on the cheek and a hug goodbye. Then when he got to the stairs: 'Do you know where you're going? Alright, take care, see you soon … Byeee!'

I let the door swing shut. *Fucking hell, what have I just done? What on earth have I just done?*

I wiped myself down below and paced about the office, wondering what to do now. *Should I go downstairs to tell Matt the first one had gone, and risk the next guy turning up when I'm not up here? Or just stay up here?* I didn't know. As I was worrying about my next move, the next guy pitched up. He came up the stairs, just like Rash, and, just as before, I switched on 'Lydia'. *Well, it worked the first time, I suppose I can just do the same again.*

'Hello, babes, good to see you. You got the money?'

Another 40 quid tucked safely under my boob, we moved on to the 'services'. But this guy wanted to kiss. I told him firmly that I don't do kissing.

'No thank you,' I replied primly. 'I don't do that.'

'Why not?'

Why not? Yeah, why not? I couldn't tell him 'because my husband says I'm not allowed to'. I felt slightly ridiculous, thinking about it. I mean, I was happy to let this perfect stranger put his dick in me but kissing was forbidden.

'I don't know you yet, darling,' I replied. 'Not the first time.'

Even so, he still tried to kiss me on the lips so I turned my head to one side. *Fucking hell! I didn't want to be doing this anyway – I've just told him no and he's still trying to do it!*

Next he wanted me to suck him and I said that was fine but I'd have to put a condom on him first. Again he objected. God, this guy was hard work! I was trying to stay perky and confident, the character I needed to portray, but he was really making that hard. Finally, I put the condom on him and started to suck him through the condom. But almost immediately his hands landed on the back of my head and he started to push. *Oh God! I hate this. I'm fucking choking here. What the hell do I say? I don't like this … do I politely let him know I don't like it or would that not be alright with Matt? Am I allowed to say that I don't want him holding my head so he can ram his cock down my throat? Am I allowed to say that?*

I didn't know so I let him carry on.

Eventually, when I thought I was actually going to vomit, I pulled back and smiled: 'How do you want me then, baby?'

'Can you do it without a condom?'

'No, definitely not.' He knew I meant it.

'Okay, let's do it from behind then.'

Now I bent over the black inflatable again and he did his business just the same as the first guy. He grabbed hold of my hips and started to pump. *Hurry up. Hurry up. Hurry up* … It seemed to go on forever this time and all the while I was doing my best to make encouraging noises. But he didn't come and I knew time was up.

'I'm so sorry I can't give you any longer,' I said, thinking that soon punter no. 3 would arrive.

'No, no, no … I've got more money with me,' he objected. 'Can I buy some more time?'

'Sorry. Not today. Do you want a baby wipe?'

He knew it was over but he kept delaying and delaying. I couldn't get him out of the door. *Christ, what a creep!*

Finally he left and now I had £80 under my left breast and I tried not to think about the disgusting things I'd done to get it. The phone started to ring. 'Hi – I'm here, you're running late, aren't you?' came the voice of punter no. 3.

I looked at the clock – 7.15pm. I wasn't late, he was early. Still, he didn't seem upset about it. I gave him directions and when he arrived I was relieved to find he didn't want to mess around with kissing or small talk and was happy to put the condom on himself. He just wanted to get straight down to it and leave. It was all over in five minutes. *Thank God!* I was grateful to see the back of him but now I had to face Matt and this was scarier than anything else I'd done that day. I didn't know if what I had done was right or wrong. No matter what I'd done, he would find fault … and then what? I counted out the £120 again – just to make sure I had exactly the money he was expecting – then I looked over at the bin filled with used condoms and baby wipes. *Should I take out the rubbish? What about the rubber sofa? Do I deflate it? Do I shut the door? Do I leave the light on?*

I'd just been fucked by three complete strangers on the orders of my husband and these were the questions that concerned me: *Do I leave the light on? Is it going to be okay with Matt if I shut the door?* But this is how I lived my life. This is what I had to think about. Everything mattered. When anything can lead to violence, every small act takes on supreme significance. There was no such thing as 'inconsequential' in my world. Everything had a consequence so I couldn't afford to let a single thing go unanalysed. I made my decisions, turning off the lights, emptying the bin but leaving the sofa inflated, then I left the room, wondering what awaited me downstairs.

Clonk, clonk, clonk – the sound of my stiletto heels on the staircase echoed through the empty warehouse. I tapped on the shutter and it didn't take long for Matt to flick the electric switch. The shutters started to rattle as the electric pulleys brought them up. I saw his feet first, then his jeans, shirt … and, finally, his face. The hint of a smile dancing in his eyes.

'Alright? How was it?' He seemed pleased, satisfied. I don't know why. Was he happy with me for going through with it? Or with himself because he had pulled it off? I handed over the money. He counted it out, folded it up and put it in his left jean pocket.

'Can I get changed now?' I asked. I wanted to put my jumper on so that I could touch my kids. I didn't want to hold them still wearing these clothes.

'Is there anyone else who wants to come and see you?' he asked in response.

'I don't know.' I handed him the phone. Now I looked at my kids, playing.

'Hello, Mummy!' Poppie shouted across the room. Matt nodded so I quickly put my jumper back on and went to give Poppie a hug. I tried not to think about what I'd been doing a few minutes earlier.

'No one else tonight,' said Matt. 'Shall we head home?' We started to pack up and I was silent the whole time. He knew I was upset. Still, he tried to make conversation.

'Come on, tell me, what did they say to you?' he asked cheerfully. 'What did their dick feel like in your hand? What were their cocks like? How big were they? What did they feel like in you?'

I gave him one-word answers, trying to shut him down. I didn't want to talk about it, I really didn't. I tried to push it all to the back of my mind and bury the feelings too – the shock, sadness, trauma, disgust, shame. Feelings were a luxury I couldn't afford.

As we pulled out of our parking space Matt turned to me: 'So, what should we have for dinner? Shall we pick up a kebab on the way back?'

I thought he meant for *them* – him and the kids – as he would never allow *me* to eat a kebab. But then he added: 'Do you fancy a kebab?'

I didn't know what to do or say. If I said *yes*, he could reply: 'You know you're not allowed food like that.' But if I said *no* he would tell me off for being ungrateful.

'I ... erm ...'

As I hesitated he decided: 'Yeah, let's get a kebab on the way home.'

A kebab! Real food! It had been so long since I'd tasted real food. By the time we pulled up at the kebab house it was dark and the lights from the shop sign bounced off the car hood. My mouth was watering just at the thought of the lovely food inside. Before we got out, Matt gave me strict orders: 'Chicken is less fatty than lamb and you'll have salad with it, jalapeño peppers – speeds up your metabolism – but no mayo. You're not having any mayo on it.' I nodded: *Yes, yes, anything! Just give me food!*

The smell in the car for the rest of the journey was exquisite, delicious and utterly torturous. It was agonising to wait any longer. My head pounded, my stomach ached with hunger. It had been three months since I last ate a proper meal and I couldn't get into the house quick enough. Now we all got plates from the kitchen and I sat in front of mine, nearly crying with gratitude. I couldn't believe he was letting me have this. The first thing I picked out was the chicken – *Oh my God, oh my God, oh my God.* That first morsel of chicken was amazing, like biting into a little piece of heaven. And yet, it had been so long since I'd eaten real food, my stomach was full before I'd even swallowed it. Nevertheless, I carried on. I ate and ate and ate, careful to hoover up every last scrap of food on my plate – every strip of lettuce, every pepper and tomato and every crumb of pitta bread. And then I sat back, full up for the first time in months, and I thanked Matt. After everything he had put me through that evening, I actually thanked him.

11

Mummy by Day, Mistress by Night

Within a few short months my life transformed. By day I was a respectable mother of two and a trainee nursery keyworker, by night I was a prostitute and BDSM mistress. After that very first occasion when he made me have sex with three people in a row, I told Matt I didn't want to do it again, but of course I got a swift beating and that knocked any further objections out of me. I was doing it and that was that. Matt had it in mind from the very beginning that our new business venture was not going to be an arcade, but my body, and those machines he had bought were just a front. They sat in the bottom of our warehouse the whole time, never touched or plugged in. Matt had never intended to make use of them except as so-called 'proof' of our business in case any suspicious officials decided to visit our premises.

Matt insisted I change my hours so I arranged with the nursery to move my 16-hours-a-week keyworker course to the mornings, which meant that from 2pm onwards I could come home, shower, change, put on my make-up and get to the office for my afternoon 'appointments'. It was always a mad rush, though, as Matt never left me enough time to get everything done before our first appointment of the afternoon. Meanwhile, Matt spent the mornings on the phone, texting punters, checking our messages online and booking people in. It was slow to begin with but it didn't take long for Matt to build up the business, ensuring a steady stream of 'work' for me throughout the week and weekends while Lindsey came round more and more frequently to babysit the girls. At this time she had no idea that our new business venture was actually prostitution but later on Matt made sure she was put in the picture.

To start with I stuck to the ground rules that Matt had outlined during my first day's work – I didn't kiss anyone, I didn't give oral without a condom on and I didn't have sex without a condom. But as soon as Matt saw there was a demand and he could charge more for these things, he started to break down the rules. It was all about the money. In the end I was snogging people, taking it up the arse, giving oral without a condom, on some occasions having sex without a condom and doing all sorts of kinky, horrible stuff that I never even imagined before. I tried a couple of times to divert some of the men from their intentions by offering them alternatives. For example, if a man wanted to come in my mouth, I would say to him: 'Do you know what, baby, I really love feeling nice hot sticky cum on my tits. Do you fancy coming on them instead?' I would much rather it be on the outside than inside of my body. Matt didn't like it if he found out.

'We are running a business,' he'd fume. 'If someone has paid to come in your fucking mouth, you have to let him come in your fucking mouth.' But a few times I got away with it. And the business got so busy that within a few short months I was seeing so many people he generally didn't have time to argue with me. As long as the punters paid and left happy, he was happy.

Matt thought he was best placed to know what men wanted as he liked BDSM himself. He knew that men would pay more for this kind of erotic practice so we started offering these services too: tying up, dominating, being kicked in the balls. I discovered that there are lots of men out there with a whole range of unusual preferences from being tied up and teased with a feather duster, to wanting hot wax poured on their dicks and some men even like to be pissed on. We kept proper books and I made a note of every punter's name and telephone number. At first my prices were quite low at £40 for 15 minutes and £60 for half an hour. But as we got more professional, increased our range of services and improved the offices, we were able to raise the prices to £60 for 15 minutes, £90 for half an hour, £160 for 45 minutes and £200 for an hour. We even introduced a loyalty scheme – after four visits the fifth was free. And we gave a 20 per cent discount for every new customer. I say 'we' – of course, none of these decisions were mine. If it had been up to me there wouldn't have been any prostitution. This was not how I had imagined married life and all I wanted was for it to stop. But Matt always spoke about it as 'our business' so I picked it up from him. And I suppose in many ways it was 'us' – his control, my body.

The money started to roll in – on one of my busiest days I pulled in £3,000. It meant working for 15 hours straight but Matt insisted on keeping me awake for hours on end so that I could earn him more. At the very peak I was pulling in around £1,500 a day, which meant our lifestyle started to change. Matt bought himself a couple of cars – a Mercedes and a Range Rover – plus a new laptop, clothes and beauty treatments for me so I looked good for work. And instead of having to cook every night we bought fast-food like pizza, kebabs and burgers or ready-made microwave meals from Tesco. Matt indulged my desire for proper food when I complained of tiredness and lack of energy. One thing he didn't want to lose was his new cash cow. Plus, he reasoned that I was burning off what I was eating from all the fucking.

Matt also invested in our offices, making them more suitable to our line of work. There were five offices in total – three large ones and then two smaller offices at the end. Thankfully, the people who ran the arts foundation were rarely in their office at the end. They came in once a week at most and in the holidays. Apart from that, they weren't around so they had no idea what was going on. But in the beginning there were no locks on the doors so when they did come, some of the kids would be running up and down the corridors. To make the offices secure Matt installed two pairs of separate doors with locks on all of them to prevent anyone wandering in accidentally. At the same time, we decorated; putting up wallpaper, painting the walls deep purple and installing a massage table and desk for me to be bent over – after all, it was an office block. Later on we exchanged these for chocolate leather sofas and a thick, luxurious white shag-pile carpet. We put in a proper bed and made it look attractive with decorative lights all around it. And in the entrance we built a bar so punters could come in and have a drink while they waited until I was ready.

Matt installed baby monitors in the rooms so he could hear what was going on, which meant I had to be careful about what I said to the punters as I knew he could be listening at any point. One after the other, I serviced their needs. Some days, I didn't even get a break in between, there wasn't time – it was in out, in out, in out. I was a robot, a machine, just satisfying punters one after another on his command. Matt's good little whore robot, doing everything he instructed me to do, no matter how horrible or humiliating. Matt wasn't just my husband anymore, he was my pimp, so when he asked me to demonstrate the blow jobs I was giving to punters, I got down and did it for him. And naturally, I did it wrong.

'No! That's not what men like … Your hands are all wrong. Can't you open your mouth wider? Stick it right down … if he wants you to choke on it, you choke on it!'

I was sick once during a blow job. Even though some men like this and actually will pay for it, on this occasion it was completely unintentional. Before we had come to the office that evening, I had eaten a child-sized portion of sweet-and-sour chicken for dinner. Then I started work and this man was shoving his cock down my throat so hard, I started to choke. He rammed himself into my mouth while at the same time forcefully holding the back of my head so my eyes watered and my make-up ran off my face. Eventually I couldn't help it, I threw up – bright orange sick all over his dick. He didn't care; he was one of those sickos who liked that sort of thing.

It didn't matter what they did to me – to Matt I was just a piece of meat and I had to take it. He listed all the services I performed on the website and asked for the punters to specify if they had any particular needs, just to check that we could accommodate them. For example, some guy might say: 'I want to bend you over, get a blow job, I want to lick your pussy, do a 69 and I want to end by coming in your mouth.' If that's what he wanted, that's what I did. To Matt's mind I had to do what they asked because that was the service they were paying for, no matter how disgusting or humiliating. He was as sick as the rest of them, if not worse. The more degrading the better as far as he was concerned. So if they wanted me to piss on them, then I did it.

Most of the men who came to see me were actually all right. With a few exceptions, most were polite, respectful and didn't push their luck. I don't hold anything against them, even to this day. They had no idea I was being forced to do this – they thought I loved sex because that's what Matt wrote on the website as 'Lydia' and that getting paid for it was just a neat way to make money out of my 'favourite hobby'. Of course, there were a couple of creeps here and there but most of my regulars were fairly decent people. Some didn't even want to have sex – they just wanted to talk because they were lonely. I had one regular who was really fat. He'd get on top of me and I could not breathe. I'd have to take a big deep breath in or I was going to die! Actually, he was a really nice bloke – respectful, kind and treated me like a human being. But when we had sex I took my life in my hands.

Matt invested in massage oils, incense and candles. And he bought me a whole wardrobe of kinky outfits from Ann Summers – I had a nurse's uniform, a pilot outfit, an air-hostess outfit, witch dress, and school-girl and secretary outfits, as well as a massive range of different-coloured basques and teddies in every colour and material you could imagine. He took pictures of me in all these different outfits for the website and, naturally, if I didn't smile enough or give the camera the right 'look' I'd get a punch in the head. Matt personally preferred the BDSM mistress look – sleek black PVC catsuits, slicked-back hair with thigh-high stiletto boots. His own preference was for something called ball busting where women kick and stamp on men's balls. He would watch videos of this on several sites online and make me watch them too. Over time, we created a whole dungeon for the BDSM side of things. The walls were painted red, the ceiling and radiators were black, it had dark-brown laminate flooring and square plates on the walls with metal hooks for ropes. There were hooks and chains in the corner, a whipping bench and torture tools.

Alongside the prostitution, Matt also signed us up to a swingers website. He told me that he wanted to watch other men fucking me who had bigger dicks than him – giving me what I really needed, apparently. He wrote a profile describing us as a happy couple, very much in love, who just wanted to spice things up a bit. According to this story, I was the sex-mad nymphomaniac and Matt just liked to keep me happy. It turned out that these so-called swingers were mostly just single men who could put up with a husband watching for the sake of a free fuck. Actually, that wasn't strictly true. It wasn't free – they had to come with a pack of fags. A fuck for a pack of fags. That's all I was worth – and sometimes not even that. When a bloke turned up without the fags Matt still had him shag me anyway because he liked watching. Pretending to be 'Lydia' on the swingers website, Matt would ask for pictures of the guys' dicks, what they wanted to do and how they liked to do it. He pushed the boundaries with some of these strangers, asking if they were up for anything naughty or out of their comfort zone. This usually involved Matt being close to 'the action' as the other guy was fucking me. There was only one rule for the swingers – Matt had to watch.

While Matt 'gave away' my services for a pack of fags just for the sake of watching, he would also try to use my body to get out of paying for anything. We had arranged for the carpet fitters to do the offices as well as the carpets in our house. On the day they came to our house we were meant to settle up with cash but Matt dressed me up in thigh-high boots, a mini-skirt and a low-cut black top and, once they were finished, I was ordered to go downstairs and make them an offer: 'So how do you want paying? A suck, a fuck or the money?'

Matt leaned over the bannister, listening, while Lindsey and the kids were in the living room. Thankfully, with the telly on and the door shut, they couldn't hear. Still, it was horrible. There was an awkward pause, then the guy looked down at his feet and said: 'Ah, well, my colleague's already in the van and we've got another job to go to so we'll just have the money, please.'

I took the cash out of my bra and paid him in full without another word. It was humiliating for both of us, and I felt horrible for putting him in that position but I had no choice. Matt's word was law.

There was never any question I wouldn't do what Matt told me to. Any objection on my part was always met with violence on his. *Always.* On the days he beat me so hard I had bruises all over my body, a fat lip or black eyes, he'd cancel my appointments, offering the clients a 50 per cent discount on their next visit for the 'inconvenience'. His weapons of choice varied: he liked to hit me with the end of the rolling pin, his baseball bat and the metal pole from the vacuum cleaner. These were his most frequent tools of punishment but quite often he just picked up whatever came to hand: a china bowl, one of the weights he lifted, a wooden ornament … anything really. He liked to hit me across the shins a lot as he knew this hurt the most and that I would cover them up with trousers or stockings. There were times he hit me so hard I thought my bones were going to break, and I probably had a few broken toes over the years. Matt was a greedy man, though – enjoying the cash that our new business generated – so stopping me from working didn't seem to keep his temper under control. If anything, the violence just got worse and worse and worse … The day after Poppie's third birthday was one I'll never forget.

On her actual birthday we all had a nice outing to a petting zoo and even though it was a really hot day, the girls loved going on the little train around the park. I always put the 'disgusting stuff' out of my mind when I was with them. It was easy in some ways – they made me so happy and whenever the bad stuff threatened to creep into my mind I learned how to push it away. It helped to ensure I was always clean when I saw them – teeth brushed, face washed, showered and in 'Mummy' clothes. It really was a double life.

The next day, I got up early as usual, with the kids, washed them, dressed them and gave them both their breakfast. Matt stayed in bed until lunchtime, so it was my job to run the business phone, taking calls and texts and booking punters in. By now I had been fully schooled by Matt in what to say and how to arrange the bookings. In between, I rushed around the kitchen preparing a roast chicken dinner. At around midday I heard the familiar sound of footsteps above my head, the bathroom taps running and the pipes gurgling in the kitchen. *Shit. He's awake.* My heart started to thud. *What the hell is today going to bring? What sort of mood is he in?* There were times I wished he would sleep the whole day away so I could have one day without him. Or even die in his sleep! If he had a heart attack and died in his sleep, I would be free. The idea of bumping him off myself always seemed too difficult and far-fetched and, besides, if I killed him and went to prison then I would lose the girls. If he was up there asleep, at least I had some room to breathe. It was alright when he was sleeping – I could look after the kids happily, without being constantly watched and criticised. Matt was like the troll under the bridge, the giant up the beanstalk … the sleeping ogre in the cellar!

The moment he appeared in the living-room doorway in his red dressing gown, his heavy scowl told me I was in trouble. *Fe-fi-fo-fum!*

He snatched the business phone out of my hand and barked: 'What's been going on here then?'

'I've been answering some texts. Getting punters booked in …'

'Where's my fucking lunch?' He started scrolling though the messages as he stomped through to the kitchen and lifted the lids on the pots of potatoes and veg bubbling on the hob. By now Matt had found a text I had sent that he disapproved of.

'What the fuck did you say that for?' he demanded to know, showing me the message. 'It's cold, not flirty enough. Why didn't you call him "babe" or something?'

There was of course no way to answer that question. Whatever I said, it would have been wrong. Matt was in one of *those* moods. Nevertheless, I did my best. In a calm, reasonable voice, I tried to explain my thinking when I sent the message. It was no good. From the moment I opened my mouth Matt jumped in. Now he set about giving me a really good telling off. On and on he went.

Sitting on the armchair, I let Matt's anger wash over me. He worked himself up into a terrible state, getting more and more irate. He picked up a photo frame and smashed it on the floor. Then another one – there was glass everywhere. I looked carefully at the floor so I knew where to clear up after his temper had burned itself out. I didn't want the children getting cuts on their feet from shards of glass. Still, Matt raged. This dragged on for around an hour and a half. I had no way of answering him that would be right so I just sat on the armchair as he told me off, quiet and meek as a child. My face remained blank, unreadable, as he railed at me ... *Well, maybe if you got your arse out of fucking bed you could respond to these bastards yourself* ... I shouted back at him, inside my head. *I don't want to be doing this anyway!*

Then he asked me a question about one of the men's penises – was it bigger than his? Did I like it better? I didn't respond.

'If you don't fucking answer me you're gonna get that pan of boiling potatoes over you,' he snarled.

So I tried to answer him ... insisting that the man didn't interest me whatsoever, which Matt already knew, but in a way that wouldn't sound fed up, to avoid a smack.

Matt went into the kitchen, picked up the pot of potatoes and came back into the living room with it, a malicious glint in his eyes. *No, he won't do it. He isn't going to pour that over me. No way. It's just an empty threat. Those potatoes have been on the boil for ages – the water must be scorching hot by now.*

Sitting on the armchair with both feet on the floor, I had my eyes fixed on my youngest daughter in her chair near the TV, my other daughter sat beside her, when Matt came over to my right-hand side and paused for a few seconds, holding the pot of potatoes with the lid clamped on top above my legs. Then, slowly, he tipped it up, pouring the boiling water from a crack between the lid and the pot slowly up and down my right leg. Out of the corner of my eyes, I watched as the steaming-hot water trickled out. And then … I felt it on my lap. *Fuck. Fuck. Fuck.* It hurt. It hurt a lot. But I didn't react. I didn't shout, move away or jump up because I didn't want to give him the satisfaction of seeing my pain. So I just sat there, biting the inside of my cheek to distract myself as the red-hot liquid burned through my thin black leggings and scalded my thighs. I didn't look at him, I didn't move. I felt the pain but I knew he enjoyed hearing me cry, yell, scream and shout. It made him feel powerful and I refused to let him have that. I just watched as the stream of boiling water ran up and down the tops of my legs, as he whispered: 'Take it, bitch.'

He was speaking, saying more stuff to me, but by now I had stopped hearing his voice. My ears went deaf as I stayed focused on the pan and the blistering heat coming off my legs, now sizzling with steam. Once he was finished he seemed satisfied and wandered back into the kitchen with the pan as I followed him with my eyes, careful to hear where he put the pan down so there was no chance the kids could reach it. I just went about my business then, pretending that nothing had happened. No, he wasn't going to have the satisfaction of seeing that he'd hurt me. It was a full hour before I went to the toilet, pulled my leggings down and saw the burns. There were long silvery mauve marks all the way up my right leg and small blobs on the left leg from where the water had splashed. I just stared at them dumbly for a few seconds: *Fuck, that is massive. Look at what that evil monster has done to me!* They were bad, really bad.

The next day, after the purply marks had turned deep red, Matt took me to the doctor, and we told the GP that I'd had an accident making up the baby bottle. The doctor looked at the burns and advised using Sudocrem where the outside layer of skin had come off, exposing the red raw and shiny bottom layer of skin beneath. So that's what I did. I treated the burns with Sudocrem and today I still have the scars on my legs.

From this point onwards, I sank into a deep depression. I didn't know it was depression at the time. I didn't know what was wrong – all I knew was that every day I woke up with the same thought: *I want to die. I want to die. I want to die.* And immediately, I felt awful about even having those thoughts. *What kind of mother thinks like this?* I had two beautiful children. I was blessed with the amazing gift of life, twice over. Some people never get to experience motherhood at all. Why the hell would I want my life to be over? And the guilt and shame at feeling so miserable and wanting to die just compounded it all, dragging me further and further down into despair. Yes, I was worthless, I was a piece of shit. I didn't deserve those kids anyway, judging by the way I felt about myself. Now, on the days he threatened to kill me the voice inside my head screamed out: *Do it. Just do it. Put me out of my misery, please.* There was no other way out for me now. I wanted it all to end.

12

The Woman in the Mirror

'Faster! Come on. Pick it up. I want to see you RUN, BITCH, RUN!'

'I can't. I can't do it anymore …' I gasped. I was done in, exhausted. It was a struggle just to put one foot in front of the other.

'You can and you will!' he yelled so I trudged on, somehow managing to pick my feet up over and over again. I'd been running for what felt like hours already and, still, Matt wouldn't let me rest. This was part of my regime, my plan for staying slim as Matt hated the idea of me putting on weight. He still kept a sharp eye on my food intake but now he maintained my weight loss by forcing me to exercise for hours at a time – making me run or skip in the park or train in the 24-hour gym. Today, he'd taken us all to the park and while the kids played on the swings and clambered on the climbing frame, I was made to run circuits around the perimeter of the park. I'd already done four circuits and I'd lost all feeling in my legs.

'I need to stop, Matt,' I panted as I passed him for the fifth time. 'I really need to stop.'

After two children, I didn't have much control over my pelvic floor and without any feeling down there, I knew that I could run the risk of peeing myself. It had happened before.

'NO!' he roared. 'Push yourself! Go beyond that pain barrier. Don't be so bloody weak-minded.'

It was too late – I felt the warm liquid oozing down my legs. *Oh God, how humiliating.* On the final lap, I stopped running and walked slowly towards Matt, my cheeks flaming, not just from the exertion but also shame, my leggings soaked through with urine.

'We need to go home, Matt,' I said quietly, timidly. 'I've wet myself.'

'It's fine.' Matt waved away my distress. 'People won't notice, your trousers are dark. And even if they do, they'll think it's just sweat.'

Even so, I couldn't run any further and by now it was time for the kids' tea so Matt ordered me to get the girls in the car. *Phew, okay, now we can go home. I can change out of these trousers, have a shower and do the kids some dinner …*

But instead of heading home, Matt started driving us down some country lanes. We were going on a 'detour', he said, his voice steady and even. Thankfully, the kids were tired and fell asleep in the back of the car straight away. My mind started to race – *Where are we going this time? How long will we be gone? What is he going to do to me?*

It wasn't the first time he'd taken me on a 'mystery tour'. On a couple of other occasions he had told me we were going out for a drive, demanding I leave the phone at home.

Then we would drive out into country lanes till it was dark. After a while he'd stop the car on a grass verge in the middle of nowhere and ask me:

'Do you know where you are?'

'No.'

'Are you sure you don't know?'

'Yes, I'm sure.'

'Okay, so if you were unconscious and woke up in the early hours of the morning in a ditch somewhere here you wouldn't know where you were?'

'No.'

He did these things to scare me – and it worked.

Now he stopped in the middle of a country lane, no people, houses or cars for miles around. The minute he turned off the engine, he punched me once, without warning, in the mouth. The inside of my lip was cut badly against my teeth and now started to bleed all over my top. Then, as the children slept, he dragged me out of the car by my hair, beat me up, threw me in a bush, winded me, knocking all the air out of me and then left me struggling to breathe in the road, all while shouting at me about how I liked the swingers' dicks more than his and how I'm a dirty fat whore. I didn't notice until I heard the car door slam but he had jumped back in the car. I heard the engine start and the lights flick on. The car was facing me directly and now Matt put his foot down, driving directly at me. The last thing I saw before I screwed my eyes shut and turned my head away was the blinding light of the headlamps coming towards me in the dark. A screech of brakes and he stopped, inches away from me. I gasped with relief. He could have hit me. He wanted me to know that. He liked it when I was scared.

'Get in the fucking car NOW!' he shouted from the driver's seat. 'I want my dinner cooked when I get home.'

So I dragged myself into the car, my face throbbing and my body sore from the beatings. I could feel my top lip start to swell from where he'd punched me. *Please, please, let's just get home so I can put the kids to bed. You can beat me to a pulp and kill me afterwards, but please, let's just get the kids to bed safely.* But instead of driving back to our home, Matt parked up at the garages at the end of our road. He turned the engine and the headlamps off so now we were sitting in the dark, lit only by the lamp posts, as he berated me for being so fat. I was only a size ten but, still, Matt was outraged. How could I be so fat still after all that running? I was disgusting, a disgrace. Why couldn't I be more like all those other beautiful women who have had children? As he ranted and raved, he pushed the cigarette lighter in. *Uh oh … that's coming for me. But where – my arm? My leg? Side of my face? End of my nose? Not one of my eyes, surely!*

I knew what was going to happen but, still, there was nothing I could do to stop it. I just had to wait. Wait … as he carried on berating me, telling me I was stupid, fat, a waste of fucking air. The lighter popped out and straight away he pushed it back in. *Fuck, he's really going for it …*

It popped out a second time and I thought: *He'll push it in a third time*. But in the time it took for me to think that he whipped it out and thrust it into the outside of my right thigh. I heard it sizzle. *Tsssuuuuuuhhh* – like the sound of a hot pan when you put it in the sink and turn on the cold tap. I felt the lighter burning through my navy jogging bottoms to my skin, as I sat there, staring straight ahead. I could feel it but I had trained myself not to react anymore. I just took it. The blood poured out of my nose, my lips swelled, my eyes and eye sockets ached from fresh bruises and my head throbbed from where he'd punched me. I could feel there was already a big swollen lump forming. (You think those *Tom and Jerry* cartoons are exaggerated? When Jerry slams Tom over the head and a great big cone springs up? It's no exaggeration – that does actually happen if you're hit hard enough!) And now, to add to my injuries, there was a great big burn in the side of my leg.

Now we were going home. *Now* he was done with me. We got in the front door and Matt ordered: 'Go upstairs to the bathroom, get your face cleaned up before Keith gets home.' So I went up the stairs as he got the kids out of the car. In the bathroom mirror, I looked at myself in the mirror for the first time that night. It was fucking horrible. Horrible. What a mess he'd made of me. Looking at myself, I wanted to cry. *This* was the worst part of the whole day. I could take the pain, the blows, the burns, the humiliation, everything – I found that in the moment when he actually hurt me, I could switch off, disconnect myself from reality. But having to look at what he'd done to me afterwards, to face the consequences in the harsh bathroom light, broke me. *Who is this woman staring back at me? This battered, bruised, swollen, miserable woman? It isn't me. It can't possibly be me. I remember a time, a long time ago now, when I was happy, when I laughed, proper big belly laughs. I had mates, I danced, I went out and got drunk with my mates and we laughed and danced till our sides hurt. Where has that Hannah gone? Where is she? Will she ever return?*

That night Matt gave the girls their tea, then put Poppie to bed while I took Katie up. Katie was still too young but

Poppie would have noticed my messed-up face. And I didn't want to scare her. I knew that if she asked the next day, I could tell her that I'd slipped over getting out of the bath or I had tripped over the stairs or fallen in the kitchen. Just like I always did. I could tell her a little white lie to make it okay and I knew she would believe me.

How did I survive? How did I get through those brutal beatings, day after day after day? Sometimes I don't even know myself. Many of my scars have faded over time but my body remembers everything. If I press the place on my thigh where he burned me with the cigarette lighter today, it still hurts. If I press my cheekbones, they ache from the dozens of black eyes he gave me. The silvery lines down my leg are evidence of the boiling-hot water he poured over them. I can place my fingers on every place that he hurt and look back now and I weep for all the times he beat and abused me. But I didn't look back then. I didn't look forward or back and I certainly didn't weep. I just lived in the moment. Day to day I carried on, pushing through, putting one foot in front of the other. Surviving.

Of course I didn't want to be with him anymore – I hated Matt for everything he put me through, for all the times he made my children watch him beat me, for all the pain and shame I was forced to endure. But how could we all escape safely without him finding and killing all three of us? I had no idea. I couldn't even leave the house on my own – he watched and tracked my every move – so I just kept my head down and got us through each terrible day. Whatever happened, as long as I could get the kids fed, bathed and into bed at the end of the day, I felt I had succeeded. You can ask me now if I think that was enough and of course I know it wasn't. This was no way to live a life. But how could I do anything else? Motherhood for me was simply a case of survival – making sure my children were safely tucked up and out of harm's way was my primary goal each day. Then, if Matt wanted to beat the living daylights out of me later, when they were asleep, then that was fine. As long as the kids were safe and in bed then today was over and my job was done. Tomorrow was a new day.

The one thing I did manage to do was to start putting money aside. What for? Well, maybe to get us out one day, to disappear, if the opportunity ever arose. It wasn't clear in my mind, I just knew that if I ever wanted to break free I would need cash. Untraceable cash that would allow me to pay for an exit without leaving any clues behind. So when a punter tipped me extra, I didn't always pass it on to Matt. I squirrelled that money away, hiding my secret stash in the bookcase in the kids' bedroom, a place that Matt never looked at. Just £10 or £20 at a time but it quickly built up.

I had saved around £2,000 when Matt asked me one day: 'Have you got any money stashed away for a rainy day?'

Instantly, I knew I had to confess. I had no choice. If I didn't and he had already found the money then he would know I was lying and that would betray my real intentions of keeping the money hidden.

'Yeah, I have,' I said.

'What for?'

'Just in case we need it. In case we have a bad week at the office.'

'Well, go and get it then. I need cash.'

Damn. He hadn't found it after all. But I couldn't risk denying it just in case he knew already. And that was it – I gave him the money and he went to buy the second-hand car he wanted. Now I was back to zero. *Tomorrow*, I promised myself. *Tomorrow, I'll start saving again.*

For me, I could take the beatings, the pain, the abuse because it was only my body, after all, and I had no feeling left for what he did to it. Every week he devised new and more brutal ways to make me suffer – there were times he woke me up by punching me in the stomach, winding me. He hit me with every object imaginable, he would wind me and then spray deodorant straight into my face, holding down the nozzle till the can was almost empty, gassing me till I coughed, spluttered and could barely breathe. Then he'd punch me in the stomach to wind me again. He bent my fingers till I yelled out in agony. He even woke me up by hitting me or pouring freezing water over me. I was under siege, all the time, whether awake or asleep, and I got through it because I managed to switch off that part of me that cared about my body. But it was when Matt's nasty, controlling behaviour impacted on the children that I hurt the most.

They were still young but by the time it was coming up to Christmas Day, Poppie was old enough to know that this was a special time. We had a tree, there were presents under it and all the programmes on CBeebies told them the Big Day was coming – there was even a TV advent calendar so the excitement built day by day.

On Christmas Day itself, Poppie awoke, a bundle of three-year-old energy.

'It's Christmas! It's Christmas!' she sang out as she dashed downstairs to the presents and picked one up with her name on it. I tried to keep her quiet as I knew Matt wouldn't appreciate being woken up but Poppie's uncontrollable excitement burst out of her.

'This is for me! Look! It says Poppie! Poppie!' she burbled, now showing me the gift and ripping open the wrapping paper. She recognised the 'P' on the gift tag and knew it was meant for her because when our neighbour had dropped it round, she had said so.

At that moment, Matt appeared at the top of the stairs, shouting: 'If I find out the kids have opened any of their presents, I'm going to put your face in.'

Quickly, I snatched the gift out of Poppie's hands and the look on my little girl's face nearly broke my heart.

'But it's Christmas,' she said, crestfallen.

'Well, maybe ...' I said, trying to keep my voice bright and cheerful. 'I'm not sure. We'll have to check with Daddy later. We should all wait until Christmas Day to open our presents.'

Then I distracted her with the TV while I Sellotaped her present back up – I felt terrible. She'd been so good, waiting patiently for the presents that she saw every day under our tree. Her disappointment at not being able to open even one of them was a dagger to my heart. I was her mother, I wanted her to be happy on Christmas Day, as all children should be. But she was a good girl, and accepted what I said ... we all waited a little longer for Daddy to get up. For Daddy to tell us what day it was.

The lights twinkled on the tree as we passed the morning reading and playing games, then we had lunch and waited while Matt remained in bed. I put the kids down for a nap in the afternoon, wondering what to do. I knew I couldn't make a Christmas dinner until Matt was awake and gave me permission. So in the evening we watched films and played some more. By the time Matt got up at 10pm, the girls were still awake but yawning, sleepy and ready for bed. Matt was in a horrible mood and he let us all know it, sulking about in his dressing gown. The girls were awake at this time still, because I let them sleep in in the morning and they had had a long nap, which again I didn't disturb. Had I put them to bed at their normal time, the noise would have either woken Matt up or I would have been wrong to put them to bed if he hadn't said it was okay first. Whatever I did was wrong.

'Daddy, it's Christmas. Can we open some presents?' Poppie asked timidly.

'No you can't. Put that down, it's not Christmas yet.'

By now I had resigned myself to the fact that Christmas was cancelled – the day was almost over anyway so I went along with what he said, trying my best to make it okay for the kids.

'It's not Christmas Day just yet, Poppie, but when it comes, we'll open all the presents and have a lovely time together,' I enthused in my most upbeat, happy voice. She nodded solemnly back at me, innocent, trusting, ready to believe whatever I told her. My heart cracked.

I took the kids to bed shortly afterwards. The next day, on Boxing Day, when our mums came round for dinner, we all pretended to the kids that it was Christmas. And finally, the girls got to open their presents.

13

Sunniboi666 and a Packet of Fags

The man worked for a van-hire company but we just knew him as Sunniboi666. He was tall with dark hair and had brought with him the required payment – a pack of fags. Now Matt made small talk between the three of us, as he liked to do with the new ones, putting them at their ease. Making our swingers feel 'nice and relaxed' was how he put it. Only this man didn't seem to relax and when the moment came for him to fuck me, he couldn't get it up. Matt was watching my every move so I tried everything I could think of to help him but it was no use.

Eventually, Matt said: 'Shall I leave you two alone for a little bit?'

He must have only been gone a couple of minutes but in that time the man managed to get himself hard. *Better not waste it or I'll get into trouble*, I thought, so I turned around in my black suede thigh-high boots and let him take me from behind. I stared down at my feet as he pumped himself against me, just waiting for it to be over. Then, a minute later, he was done. He wiped himself with a baby wipe, I did the same and then we left the room, walking down the corridor to the bar area where Matt stood, tapping out a message on his phone.

He looked up briefly, Sunniboi666 shook Matt's hand, thanked him and then left while I went through to the office.

'What happened?' Matt followed me.

'When you left the room he relaxed, got it up, he did it. And that's it, he left.'

'WHAT? WHAT THE FUCK? YOU FUCKED SOMEONE BEHIND MY BACK? YOU'VE FUCKING CHEATED ON ME!'

'You left the room, Matt …'

'I LEFT THE ROOM SO YOU COULD HELP HIM GET IT UP. YOU SHOULD HAVE CALLED ME SO I COULD COME BACK IN. I WANTED TO SEE HIM FUCK YOU. THAT'S THE WHOLE FUCKING POINT, YOU STUPID BITCH.'

For the rest of the day, I didn't hear the end of it – shouting, swearing and calling me names. I was almost relieved when the next punter came. At least it was a break from Matt.

Later that evening, we were back in the main room with the shagpile carpet and he was still going on about my 'cheating', insisting I had willingly fucked someone behind his back. *Cheating?* I wanted to laugh. The whole idea was ridiculous – *he* was the one who set up these meetings, *he* was the one who insisted I fuck a load of strangers for fags. I didn't want to be doing any of this anyway! *I just do what you tell me to do*, I wanted to scream back at him. *I only ever do what you fucking tell me cos I'll get fucking hurt if I don't!*

'You waited for your chance and then you fucking grabbed it ...' he snarled.

'Matt, you left the room,' I sighed. 'What did you expect me to do?'

'I bet you love the feel of his cock in yer ...'

'Whatever I do is wrong!' I wailed. 'If I hadn't done anything you would have told me off too.'

'YOU FUCKING BITCH!' Now he lifted me up by my hair and dragged me round the room. A punch to the face, one to the stomach and another in the face again. He picked me up and flung me into the wall so hard I hit the plasterboard wall with a crack. It had come away from the other piece of plasterboard that joined the wall together. I lay there, my arms raised up over my head to protect myself, as the punches rained down on me – head, cheeks, stomach, shoulders, arms, head, face, cheeks, stomach, face ...

'Right,' he said, straightening up, panting from the exertion. 'There's another punter coming. Get yourself sorted the fuck out.'

Then he left the room.

I limped back to the office to find my mirror and make-up bag. Everything hurt. Sitting there, shaking, I stared at myself in the mirror – what a mess! I wiped away the mascara running down my face, then, with a quivering hand, tried to reapply my eye shadow and liner. *Tsk. Why won't my damn hands stop shaking?* I put the liner down for a second, sat back and stared at my half made-up reflection. *What the hell am I doing? Redoing my make-up so that the next person who comes to fuck me doesn't know that my husband's just beaten the living crap out of me?* This was my life now. *I can never leave. Never, never. The only way I can ever get out is if he kills me.* I finished my make-up and changed my outfit. *At least there is some let up … if only for fifteen minutes at a time.*

The punter texted to let me know he was downstairs and I replied that it was fine for him to come up. I heard the door click downstairs. *He's here. Okay. Deep breath, here we go again.* The door creaked open and I switched to 'Lydia'. *Here she is! Here's Lydia!* The mask firmly back on, I allowed bright, cheerful, jolly Lydia to take over. Lydia who is willing, Lydia who loves sex, Lydia who never gets down or depressed. Lydia the 'Happy Whore'. Actually the next guy wasn't a stranger at all – Jack was a regular of mine. Middle-aged, slightly overweight, with glasses and a lonely life outside these walls, Jack was typical of many of my punters. He had been coming to see me from the start of this whole enterprise so Matt rewarded his loyalty by letting him remain on the old rate of £40 for 15 minutes. He was here at least once or twice a week, enjoying the company and the small talk as much as the sex. I acted like nothing was wrong. Did he notice the fresh bruises and cuts? I hoped not. Besides, the room was dark, lit only by a couple of candles, so I managed to hide my face from him and we carried on as we always did. Jack was polite and respectful, he asked me how my week had been, I did the same and then he bent me over and fucked me from behind. It didn't last long – a few minutes and it was all over.

By 7pm, it was dark and we were alone again, just me and Matt. He was giving me the silent treatment. No more clients to see tonight so we turned off the lights, blew out the candles and locked up. A horrible, awkward silence filled the car on the way home. We stopped to pick up fish and chips for dinner and when we arrived back, Lindsey could tell something was wrong. The way he moved, gave one-word answers or didn't answer at all, refused to look us in the eyes, snapped at the kids ... It was obvious. Matt didn't bother to hide his bad moods. We unwrapped the dinner and everyone tucked in. I had my usual child-size portion, a small piece of fish and five chips.

Lindsey was now living with us full-time. A month earlier her cousin told her he needed some extra income so he planned to rent out his house that she lived in and she asked if she could come back here, with us. It turned out that we had actually been living in Lindsey's rented council house all along. I hadn't realised it but this wasn't Matt's house – he had chucked her out years earlier and she had gone to live in her cousin's home. It was just one of the many lies Matt had told me when we first got together. I wondered too about all the things he had told me about his former partners and how they had cheated on him, their so-called 'betrayals'. I'm sure he had lied about that too. Now Lindsey had nowhere else to go and needed a roof over her head. Could she stay with us?

'Yeah, course!' Matt said, laughing and enjoying the sense of power this gave him, hearing his mum beg to live in her own home.

'Anyway, that makes perfect sense,' he went on. 'With the business picking up, you can look after the kids more.'

So Lindsey had moved in a month earlier, and shortly after Matt insisted I tell her the truth about our thriving new business. It was after I came home from nursery one day and Lindsey was about to leave the house when Matt called me upstairs.

'Sit my mother down and tell her – *you do realise I have sex with people for money? I am a prostitute*. Just tell her that so she knows what we're up to.'

'Really?' I laughed, thinking he was joking. I *really* didn't want to do that.

'Just do as you're fucking told!'

So I went downstairs, took Lindsey away from the girls, and said quietly: 'Regarding us going out and earning money and our new business, which isn't anything to do with arcades, you do realise I have sex with people for money? I am a prostitute.'

I used the exact words he gave me, knowing that even one wrong word could earn me a smack in the face.

'Hmmmmm ...' She made a funny noise, like she was surprised but she wasn't. She knew Matt too well to know this was no joke.

Tonight Lindsey also knew that something was brewing. She glanced from me to Matt and back again and kept her mouth firmly shut. We ate in silence. Later, I put the kids to bed while Lindsey washed up, then I went into our bedroom. Matt lay on the bed, still brooding. He started on at me again – I'd made a fool out of him, did I think he was stupid? I sat down on my side of the bed and hoped a conciliatory approach might calm him down. Yes, he was right. Yes, I knew I'd made a fool out of him. No, I didn't think he was stupid. Yes, I was very sorry. Quickly, he rolled on top of me on the bed, pinning me down. I stared up at his black polo shirt and out of the corner of my eye I caught sight of a can. Lynx deodorant. I knew what was coming so I took a deep breath in and held it as he unleashed the spray can into my face. I had my eyes and mouth shut, as he sprayed and sprayed and sprayed. Then he punched me in the stomach, knocking the air out of me, and I had no choice, I gasped, taking in clouds of Lynx. Urgh, my lungs flooded with chemicals. I choked, coughing and gagging from the foul-tasting mist.

Now he half-dragged, half-pushed me off the bed.

'Get up on that windowsill!' he ordered.

Do as your told, Hannah. Just do it.

The window was wide open to the night sky as I found myself kneeling on the frame, looking down to the garden below. Scattered directly underneath me, 20 feet down, I knew there were a handful of wooden planks with nails sticking straight up, though I couldn't see them in the dark. They were meant to be planters for flowerbeds but Matt hadn't yet got round to putting them in the ground and they'd been sitting there on the patio for months, the nails gradually rusting to brown. My hands clung to the side of the window frame and the ledge dug painfully into the tops of my knees. Behind me, Matt pushed at my back and spat: 'If you feel sorry about what you've done, you'll let me push you out this window. You'll let me. If you're remorseful about what you've done, you'll let me do it.'

'I'm sorry. I'm sorry, Matt. I really am …' I said, frightened now. I didn't want to fall onto those planks, I really didn't.

'Then get your fingers off,' he snarled, pulling back my fingers. 'Let go of the window frame. Let go. LET GO!'

He punched me in the back, pushing me forward till I almost lost my grip and tumbled out of the window. I looked down again. *Just let go, do as you're told. Let go, Hannah. He won't stop till he's broken your fingers and made you let go anyway. If you let go you'll still be hurt but you won't have broken fingers.*

'LET GO, YOU STUPID BITCH!' he shouted again. I felt sure the whole neighbourhood could hear him.

Let him do it. You'll go down, you'll hit the patio, you might have nails in your body but you'll go to hospital and they'll make you better. You'll come home and all this will be over …

My left hand was off the frame, I was clinging to the windowsill now with just my right hand and Matt had hold of my wrist and was trying to bend my fingers back, pushing me in the back at the same time, forcing me out. My body rocked back and forwards as he pushed and pushed. And all of a sudden, I was ready. *Okay, I'm going to do it. I'm just going to let myself fall.* I was about to take my hand away, when Matt yelled out 'URGGGH' and staggered back towards the bed, clutching his chest.

What? What the hell just happened? I looked round to see him rolling around on the bed, clasping his chest as if he was having a heart attack. Slowly, I got down off the windowsill and went towards him.

'Matt, are you alright?' I asked, playing 'the concerned wife'. I had to. I mean, I *really* fucking hoped he was having a heart attack but everything about this over-the-top performance told me it was fake. Maybe he'd had second thoughts, maybe it occurred to him that pushing me out of a window wasn't the best idea he'd ever had – especially if he wanted me to work – or maybe he just didn't feel like taking me to hospital. Matt looked at me, scrunching up his face as if in deep pain, but he didn't say a word. *Please, please, God, let this be real.*

I called downstairs to Lindsey: 'Lindsey! Can you come quick?'

She came upstairs and we both stood there, looking at Matt.

'Does he need an ambulance?' I asked her.

'I don't know. What's wrong with him?'

'I don't need an ambulance,' he grunted. 'I'll be alright in a minute. Just leave me alone.'

So we did, we went downstairs and when I went back to check on him, he'd put himself to bed. In time Lindsey also went to bed. I didn't know what else to do so I stayed downstairs in the armchair, fully dressed. I didn't want to go up to bed. *What the hell is waiting for me up there? He just tried to push me out of the fucking window. What will he do next? He might attack me in the night while I'm asleep. He's done it many times before. What if he gets the urge to put a pillow over my face and hold it there till I stop breathing?* I was too fearful to go and lie down next to him so I stayed awake in the chair, thinking, watching, waiting for whatever was coming next. At some point in the early hours I must have dozed off because I woke the next morning, still fully clothed, my back sore from where I'd slept with it pressed against one arm of the armchair, my legs hanging over the other arm, and a heavy sense of dread that this was far from over.

14

It's Gone In

Just as I had feared, Matt's bad mood from the day before carried over into the morning. I'd woken up as the girls tramped downstairs in their pyjamas and turned on the TV in front of me. I was still in my Kingfisher-blue velvet hoodie, black strappy top and matching bottoms from the night before and after I'd greeted each one with a kiss, I set about making their breakfast. Lindsey came down with them. We exchanged a few words. She made her own breakfast and told me she was going into town this morning to meet her friend. Unlike me, Lindsey had the freedom to come and go as she pleased. I wasn't allowed to leave the house alone – even just popping out to the shops alone or taking the kids to the park was out of the question – so it didn't cross my mind to leave that day, to just pick up the kids and go. Go where? There was nowhere for me to go except my mum's and he knew where she lived. So he would find me, take me home and my life wouldn't be worth living … not that it was worth much anyway. The only things that kept me going were my beautiful girls. I never thought for a minute there was any way for me to escape safely with the girls and to stay away from Matt. Besides, nobody would believe me, that's what Matt said. I'd already lied repeatedly to the police, in court and to the authorities. Matt even had evidence I'd committed fraud. Why would anyone believe a word I said? That was what he had told me for so long I honestly believed it was true.

Just after 11.30am I heard his footsteps overhead. *He's awake!* I recognised the heavy stomping and the familiar route of his footsteps as he walked to the bathroom and back again. I was in the living room, sat on the armchair, when he appeared at the door in his red dressing gown, hair dishevelled – a murderous glare for me, a cheery 'good morning' for the girls. My stomach cramped in dread of what might be coming. I had to be ready.

'You having a cup of tea?' I offered.

He ignored me, turned around and went back through to the kitchen, muttering to himself. I hovered for a second in the hallway, wondering what to do next. What could I do to make things better? How could I defuse the situation?

He made himself a cup of tea and all the while he grumbled indignantly under his breath. Then he came back into the living room, his voice rising in anger.

'Don't look at me like that,' he snapped. 'You know what you did, you cheating bitch!'

'I said I'm sorry, Matt. I didn't mean to. I really didn't. I thought it was what you wanted. I'm sorry. I was only thinking of you.'

'Fucking liar! All this fucking time and you'd rather have some other cock in yer. You whore!'

He pushed me back into the living room and onto the

middle of the sofa, shouting at me, hitting me and calling me a 'whore', 'bitch' and 'fat slag'. The girls just carried on playing with their toys and watching CBeebies – they didn't even look up. For them, this was just a normal morning and they were used to seeing Matt attacking me. In the past Poppie might have said: 'Daddy, don't do that to Mummy. It's naughty.' But Matt had contradicted her – no, it was alright to hit Mummy, he had told our daughter. *See! I hit her all the time and you can hit her too. Go on, hit her! Hit Mummy! Hit the bitch harder!* Then Matt would laugh. Poppie hadn't wanted to hurt me but she accepted what her father said so when she saw Matt hitting me she honestly thought that this was okay.

Now Matt picked up the small wooden chair which Katie had been sitting on at her toddler table to eat her breakfast and started smashing it over my head and arms. I scrunched myself up into the foetal position, knees and arms over my head and face as Matt brought the chair down on me over and over again. Lindsey heard the commotion from the hallway and came into the living room, already dressed in her coat and shoes.

'Matt! Stop it! Matt, don't!' she yelled as she opened the living-room door.

'You shut the fuck up,' he shouted back. 'Or you'll get this over your head as well.'

Lindsey didn't say another word. She knew he meant what he said. She shut the door behind her and then I heard the sound of the front door clicking and slamming shut as she left. *Oh God, she's gone!* All of a sudden Matt flung down the chair and ran out to the kitchen. And that's when I heard the noise – *clang*.

Clang. If there's any sound that comes back to me stronger than any other from that day it is that clanging sound, the one Matt made as he rummaged inside the box of tools by the back door. And just before that, the sound as he yanked the toolbox open, the *rattle* of the tools as he rummaged through then – then *bang*, the sound of him closing the toolbox. *Clang*, *rattle*, *bang* … Just three little sounds that in ordinary life you might not notice but I was on high alert, I was listening, watching, observing, trying to work out what was going on. Every sound told me something I needed to know, each noise was a vital piece of information that could make the difference between getting hurt a little or getting hurt a lot. So I listened for the sounds he made when he disappeared into the kitchen and every time I have thought about that day since, they have come back to me. *Clang*, *rattle*, *bang* – and then the sound of his footsteps drawing closer to the living room, then him appearing in the living room, brandishing a screwdriver, shouting: 'I'M GOING TO FUCKING KILL YOU!'

Terrified for my life, I scrambled into the right-hand corner of the sofa. Now he jumped on top of me, slamming his knees down onto my body, which was turned over to my left side, pinning me there. He brought the point of the screwdriver down towards my chest with both hands on the handle and I grabbed hold of the tops of his arms, trying to push him away. The tip of the screwdriver touched my skin through my clothes. He leaned down harder and I could feel the sharp point digging into my flesh. I pushed back with all my might.

'YOU FUCKING WHORE. I'M GOING TO FUCKING KILL YOU. FUCKING OTHER MEN BEHIND

MY BACK. YOU LOVE THEIR COCK MORE THAN YOU LOVE MINE …'

His face was so close now flecks of spit flew out of his mouth and onto my face. He pushed the screwdriver harder and harder down into my chest. My arms were shaking with the effort of pushing so hard against him, trying to keep the screwdriver away. For a second, our eyes met and all I saw was hatred, pure hatred and pure evil. He gritted his teeth, pushing down harder and harder … *I can't stop it. I'm not strong enough … the screwdriver is going to go in me. Relax. Relax, Hannah. If you relax it won't hurt so much* … And in that split second I relaxed all the muscles in the top half of my body and released my grip on his arms … *Bang*, it went in. He pushed the screwdriver into my left-hand side between my ribs.

There was a popping sound as the metal sank into me, like air escaping after piercing a roll of cling film stretched taut over the top of a bowl. I could feel something deflating inside me. The screwdriver had gone right through my skin, my fat, my muscles and to whatever was below. My mind raced: *It's gone in, it's gone in, it's gone in, it's gone in, it's gone in, it's gone in … How far? How deep? Two inches? Three? More?* Matt pulled the screwdriver out, then he got off me, walked backwards away with the screwdriver still in his hands and he turned to go through to the kitchen. As soon as it was out, I slapped my right hand over the bleeding and put my left hand on top of that. Within seconds, both hands were covered in blood – it was spurting out everywhere. I tried to get up but I couldn't use my hands on the sofa to push myself up. Then Matt appeared in the living room again, without the screwdriver on him. *Where is it? What's he going to do with it? Is he coming back to finish me off? Has he tucked it into his dressing-gown belt behind him?* I rocked myself forward and stood up.

The kids were still playing with their cars on the living-room floor – I watched them now, making '*brrrrm, brrrrm-ing*' noises as they sped their little plastic toys across the carpet, Poppie still wearing her pink-and-blue *Octonauts* pyjamas, Katie in an emerald-green *Snoopy* set. *Is this it? Am I going to die now?*

'What do we do?' I asked Matt. 'What do we do? What do we do?'

I needed to know what was going to happen next. Was I dying? Would Matt try and stitch me up at home? Would he let me go to hospital?

'You alright?' Matt asked, casually. He knew the answer.

'Matt, seriously, what are we going to do?' I was trying to stay calm, but inside I was panicking. Time was of the essence now. We really did need to do something.

Matt seemed relaxed, casual, unconcerned.

'Right, I think you need an ambulance,' he said slowly.

He walked past me to get the phone, which sat above the windowsill on a dock on the side of the wall, picked it up, walked back over, facing me, then paced up and down the living room, the phone still in his hand. *Please, please, just dial it ...* He stood by the dining table, thinking. I watched him as the blood ran through my fingers, down my sleeve, off my elbow and onto the carpet. Everything was covered in it, my hands, hair, clothes, sofa. *How could there be so much blood?*

'Right,' he said, 'we'll say that you were fixing the kids' bookcase or something and you slipped.'

'Yeah, yeah, okay …' I nodded quickly. *Yes, anything.*

'NO!' he shouted back. I clearly hadn't paid enough attention. 'This is what we're doing. Okay? Or I'm not calling the ambulance.'

'Yes, Matt. Sorry. That's what we'll say – I was fixing a bookcase …'

He nodded once, then he dialled 999.

As soon as the handler at the other end picked up, he switched. Now he was the concerned husband, desperate for help: 'Ambulance, please … it's my wife. I … er … I don't know what's happened, I've been in bed, she's had an accident with a screwdriver, she's bleeding quite badly from her side.'

It felt like I had really tight clothes on. I could feel my heart beating through my palms and my hands getting warmer and wetter with the blood as I paced up and down. I looked at the clock on the wall – 11.37am. Matt was taking instructions from the call handler, grabbing a towel that had been drying on the radiator. An Egyptian-cotton king-size bath towel, part of a set, a wedding present from my granddad and nanny. He threw it at me and told me to place it over the wound. The moment I took my hands off the wound to put the towel over it, blood spurted out over me.

Matt was on the phone still.

'Sit down,' he ordered. 'They're saying you should stop walking.'

So I sat down on the sofa, my eyes resting on my children. They were still glued to the telly, blissfully unaware of the seriousness of the situation. Every now and then they glanced back at me and I smiled, trying to reassure them. *Is this the last time I see my children?*

Within a couple of minutes, the paramedic car arrived, then the road ambulance. At some point a helicopter came too and I heard the unmistakable whirring noise overhead. The first person through the door was a paramedic called Nick, and not long after, two more arrived, one called Laura and another guy whose name I didn't get. They all seemed really nice. So now we had three paramedics in the house, kids in the corner and me, sat on the edge of one of our cream leather sofas, blood everywhere. One paramedic tied my hair out of the way while Laura squatted down on the floor in front of me and asked to see the injury.

The towel came off and she put a large white plaster over the top with a valve attached to it. It was meant to let air out and stop the air coming in, but it didn't stay stuck to me for long because I was bleeding continuously. Things were starting to get a little blurry. At some point all three disappeared – to the ambulance to get more equipment, I assumed, or so they said. I can't remember but later I realised they must have been talking among themselves, asking each other: 'Is this injury consistent with falling over?'

Now Lindsey appeared in her long cream coat – she had been out and come back again, following the blue lights of the ambulance up to house. She stood at the living-room door.

'What's happened?' she asked the group of paramedics huddled around me, all working quickly and quietly to stem the bleeding. 'Is Hannah okay?'

Nobody spoke, they were too busy at this point trying to find my pulse.

Then she looked over at Matt: 'What's happened?'

'She's had another funny one,' he replied. All of this within earshot of the paramedics. A deliberate strategy, I realised, a back-up plan in case the 'I stabbed myself accidentally while fixing a bookcase' excuse didn't work. *Plan B: he was going to make out I had had a mental breakdown and done this to myself deliberately.* Lindsey knew not to say anything further in front of the paramedics. Instead she looked at me and said: 'Hannah, why are you so white? What's happened?'

'Ask Matt,' I replied, too tired to realise how incriminating this sounded.

Now Nick asked Matt to show him the screwdriver. Matt took him through to the other room to the bookcase – our pristine light-coloured carpet beneath it was completely blood-free at the spot where I'd supposedly had the accident. The screwdriver too was clean of any blood. I suppose Nick must have been wondering how I was meant to have slipped in such a way as to have stabbed myself without leaving a drop of blood on either the screwdriver or the carpet next to the bookcase, but had covered our couch in the other room with the stuff instead. Still, I wasn't really concerned about getting our story straight at this point. I was more worried about staying alive.

'If you're going to hospital, I'll take the kids upstairs, get them washed and dressed,' said Matt. So Matt disappeared upstairs with the girls. *How strange. Matt wouldn't normally leave me on my own with paramedics. Oh well, no time to worry about that now.*

All three paramedics were lovely, and I was grateful for their care and compassion as they patched me up and reassured me that they were going to look after me. But first, they needed to get me into the ambulance.

I shifted forward, ready to stand up: 'Okay, let's go.'

They gave me a funny look.

'What? Is everything okay?' I asked. 'I thought you said we need to go.'

'Yeah, but we'll put you in the stretcher, we'll carry you out,' said Laura.

'No, it's fine, I can walk.'

'No, really, Hannah. You can't. It's for the best. Just stay there a minute and we'll get the stretcher.'

The next thing I found myself being carried in an upright stretcher – a bit like a chair – with Laura in front by my feet and Nick behind me. As I was carried over the threshold of the front door, the blinding sunlight hit my eyes. I shut my eyes tight against the light and all I could see were white dots. *Why is the sun so bright today?*

'Hannah? Hannah? Are you okay?' Laura's voice. 'Open your eyes, Hannah.'

'I'm fine, the sun's just really bright.'

'It's because you've lost a lot of blood. What can you see?'

'Lots of white dots. Like looking at something black with loads of fuzzy, glittery white dots.'

'It's because you've lost a lot of blood, honey, but we're going to get you sorted.'

They loaded me into the back of the road ambulance, transferred me to the bed and placed an oxygen mask over my face. By now two more people had arrived dressed in red jumpsuits – they were the helicopter doctors, I was told. *Am I dying? I didn't get to say goodbye to my children …*

I shut my eyes again and when I opened them, a policeman had appeared at the bottom of the ambulance doors. *I didn't know anyone had called the police. Maybe they are here to shut the road off to let the helicopter land.* A second later Matt appeared at the bottom of the ambulance doors, looking at me with the oxygen mask over my face. He raised his eyebrows and gave me a small, knowing smirk, as if to say: *Look what I've done to you.*

But out loud he said: 'I'm going to follow the ambulance. Mum's going to stay at home with the kids.'

I saw the policeman standing behind him.

Someone said: 'Right, we need to get going.'

Bang, bang – the ambulance doors closed behind us and we were off.

Sirens on, blue lights, we sped down the motorway towards the hospital.

'Can we cut your clothes off?'

'Yeah …'

'I need your arm. Hannah. Can I just take it out of the blanket a second?'

'Yeah.'

Prodding, poking, things going on … I felt like I was half asleep.

'It's okay, we've finished with your arm now, you can tuck it back in.'

But I had no energy so I left it there, hanging out the bed. Someone wiped me up, someone turned the oxygen up. As we pulled into the hospital the air-ambulance doctor said to me: 'I just want to warn you because I don't want you to be frightened that when we come out of the ambulance and we go into the hospital, there will be 30 or 40 doctors and nurses around you and they will come up and do things. But don't worry. Sometimes people get a bit anxious with that many people around. We don't want to frighten you, we just want to prepare you. Okay?' I nodded.

My God, he was right! There were doctors and nurses everywhere – all in different-coloured uniforms. I was wheeled out of the back of the ambulance and through the doors into resuscitation.

Above me, a voice announced: 'All right, everybody, this is Hannah, 22-year-old female …'

Everywhere I looked there were faces. A small, plump lady with brown hair, around her late forties, came up to the left of me and stuck a needle in my arm. Morphine. Someone else put a monitor on my finger. 'Can't find a pulse … found it.' Wires everywhere … people everywhere. *Where's Matt? Wasn't he following in the car?* A nurse came over with a massive bag of blood hanging off a big stick.

'Oh, is that for me?' I slurred, drunkenly.

'We've just got this here just in case. Don't you worry about that for now, darling.'

By now my top half was naked with a sheet half covering me for modesty. In the background somewhere a darkly dressed figure loitered. The policeman.

The consultant now came up to the left of me: 'Can you lift your arm up, Hannah?'

I lifted it and placed my hand on the back of my neck to give him access to where they needed to get to under my armpit. Someone wheeled over a trolley and on it I saw a scalpel and lots of other medical instruments. The consultant explained they were going to cut me open and put a drain in. I nodded. *Everything is hazy. I sort of understand but not fully. I'm drifting a bit. At least I'm in the right place. They know what they're doing, just let them get on with it.* Someone numbed my side and now they cut me open but, to my alarm, I could actually feel the doctor's fingers inside my body.

'GET OUT! GET YOUR FINGERS OUT OF MY BODY! GET THEM OUT!' I screamed.

Another doctor was called, a couple of seconds later, someone came and squirted something into my veins through a cannula. I could still feel his fingers wriggling around inside my ribcage. *Stop … stop … I can feel … I can feel … I can …*

Darkness.

15

Mr Policeman

I blinked open my eyes, my head thick and woozy from the drugs. The world came into focus, slowly – white walls, beeping machines, wires, tubes, people beside me … *Where am I? What's happened?* My eyes landed on a pair of heavy black boots. *That's funny. I wonder whose boots they are.* Gradually, my eyes travelled upwards to reveal that they belonged to a policeman – the same policeman I had seen when they hoisted me into the ambulance and, in a flash, the events of the morning came back to me.

'Hello, Hannah. How are you feeling?' said the policeman kindly.

There was a doctor sat beside my left arm, just finishing stitching me up, and a nurse holding my arm above my head and keeping my hair out of the way.

'That's it,' said the doctor. 'All done!' He cut the thread attached to a long scar across my wound, out of which ran a fat tube that hung down to a bucket by the bed.

'That's the chest drain,' the doctor explained. 'Your lung was punctured so that's why you've got the drain in, to re-inflate the lung. We've stitched you up and the drain needs to stay in for another 12–24 hours.'

I felt the tears prickle behind my eyes. *Look at the size of that wound! Look what he's done to me!*

'Is it okay to talk to Hannah now?' the policeman asked the doctor.

'Yes, that's fine,' he nodded, got up and left us alone. The nurse now brought my arm down gently and he too made himself scarce.

The policeman stood to my left side.

'I'm PC Williamson. Would you mind just telling me what's happened to you, Hannah?'

'Where's Matt?' My eyes darted around the resuscitation ward.

'Mr Gower has been arrested. He's at the police station. We're trying to establish what happened. You've had a very severe injury here.'

Thank God for that … he deserves to be locked up for what he did to me today but … oh my God, Matt's going to be so angry at me …

'We just want to ask you what happened …' he went on.

'I was tightening a screw on our children's bookcase when I slipped,' I repeated, robotically. That was our story and I had to stick to it. I didn't know what else to say. How could I possibly tell the truth when I had to go back home and face Matt? The policeman took all my answers down on a little notepad, then asked me to show him what I did with my hands when I slipped …

'My hand came forward towards my side like this,' I said limply, realising for the first time how unlikely it would be for me to have the strength to drive the screwdriver in that hard. Nevertheless, he nodded and wrote that in his notebook too. He asked me to read and sign it, which I did. Then he asked if he could take some photos of the injuries and I agreed. I would be made to pay for that later down the line.

PC Williamson got his little camera and I pulled the sheet down a little to show him the wound. He took one close-up of the injury and another photo with my face in it.

'Okay, thank you,' he said, smiling, and I pulled the sheet back over me.

A moment's silence … then: 'Is there anything else you'd like to tell me, Hannah?'

'No. Like I said, it was just an accident.'

'If Mr Gower has done this to you we can look after you and we will take it seriously.'

'Where are my kids?'

'They're at home with Mr Gower's mother.'

'Are my children okay?'

'Yeah, they're fine.'

'Well, when are you going to let Matt out of the police station? Cos he hasn't done anything wrong.' I had to cover for him, make it sound genuine.

'Okay, Hannah, I'll leave you to it but if at any point there's something you remember you can contact us.' The policeman was so nice.

After he left I realised I was starving hungry. I hadn't eaten anything all day and asked one of the nurses for something to eat and drink. She brought me a sandwich and the best cup of tea I have ever tasted in my whole life. Shortly after that, they wheeled me up to the ward, dosed me up with morphine and let me doze for the rest of the day. Mostly, I stayed still, lying on my back, unmoving. At one point I shifted to the right but I felt the drain pull, which alarmed me so I resolved not to move again, instead just closing my eyes, letting myself drift off. Later that afternoon, I asked to call home on the hospital phone. Lindsey answered and she put me on to Poppie.

'Mummy's okay. Mummy's getting better,' I told her in as cheerful a voice as I could muster. 'I'll be home as soon as I can.'

Then I spoke to Lindsey. She told me that after I was taken away, the police cordoned off the whole of the downstairs and she and the girls were instructed to stay in the bedroom upstairs for two hours while they took forensic samples from the 'crime scene'.

'They came and took photos all over the house,' she said quietly, keeping her voice low so the children couldn't hear. 'Then the police went door to door, asking all the neighbours questions. I didn't know what to do about telling your mum but one of the neighbours said I had to let her know so I called her and she came round here. And then Matt turned up after the police let him out, wearing the paper suit that the police gave him. They had taken all his clothes off him, even his dressing gown. He says he wants to come and see you tonight.'

'Okay … okay …' My mind raced. *What would he say? What would he be thinking?* I had to be ready.

At around 7pm, Matt arrived on the ward with a pack of Oreo cookies and some Go Ahead! yoghurt bars. In that moment I hated him, I hated everything about him, including the way he breathed, talked, moved and coughed even. I had no fear of him inside that hospital, knowing he'd never do something in front of other people.

'I brought you these, thought you might have been hungry,' he said, showing the concern he knew was expected of him. I recognised the packets from our cupboard at home – he hadn't even bought them. I was starving but I didn't want the biscuits. I didn't want to take anything from him. But of course, I thanked him and ate a couple of the cookies, knowing full well that he would be offended if I didn't. Funnily enough, I haven't touched an Oreo cookie since.

'Let's have a look then,' he said, nodding at the wound. I lifted up the hospital gown and showed him the 1½-inch scar.

'Oh for fuck's sake!' he muttered, shaking his head. Was he complaining? He was the one who had done this to me and now he was complaining about the work the doctor had to do to repair the damage! Perhaps it was because he knew I wouldn't be able to go to the office for a while. Matt shifted in his seat and looked around at the other patients on the ward and the nurses moving between the beds on their drug rounds.

'Right, should we go out for a fag?' he said, more of an order than a question. I had a punctured lung but this didn't seem to worry him – he wanted me away from all the people. So I called over a nurse and asked if it was okay if Matt took me outside for some fresh air. She agreed so I climbed carefully out of bed, wrapped a dressing gown around me and walked outside, carrying the drain by my side.

Once outside, we headed to the car and sat on the cold leather seats of Matt's Range Rover. Matt lit a fag and handed it to me. I took it and shivered: the sun was setting now and my hospital gown was thin. Matt lit a fag for himself, took in a long pull, then blew out the smoke.

'Well, you know I'm capable of anything now I've done this to you,' he said slowly, staring straight ahead. 'So you better fucking do as I tell you. What happened with the police?'

I told him everything I could recall about the interview in A&E, including how the PC wrote down my statement on his pad.

'You better not have fucking signed it,' he growled. *Oh God …*

'I don't know … I don't know if I did. I might have done. I don't know. It's all hazy …'

'If I find out you fucking signed it, I'll fucking put you back in this place again. You know I'd do it. Look what I done to you already.'

Later, back on the ward, I lay down, more depressed than I had ever been in my life. He was going to kill me, I knew that. It wasn't a question of if, but when. At least in hospital, I was away from him, even just for a little while. I could sleep, I could rest and recover a little … until he did it again.

The next day, I spoke to my mum on the phone. She was obviously upset that I was in hospital but didn't suspect for a moment that I was lying about how it happened. The social worker called too, wanting to speak to me about 'the accident' but Matt insisted I refuse unless I could be sure the call was recorded. We had managed to keep them away until now. They had written to us once towards the end of my pregnancy with Katie but Matt insisted they had nothing on us and told them to leave us alone. A few weeks later we had received another letter stating that they had had a meeting and didn't feel that there was any need to be involved with our family at this time. Now they were back.

Matt told me to discharge myself.

'Get that drain out and get yourself home,' he instructed.

So when the doctor came to see me on his ward rounds I told him I wanted to be discharged. Of course he tried to talk me out of it but I was adamant, even though I was still fairly drugged up. At around 3pm, just one day after being admitted, Matt came to collect me – he walked me out of the hospital and put me in the car. It was sunny and just as we pulled out of the hospital car park it hit me: *That's my break over. Back to reality now. Back to the nightmare of my life* … My one consoling thought was that at least I would be reunited with my children.

The stitches stayed in for three weeks. I had to go to an appointment at the GP surgery to have them taken out and, naturally, Matt escorted me into the room for the appointment. He had been released on bail, pending further investigation. Mum came to see me and when I showed her the scar she gasped, her eyes widening in horror: 'Hannah, what have you done?!'

'Yeah, I know. That's why I need to be more careful next time,' I said quickly.

Matt was furious about the pictures I'd let the PC take of my scar.

'Why did you let them take a photo? You should have said to them no, why the fuck do you need a picture of my injury?'

When social services came to the house for my interview, they insisted on speaking to me alone so Matt bugged me, putting a Dictaphone in my bra to record the conversation.

'We just need to give you an opportunity to tell us if anything has happened that you haven't already told us,' the social worker said meaningfully as we sat outside in the front garden. But I feigned annoyance and just repeated the story we had rehearsed. How could I possibly do otherwise? He was listening to every word. Nobody else challenged me about what I'd said, the police didn't interview me again and I wasn't given any other information. I knew that our story made no sense at all but, as Matt said over and over, as long as we both said the same thing, they couldn't prove otherwise. He even wrote a letter of complaint to the police for arresting him at the scene, which he made me sign. This obviously did the trick because soon the police closed the investigation with 'no further action'.

I went back to work and a few months later Poppie started at a private school in a nearby village. Nobody questioned this. To the outside world we were a respectable family who ran a successful arcade business. Matt had even made a website for our so-called arcade business so that we looked completely legitimate. They had no idea where our money really came from. She was there for a week before the school called us in for a meeting. Since Poppie hadn't had much interaction with other children and was still so young – she had only just turned four – they recommended a six-month stint at nursery, to improve her social skills. Then they would take her back. So we found her a private nursery and put both girls in. At first Katie was only doing two days a week, but as the business built up they both went full-time.

By now the business was busier than it had ever been and Matt had also increased the range and frequency of our swingers' meetings. If we had an hour free in the afternoon, he would put a status update on the swingers' website: 'Gang bang this afternoon, message for details.' Then maybe ten men would turn up, all with a pack of fags. Some would stand and wank while the others would fuck me. I was a robot, I did what I had to do. I didn't allow myself to have feelings. Drink helped, and Matt knew it. We had started to throw swingers' parties and Matt always made sure I'd had a few drinks before they got started. He knew that made me looser and more willing to do all the disgusting things required of me. If my drink was running low he'd come and top it up. After all, there weren't any other women involved, it was just me. I had to satisfy everyone, no matter how many people turned up. I was happy to drink myself into oblivion those nights, thankful that at least when I woke up the next morning I wouldn't remember what I'd done the night before. Drink gave me that small mercy.

Now we converted the downstairs into a bar too – the arcade machines were still in one half, but in the other half we put in sofas, carpets and a bar. We expanded our business, running the swingers' parties with a new business partner called Ben, for which we were paid in cash, not just fags. Matt also started to record me on the video camera to put it on the website, which people would pay to watch, creating another revenue stream.

That Christmas was a whole lot better than the one before – at least this year we were allowed to celebrate on the day itself. Even so, Matt decided to take his mum and go to the neighbours just before I was about to dish up. He just disappeared, leaving me wondering how long he would be gone and what to do about the girls. They were hungry and we didn't know how long he was going to be gone for. They returned at around 6pm, Matt acting as if nothing was wrong.

'Can I dish up now?' I asked and he nodded.

Lindsey got up to follow me into the kitchen: 'I'll give you a hand, Hannah.'

'NO!' Matt yelled. 'Leave her to do it, that's her fucking job. She's the slave.'

So I served it up by myself and the girls got to open their presents.

By now Lindsey was aware of everything that we were doing and my mum knew about the parties too because my sister had been told by one of her friends about my listings on the adult websites. When she brought it up I was horrified but I confirmed that they were swingers' parties and she didn't question me further. Matt liked to drop little comments in front of the family, pretending I was the inspiration for starting up the business, that I was the one with the 'insatiable appetite'.

'I just go along with it to keep her happy,' he laughed. Plus, of course, there were tonnes of unopened packs of fags lying around the house, all in separate boxes. It was just odd. My mum would come round and see them all, piled up on the tables, in the corners, lying about in the bedrooms, corridor, everywhere. One day she wondered out loud: 'Why's there so many packets of fags here?'

I told her that they were gifts for special parties that we held for our customers. She just accepted my answer. She never challenged me about whatever I said.

After the screwdriver incident, social services claimed there were reasonable grounds to suspect domestic violence in the home and put the girls on a child-protection plan, visiting every ten days to make observations and write reports. The social workers came and after several months they told us they were happy enough with everything they saw. They were on the point of closing up the case but just needed to speak to the nursery to finish their reports and take the girls off the plan. But Matt, uncooperative as ever, refused to tell them which nursery they attended.

'We don't have to tell you anything,' he blustered. 'Take us to court if you like!'

Of course, we really didn't have much choice and in the end we told them the name of the nursery. To explain the intrusion from social services, we called a private meeting with the nursery manager and spun her a story about how I had been attacked and raped in our home, in front of the girls, and that's why social services were sniffing round. The nursery manager was sympathetic.

'Oh that's awful. I'm so sorry to hear that.'

Matt thought that this would be enough to keep them from thinking the worst when social services visited. Little did we know that the nursery had some revelations of their own.

One day I arrived at the office to a message on the answerphone. It was from my solicitor: 'The local authority have issued proceedings. They want to remove the children as they suspect domestic violence in the home.'

I started to shake violently. Quickly, I headed to the bar and got myself a large glass of red wine. My heart was racing at a million beats a second. I couldn't think straight. It was my worst nightmare come true. My babies! My beautiful children! They were everything to me, the only reason I got up in the morning. The only reason I had to live. It was such a shock after everything social services had said to us.

What had changed? What did they know? What had they found out? We prepared for the first hearing as best we could but it wasn't until we were in court that we discovered the reason for the sudden change of heart.

I sat in court listening intently as the representative for the council outlined the reasons for the application for an interim care order. The case they had built up against us was strong. They quoted numerous hospital appointments for so-called accidents as well as the screwdriver incident. But it was the words that had come out of my children's mouths that were most damning. Unknown to either of us, Poppie and Katie had been quite open about the things they heard and saw at home. And why would they lie? Having nothing to compare it to, they assumed our behaviour was perfectly normal.

I read the reports from the nursery with tears in my eyes and a heavy, heavy heart.

One day Poppie had told a nursery keyworker: 'This morning Daddy said he was going to rip Mammy's face off but it's okay because Mammy's face is still there.'

A large lump came to my throat. I had no idea. In my desperation, in my quest to keep us all alive, I hadn't realised the daily impact all the threats and violence was having on my daughters.

A quote from Katie: 'Daddy bangs his fist on the table and gets angry at Mammy.'

And another: 'Daddy shouts and swears and spits in Mammy's face.'

Kids don't make up stuff like that. They just don't.

Since it was only the first hearing and we would need time to prepare our defence we knew the case would be adjourned. But what would happen in the meantime? There was at least a week before the next hearing. The local authority told the court they would be happy for the children to remain in the home with the mother at the exclusion of the father. This was agreed with our representatives and so that very day Matt was forced to move out. He went to live in our office, which he was not happy about but there was nothing much he could do about it. The children stayed at home with me and Lindsey and Matt was not allowed back in the house. Every day a social worker actually came round to the house to ensure Matt wasn't there and at weekends the police did it – even checking the cupboard under the stairs to make sure I wasn't hiding him!

Naturally, I was fearful. The prospect of losing my kids was unimaginable but at the same time, this new arrangement gave me a glimmer of hope. *Perhaps the local authority are on my side? Even if we lose the application for an interim care order, perhaps the court will allow me to keep the kids on my own without Matt? Then we'll be safe from him and I won't have to give evidence against him and risk him killing me.* It felt like there was light at the end of the tunnel. The whole thing was horrible, of course, and it kept me up at night, worrying and fretting … but even so, in the back of my mind, I was hopeful. Was God showing me a way out? It certainly helped not having Matt at home for eight days before the next hearing, a taste of what our life could be like without him.

Still, the night before the start of the hearing I worked on my statement till the early hours, checking it over and over again against Matt's statement and making sure everything tallied perfectly. According to Matt the only way they could justify taking the kids was if they had evidence – so if we both stuck to the story, what could they prove? We described ourselves as a normal, happily married couple and that I was into 'sparring', which is how we explained the injuries. What the kids saw at home was just play fighting, we said, nothing more serious than that. I spent hours on the computer, typing up the statement, talking on the phone to Matt and then driving up to the office to print it off. *It's going to be fine*, I told myself the night before it all kicked off ... *the judge will read our statements. He'll take a view and, if the worst comes to the worst, they'll let me keep the children without Matt.*

Whatever happens, it will be fine. Everything will be fine.

16

The Siblings Who Sailed Away

The day is etched on my mind like no other. I wish it wasn't. I wish I didn't have to ever think about this day again. I try not to. After all, what good does it do to keep going over the most painful parts of a person's life? But I can't forget. For as long as I live, I'll never be able to forget …

We woke up early on the Friday morning, the last day of the trial and the day the judge was due to give his judgment. I had given evidence the day before on behalf of myself and Matt. After our witness statements had been submitted to the court there had been some discussion among our representatives about who would go into the witness box. Matt wanted to do it himself. He said he would make a better job of it, put our side of the story more convincingly to the judge. But our two lawyers – Matt and I each had to be represented separately – insisted it was a good idea if it came from me. After all, it was me who had the kids and it was Matt that social services had accused of violence. I didn't want to do it but secretly I was relieved it wasn't Matt. He was unpredictable and likely to end up ranting. Also, I knew that he would probably become aggressive under cross-examination. Over the last few years with Matt I'd learned how to hold my temper, how to remain calm in the most extreme circumstances and under intense scrutiny, so I trusted myself not to get overly emotional.

So the day before I had gone into the witness box and, led by my brief, I described what a kind, loving husband and father Matt was and how social services' suspicions were entirely wrong. Then, when the brief for the local authority asked me questions, I had to try to explain the children's comments to the nursery workers.

'Kids pick up all sorts of things from television,' I insisted. 'They watch these cartoons like *Tom and Jerry* where they're hitting each other and they repeat what they see. I think they just got mixed up when they said it was Mummy and Daddy.'

The council's solicitor paused, leaving my answer hanging in the air, inviting me to go on. But I didn't say anything more, knowing how guilty it looked to keep talking and talking.

'And the violent displays and gestures, Mrs Gower? Poppie has hit other children, she spits in their faces, she is physically aggressive. And when pulled up on her behaviour she has told the nursery staff it's okay because "Daddy does it". Does Daddy do it, Mrs Gower?'

'No.'

'Why would your daughter say that he did then?'

'I don't know … I wasn't there but maybe she was fibbing to get out of being told off.'

'Does your child lie, Mrs Gower?'

'All children tell fibs. I don't think my child is any different.'

Another long silence. Later that evening, in the office, Matt berated me. He said I had come across as cold, unfeeling. I honestly didn't know how I could have done things differently.

Now, on Friday morning I was up early to get the kids washed, dressed, fed and ready for nursery. The court had ordered they attend nursery every day from 8am during the course of the trial but today was different. We had to be prepared, our lawyers had warned us. If the judge found that the threshold criteria for the granting of interim care orders had been met then the orders would be granted straight away. The criteria is met when it is proved that the child is suffering or is likely to suffer significant harm and that this harm is a result of the parenting. That meant either we were coming back to collect the girls later today – or the council was.

Lindsey and I drove the girls to nursery that morning. We hung their bags up on their pegs, greeted the nursery staff and then I bent down to say my usual goodbyes. The children had no idea of course what was happening; they didn't know the significance of the day and both simply wanted to run off and play. I said goodbye to Katie first, giving her a massive squeeze.

'You have a nice day today, won't you,' I told her, smiling to hide my heavy heart. 'You go and play and I'll see you later.'

Next I said goodbye to Poppie. She was wearing her sun hat and the suncream I'd plastered on her before we left the house. Now, as we hugged, I felt her sticky, suncreamed cheek against mine. I held onto her for a little bit longer than normal, a bit longer than she wanted. She squirmed in my arms, desperate to run off and play.

'Have a nice day,' I told her, trying not to cry. 'Have fun at nursery and be good.'

Then I gave her one more extra-big cuddle. I didn't want to let go.

Next I said goodbye to the nursery nurses – Sam and Michelle – and told them about the car seats, which I had left in the hallway, just in case I wasn't coming back to collect them. It occurred to me then to give them each a big hug. I felt like it, especially since they had been so lovely to me during this whole hellish period, but I didn't. I regret that now. As we left the thought flashed through my mind: *This could be the last time I touch this door.* But I quickly dismissed it. *No, you can't think like this. Stay positive, Hannah. It's going to be all right.* We walked out and towards the car, my eyes on the outside play area where the children were running about. Some mornings the girls would wave to us from the fence as we drove out of the car park – and today I was heartened when Poppie came to wave us bye-bye. Lindsey looked at her happy little face and it was all she could do not to break down right then and there.

'It's going to be okay,' I whispered. 'Come on. We'll see them later.'

Now we drove to the office to pick up Matt. He was ready for us, wearing his three-piece suit and a nasty scowl. *Horrible face* … I thought to myself. *Horrible face, horrible mood, horrible man* … Together we drove for an hour to the family court, parked down one of the side roads, and walked into the court building where we met our briefs. My barrister was kind and supportive but she was honest too and said that she didn't think things were looking good. Despite this, I was still hopeful. We took our seats in court; Matt sat to the right of me, holding my hand, and on my other side was the social worker. Our legal team sat in front of us.

'All rise!' the court usher instructed us to stand as the judge took his seat at the front of the court. It was a brief hearing, during which he read from his prepared judgment: 'We've heard oral evidence from the mother, Mrs Gower, we've heard from the local authority, from the social worker as well as written evidence, and I am satisfied that the threshold criteria has been met.'

Matt pulled his hand away. I felt myself falling, falling, falling …

'So it is the order of this court that interim care orders are granted. Court rise. Thank you.'

And that was it. The judge left. We had lost our children.

No, no, no, no, no … What do I do? What can I do? I was breathing hard, my eyes filling with tears, trying to keep myself from breaking up, desperate, helpless, devastated. I grabbed the social worker by her arm.

'Please,' I gasped. 'Please make sure my children go to a good home.'

'I will,' she replied, nodding gently, and I crumbled. I hadn't expected this. I thought that if Matt was forbidden from coming into the house I'd be allowed to keep the kids. But the lawyers had warned us that this could happen. They had said that if the threshold was met, our continued denials in the face of strong evidence might leave the judge no choice. By us failing to give any insight into our relationship difficulties or agreeing to attend counselling sessions, our children remained at risk of further harm. Now we were told the arrangements: two nursery care workers would drive the girls to the adult social care centre where they would be placed with a temporary foster family.

I came out of the courtroom in floods of tears. Lindsey was there to greet us. She hadn't been present in court for the hearing but she could see, just from looking at us, that the judgment had not gone our way. She put her arms around me and we wept together. Matt stood next to us, silent, grim-faced, scowling. Our lawyers came to speak to us and we had a few snatched words – we could appeal, they said. This wasn't the final hearing. There would be opportunities now to put our position. Yes, we would have visitation rights ... but I didn't have long to speak as Matt was impatient to leave, bundling us all out, ignoring our lawyers.

We walked back to the car, Matt in front, still fuming, refusing to speak to either of us. He was certain we were responsible for everything. I had given evidence badly and Lindsey had given the game away on the day he had stabbed me. None of this was his fault, of course. He took out the toys, change bag, everything to do with the kids, and dumped them on the side of the road. Then he looked at us both, standing there, too defeated to move or speak.

'You two can make your own fucking way home,' he spat, then got in the car and drove off. I stood there, surrounded by all my children's possessions, and for a minute I wondered what the hell to do next. Then I realised, I didn't care. I didn't care what happened to me now. What more could he fucking do? I didn't have anything left in the world. He had taken it all. So what if he drove off without me? It was the very least of my worries right now.

But we didn't stand there for long. The thing is that Matt drives like an arsehole. A couple of months earlier he'd cut up an unmarked police car and they had pulled him over to find he didn't have a driving licence or insurance. He was banned from the road. So five minutes after leaving us in that side road, he came screeching back round the corner and pulled up on the curb.

'Come on ... get in!' he shouted as he got out of the driver's seat and went round to sit in the passenger seat. 'I don't want to get pulled by the police if I'm driving. Get in this fucking car. NOW!' So we put the stuff back in the car and I drove us all home.

I drove in a dazed, zombie-like state. It felt like someone had chucked a double-decker bus at my head. I was in so much shock. But despite the pain and the grief, there was relief too. *At least they're safe ...* I told myself. *They're gone but they're safe and they don't have to put up with him anymore. I don't have to worry about protecting them all the time. They got away, they escaped.*

I knew too that without Matt as a father they had a better chance of turning out to be decent girls. I wasn't a fool; I could see what a poor father he was. I wanted to raise fine young girls for daughters but with Matt as a father I knew that this would be nearly impossible. I didn't want them growing up thinking it was okay to hit and punch others. As little girls they behaved well at home and they both loved me deeply but Matt was teaching them bad things. How long before they turned into bullies themselves? I hated the fact that Poppie had been violent at nursery. I hated how normal it had become for them to see me with black eyes, bruises and scars, and how casually they repeated Matt's nasty threats. But the girls were everything to me; they were my world. Without them, I didn't know what reason I had to live anymore ...

Back at home, we were tasked with a grim job. Social services had asked us to pack up some of the girls' clothes and toys to take to their new foster home. Neither Matt nor Lindsey said they could face doing it, so it fell to me. I didn't hesitate. It was the least I could do, no matter how hard it was. Just going back into their bedrooms, looking at the beds they'd woken up in that morning and realising they were not coming back broke my heart. But I couldn't afford to be self-indulgent. No matter how painful this was for me, I knew it must be a hundred times worse for my children. And the guilt that we had done this to them overrode all my own emotions. My girls weren't just losing their mum and dad but also their grandmothers, their home, everything they knew and that was familiar to them. And whose fault was that? It was ours! We had created this pain, we had engineered this massive tragedy in their lives. Matt was full of bitterness, blaming everyone else but himself – it was my fault, social services, the council, the police, his mum ... the list went on. But I knew the truth was that it was our fault. And I didn't know if I could ever forgive myself for that.

Now, when our children needed something familiar, something recognisable to cling to, how could I deny them these small comforts? Their teddies, their pyjamas and blankets – they needed them. I got a black bin liner from the kitchen and set about packing away anything they might need in their new home: clothes, shoes, coats, pyjamas, toothbrushes, hair brush, favourite shampoo and conditioner, toys, cuddly teddies, books and their Bibles. I took my time, looking at everything carefully, taking photos of their things, smelling their clothes, holding them close, trying to imprint their scents into my mind forever. *I won't give up.* I made a silent promise to them both. *No matter what happens, I will fight till the last breath to get you back. And one day, with or without Matt, I'll bring you home.*

Then I drove the bags to the local authority building and dropped them off. Back home again, I was restless, uneasy. I tidied up, clearing up the kitchen, hoovering, dusting, cleaning. In the bathroom my eyes landed on a familiar object – an old inhaler. Poppie's inhaler! Now I remembered I had packed one inside a black bin liner and I wanted to let the social worker knew where it was, in case Poppie needed it in a hurry.

So I called to tell her that Poppie needed her inhaler and where she could find it. She was kind and very sympathetic, noting the panic in my voice, and thanked me for the call.

'When do I get to see the children?' I asked, now desperate. It was Poppie's birthday tomorrow – I had a stack of presents and cards all ready for her to open. *When would she get to open them? How could she celebrate her birthday without us?*

'Well, I think we can make arrangements for a visit on Monday. I'll text you the details.'

'Okay, thank you,' I replied and put down the phone. *Monday? How on earth could I wait till Monday?*

That turned out to be the longest weekend of my life.

17

The Crossroads

The children were already in the contact centre when we arrived and ran towards us the moment they set eyes on us. Now both girls buried themselves into my arms, sobbing. I tried to hold my own tears back but it was too hard and I was a wreck. I'd spent every single second of the last two days yearning for their touch, their sound, their smell, not knowing what to do with myself or how to fill up the time. I'd missed them so much I couldn't even begin to put it into words. The girls were my life, my breath, my blood, my bones. Until now I hadn't realised how much I physically needed them, how empty my arms felt without them. Now I breathed in the smell of their hair, drank in the feel of their soft hair against my cheek and squeezed them both as tight as I could. I didn't want this moment to end.

'Mummy, I want to come home,' Poppie wept in big snotty sobs. Her whole body shook as she begged: 'Please, please let me come home. I'll be a good girl. Promise.'

'Oh sweetie,' I struggled to compose myself as I wiped away her tears. I couldn't let them think this way.

'You haven't done anything wrong, either of you,' I said seriously, looking them both in the eyes. 'You mustn't think like that. You're both very good girls and this has nothing to do with you. There's been a mistake, that's all, but Mummy and Daddy are doing our best to sort it out and get you both back home as quickly as possible.'

They started to cry again.

'But why can't we come home *now*?' Poppie wailed. 'I miss you. I miss Daddy and Granny. I want to come home …'

'It's going to be okay,' I said, putting on my most reassuring voice. 'Really, it's going to be fine. You're going to see us again … Now, tell me, what's your bedroom like in your new house?'

For the next 90 minutes I tried to be as happy and enthusiastic as possible, even though it killed me. I had to show them we were okay with things. I knew this would help them settle and make the transition easier.

'Tell me about your bed! What toys have you got there? Are there any other children in the house?'

All I wanted was to be supportive of the situation, to reassure them about everything, but Matt seemed distant and unengaged. The Saturday after they had been taken away Matt had done nothing but blame me and Lindsey for the situation – it was mainly my fault, he said, for the way I'd given my evidence in the witness box – but by the Sunday he had calmed down a little and he started to plan how we could get the children back. Now, at the contact centre he seemed pleased to be reunited with them but remained quiet and uncommunicative throughout the session. Fortunately, I knew I would have some time on my own with the girls on Wednesday so I could talk to them more then. It had been arranged that Matt and I would have one joint visit on Mondays, I would see them alone on Wednesdays and Matt could come on Friday with his mum. All supervised of course – from this point onwards we weren't allowed to be alone with our children.

We had lunch with the girls, gave Poppie her birthday presents, then cut her birthday cake. We played with them until the social worker came to say that our 90 minutes were almost up. So now I helped Poppie and Katie put away the toys and then I bent down to speak to them.

'Mummy and Daddy have to go soon,' I said. 'But you're going to see me again on Wednesday – that's not tomorrow but the day after, okay? Just two more sleeps. Two more sleeps and you'll see me again.'

Poppie and Katie both looked worried. All they wanted was to come home with us.

'What about Granny? Is Granny coming too?' Poppie asked, her bottom lip wobbling.

'Yes, you'll see Granny on Friday with Daddy. So that's in four sleeps' time. Not long at all. Now you be good girls at your new house, remember to say your prayers and I'll see you in two sleeps. Okay?'

I reassured them as much as I could. Then I got my handbag together and it was time for kisses and cuddles. The social worker returned to close up the visitation and I bent down for one last kiss. The girls knew we were leaving and they panicked. They started climbing up me, locking their arms around my neck, refusing to let go.

'Come on, girls,' I whispered gently, trying to unhook their little fingers from around my neck. 'Come on, let go.

Mummy has to leave now. You're going to see me again another day, I promise, in this building ...'

But they clung to me even tighter. I didn't know what to do. I didn't want to leave either but I had to get up because I didn't want to be accused of not cooperating with the local authority. Eventually the social worker said to me: 'Hannah, can you just get up and leave, please.'

So I did. I stood up. Neither could hold on any longer; the social worker took each girl's hand, to hold them as I left. I looked them in the eyes and said: 'You'll see me again on Wednesday. I promise. I promise.' Now both girls started crying and screaming and I left the room with the sounds of their agonised wails following me out.

We couldn't go home. Neither of us could face being in the house without them – looking at their toys, their clothes, their teddies that were left behind. The place felt empty without them, so we moved into the office full-time. There was a bed there, shower, our clothes ... all the things we needed. If we popped back to the house, it was only for an hour or so to get something we wanted. Lindsey remained in the house on her own – Keith had moved out some time ago into a residential home – and I felt sorry for her, alone like that, but I really didn't have the heart to look at my children's things all the time, to be reminded constantly of their absence. It was too much.

As soon as we lost the kids, I was fired from my job. The nursery had no choice – if I had lost my own children, how could they be sure I was safe around other people's kids? I was suspended until an Ofsted report was concluded. In the meantime, I did what I could to stay busy. Matt lined up the punters and swingers' parties, and I threw myself into my online childcare courses that Matt had arranged for me. He said it would look good if I was qualified in these matters and I was grateful for something to occupy my mind. We battled on with the case, just as we had been doing before the children left, on the basis that there was no domestic abuse. What else could we do? The council wanted to bring permanent care orders for the children and we fought to have them returned. To make his assessment, the judge ordered that each of us see a psychologist individually and also an independent social worker, who assessed our attitudes, parenting and relationship.

I stopped speaking to my mum. The social worker had spoken to all the family members after the interim care orders were granted to assess whether it might be possible to place the children with them. But they decided all our family members were unsuitable. My mum had my little brother to care for and he wasn't in the best of health, plus Matt knew where she lived. On top of that, when the social worker spoke to my mum, she had talked honestly about how she hardly ever saw us. She also told the solicitor about my having troubles as a teenager, which Matt thought social services would use against us. He rang my mum up and gave her a hard time down the phone about how she hadn't supported us. After that, I wasn't allowed to talk to her again. Matt said she wasn't on our side and she didn't care if we got the girls back or not.

The case was a lengthy process because we had to wait for all the professional reports to be filed and although we had legal representation Matt fired our solicitors on more than one occasion, which caused delays as our new legal teams had to be briefed from scratch. Matt researched the procedures for making care orders and was convinced that the proper legal processes had not been followed. He wanted our solicitors to challenge the court on this but they weren't prepared to do this and Matt fired them. My next solicitor told me in a private conference that after looking at all the files and case history he suspected that domestic violence was taking place.

'Hannah, if there was violence in the home I'd like to think that you would tell me,' he said. But I denied it, in a forceful manner. I was so deep into the lie by this point I couldn't imagine telling anybody the truth. When I relayed this conversation to Matt, he was fuming and that solicitor got the sack too. The violence hadn't stopped, of course. I was still getting beatings on a regular basis. One time Matt put his hands around my throat so I had to go to a contact meeting with the kids in a roll-neck top to stop anyone seeing his finger marks around my neck.

Just before Christmas the independent social worker shared his report and I was pleasantly surprised. He had seen me interacting with the children and given me a glowing write-up, noting the close bond between us. One sentence struck me in particular: '*If Mrs Gower is suffering domestic abuse and breaks free from the relationship, she should be given the opportunity to parent the children independently.*'

I read that sentence over and over again. It played on my mind. The independent social worker was saying that if I managed to escape, I should have the chance to get the children back on my own. He was trying to tell me something here – the question was: how? How do I make it happen?

By now the girls had settled into the weekly routine of seeing us at the contact centre and it helped that we kept to the same days each week. They were already close as sisters but I noticed that being apart from us brought them even closer and they squabbled less and comforted each other more. I thought about them constantly, wondering what they were doing and what I was missing. If I looked at the clock I'd be reminded of the things I might be doing with the girls at that moment – midday, lunch, afternoon, nap time, 6pm, bath time. As the weather turned colder I started to worry more. Were they warm enough? Did they have the right coats? Were they being kept warm at night? The anxiety would have driven me mad if it wasn't for Matt keeping me busy in the office, and I filled the rest of the time working on my online courses. Time was my worst enemy now – it sped by during my visits with the children and dragged intolerably in the days in between.

We were allowed a visit at the centre on Christmas Eve and, once we arrived, we decorated the room, putting in a little Christmas tree, some balloons and tinsel to make it more cheerful and festive. We also bought loads of presents, letting the girls unwrap them right there in front of us since we wouldn't see them on the actual day itself.

'Make sure you have a wicked Christmas Day tomorrow!' I told them before we left. 'Eat lots of Christmas dinner, lots of cake, watch lots on telly and you might get extra presents from Santa this year!'

They cuddled us and gave us little presents too – home-made calendars, plasticine figures and framed photos – then we waved them off to enjoy Christmas Day with someone else's family. I felt sick at the thought. *It wasn't fair. It just wasn't fair.*

By the time we left the contact centre at 5pm it was dark and we drove back to the house in silence. Back at home, I went upstairs and looked at the dismal sight of our children's abandoned rooms. Six months! It had been nearly six months since they left. Now I let the sadness wash over me as I noted their little beds, all made up ready for their return with the same bedding they had slept in the night before they left. It had not been washed since and still retained their childish smells. I looked at their toy boxes, bursting with toys, teddies, trains and games they hadn't touched in all that time. I opened Katie's cupboard, pulled out an old perfume box from the back and very quietly, without alerting Matt, I stuffed a roll of notes inside. Another stash that I'd managed to hide from Matt – hopefully, he'd never find it.

That night we stayed in the house. It was the first time we had been at home for any length of time since the girls were removed. We ate a Chinese takeaway with Lindsey, trying to ignore the sadness of the occasion. Afterwards, I worked on my childcare course on the computer, while Matt went off with Ben. I don't know where he went, to do some work with him somewhere; I didn't care. I just threw myself into the coursework, trying to keep my mind off the fact that it was Christmas Eve. Just past midnight, I glanced at the clock: *it's officially Christmas Day now.* No stockings to put out, no sherry for Santa … there was really no point celebrating Christmas without the children. The next morning, Lindsey went out for Christmas dinner with her friend and Matt worked with Ben. I stayed at home all day on my own. I had no punters to see so I just kept myself busy, working on my childcare course. By now we had a date set for the final hearing in a few months' time.

After Christmas, I was straight back to work and Matt made sure I serviced as many punters as humanly possible, keeping me up for days at a time, refusing to let me sleep. Sometimes I'd close my eyes for 30 seconds while I was in the chair waiting for the next punter, and accidentally doze off. But that was a risky business. If I fell asleep Matt might wake me up by throwing something at me or punching me. One night, before a swingers' party, he was attaching a black sheet to the ceiling, stapling it to the polystyrene ceiling tiles. He was up the ladder and I was sat in the chair, texting a punter, watching him for a while before I dropped off. The next thing I knew I felt a searing pain in my big toe.

'Oww. Fuck!' I yelled. He'd shot a staple into my foot. My punishment for daring to sleep.

In the early hours of one morning I had just waved off a punter and was ready to hit the sack so I sat down in the office and clicked open my mirror. Matt hadn't mentioned anyone else coming to see me so I was about to start removing my make-up when Matt stopped me.

'There's another person coming,' he said. 'They'll be here in 10 minutes. They've got a pack of fags.'

I had to stay awake for a pack of fags!

There were times I was allowed to go to bed – because Matt wanted sex or because he thought I looked too rough and run-down.

'Look at you, you're a state,' he would say. 'The punters can't see you like that. They're paying for a service and won't come back! They want their money's worth.'

This night was not one of those nights though. Forty minutes after the punter had arrived, I flopped down in the office again, my limbs weighed down by fatigue. I was so weary all I could think about was sleep. So I sat down to take my make-up off again, clicked on my light-up mirror and prepared to get ready for bed.

'Is that it?' I asked Matt as he sauntered in, a drink in his hand. Ever since the kids had gone, we both drank most nights. It helped in a lot of ways.

'No, there's someone else coming.'

Rage surged up in me. I wasn't allowed to get angry with Matt but suddenly I was furious and I couldn't keep it in. All I wanted was to get some bloody sleep.

'I'm not fucking doing this, can we not just go to bed?' I said slowly and deliberately.

Occasionally, I could speak to Matt like this and he wouldn't get mad.

'Let's just bag another packet of fags and then we'll both go to bed,' he replied.

But I couldn't. I just couldn't do it. My mind was made up. *Whatever happens, I am not going to have sex with another person tonight. I don't care if he fucking kills me. I don't care what happens to me anymore. The kids are gone. What more can he do?*

A couple of minutes later Matt got up to go to the toilet. *Now's your chance, Hannah. Just go.* I grabbed my bag, ran down the stairs, out the door and onto the main road. As luck would have it, there was a taxi parked out on the main road. I ran to it, just as I saw Matt coming out of the door after me. Now I grabbed the handle to the back door behind the driver's seat and tried to open it. But the doors were locked.

'It's okay, I've got money,' I said urgently. 'Please, just open the door.'

I don't know where I wanted go. All I knew was if I didn't get in that taxi in the next ten seconds, it was all over.

'Please, I've got to be quick,' I begged. 'I'll pay you the money now if you want. Let me in! Let me in!'

But it was too late. Matt came up behind me and said to the taxi driver:

'No, it's all right, we don't need you. Go on, off you go!'

And the taxi drove off. I couldn't believe it – I was a desperate woman, clearly in urgent need of help, and he had driven off. If Matt had killed me that night that taxi driver would have had my death on his conscience.

I watched the rear taxi lights disappear up the road, then, enraged, I turned to Matt.

'I'm not doing this anymore. I want to go home.'

Until this moment it hadn't even occurred to me to go home but I realised that as much as it hurt to be there, I hated being at the office. I wanted out. It was late, I was exhausted and I'd probably had too much to drink but I no longer cared about the consequences. I just wanted to go home – so I set off running towards the end of the road, no shoes or socks on my feet, desperate just to get away from Matt. My feet were numb, like blocks of ice, and I was shivering in my skimpy little negligee and thin zip-up cardie, but I didn't care. I just had to get away from him.

Matt shouted after me: 'Get back in here.'

'No! I'm not doing it. I want to go home,' I repeated. But our car was in the garage so we couldn't drive home. Instead, I stood at the end of the road, trying to flag down a passing car.

'He'll be here any minute with the fags so just get … back … inside,' Matt growled through gritted teeth.

'No, I'm not doing it. I've had enough. You're always making me do things like this. Give me a fucking break.'

God knows how many people I'd seen that day already. I was tired!

A couple of cars drove past. I was distracted, looking out for any more cars I could flag down. That's when Matt came at me. He punched me in the stomach, winding me. I folded, bent over with all my hair hanging down, and a car drove past at that moment. It started to slow down. Matt panicked, thinking they were going to stop. I tried to get my breath back, at the same time, crying: 'You're telling me you want me to get back inside and you've just hurt me again!'

Now a car pulled up outside the warehouse. It was the person who'd come to fuck me for a pack of fags. The phone started to ring in Matt's hand – it was him, the punter.

'Come on,' Matt snarled. 'Just get back inside. I'm telling you to get your arse back inside NOW.'

'NO. NO. NO. NO …' I repeated over and over. I wasn't going to do it. I didn't care. I'd had enough – I'd lost my children, I hadn't slept. I'd had enough. What more could he do? He could kill me but I didn't care anymore. I was ready to die.

After 20 minutes of waiting, the punter drove off. Matt couldn't do a thing about it so he said: 'Okay. We'll go home. Come on, let's get our stuff and lock up.'

Really? Was he *really* going to let me go home? Or was he just saying that to get me to go inside? I didn't trust him. I knew the moment we stepped through the door he could turn and beat the shit out of me … But, remarkably, he didn't. We went upstairs, got all our bits together and walked home. Too tight for a taxi, Matt forced us to walk half an hour in the early-morning chill to get home. Actually, it was okay. I could smell the fresh air, hear the birds cheeping in the pitch black and soak up the coldness of the night. We went straight to bed and the next morning when I got up, I was still in shock. I couldn't believe I had stood up to Matt last night. Yeah, I got winded for it but I ended up coming home, which is what I wanted. I felt something shifting between us – in some small way, he was losing his grip on me.

The last time he hit me was early in the New Year. I didn't know it was the last time. I didn't know what I was about to do until it happened, but I suppose I could feel something changing. The report from the independent social worker played in the back of my mind. I'd stood up to him once and got my way and I had that feeling that there really was nothing left to lose. He could kill me, but I wasn't afraid of dying anymore. My children had gone. It couldn't get any worse than that and Matt was never going to change. I had come to a crossroads, to a point where I had to decide – was this really the life that I wanted? I didn't have to worry about taking the girls with me, they were already safe. I thought about the few grand I had stashed up … Even if we won the case and got the girls back, how much longer before I was back in hospital or the children said something that alerted social services? Or worse … What if Matt killed me? Then what? Then he would go to prison and my girls would be left all alone in the world. Or, in the worst-case scenario, nobody discovers he is the killer and the girls are left in his care. That last punch, that was all I needed. One final push …

It was around 7.20am on a Saturday morning and I'd been awake the whole night, seeing punters. The last had arrived at 4am. This was one of my regular clients and before he'd arrived Matt had said not to rush him since we hadn't got any one else booked in. So we sat and chatted, had a drink, chatted some more. He was a nice guy and I was happy in his company, especially as the lengthy session kept me apart from Matt. A lot of my regular clients came as much for the company as the sex. But I knew something was wrong when Matt kicked the door of the bar to get my attention. *Uh oh – that doesn't sound good.* So I told the client his time was up, we cuddled goodbye and he left.

Back in the office, Matt was seething.

'How much time have you gone over with him? We're not running a fucking charity here. When I said 'don't rush 'em' I didn't mean give them *that* long.'

I sighed. Whatever I did was wrong. As usual. We walked down to the bedroom where we slept and I yawned: 'Matt, you told me not to rush him.' And *bam*, he punched me on the right side of my face with his left fist.

'I'm your husband. You fucking do as I say,' he snarled. 'I had arranged for more people to come round but I couldn't fucking give them a time because I didn't know how long you were going to be.'

I went to say something else and *bam*, he punched me again in exactly the same spot.

Three days later I left.

18

The Bravest Day of My Life

Tick tock … Tick tock … tick tock …

The clock on the business phone clicked slowly past the minutes as I waited for Matt to wake up. It was a few months before the hearing, an ordinary day, or so I thought when I got up and went through my morning routine. I had an appointment with my solicitor in town at 10am to go through my statement. I'd discussed it with Matt the night before and had offered to get the train but Matt insisted on driving me to the appointment instead. So now I sat there as his bowl of porridge slowly cooled and congealed on the desk in the office, waiting for him to get out of bed. I had been into the bedroom once already to tell him that his tea was made and it was time to get up but he hadn't moved. I knew not to go in a second time – it would only make the situation worse. The more I asked something of him, the more he would refuse to do it. So I just sat and waited … and waited and waited. My eyes were fixed on the clock – 9.45am – I would never make it on time. I sighed. This was typical Matt. He always made sure he turned up to his own appointments on time but for mine he really didn't care. I could have taken the train but I wasn't allowed, so instead I called the solicitor and told her I was running late.

Finally, Matt rolled out of bed at 11am and took his time getting washed, dressed and breakfasted. Then he insisted we stop on the way to the solicitor's office to put air in the tyres. As if he couldn't have done that on the way back! It was all deliberate, of course – another delaying tactic to show me who was boss. By the time we arrived it was 12.30pm and I was two and a half hours late.

'Do you want to go in to check she's still happy to see you?' Matt suggested as I got out of the car. 'If not, we'll go back.'

So I walked into the office to meet my solicitor, apologised for being late and asked: 'Are we still alright to go ahead?'

'Yeah, it's fine,' she replied. 'I'm not seeing anyone else today so we've got as long as we need.'

I walked back to the main door, gave Matt the thumbs up and he drove off.

We went through to her office and spent the next 20 minutes going through all the 'points of concern' that the local authority had brought up in their statement: the girls' behaviour at nursery, various hospital appointments as well as Matt's behaviour towards the professionals. Then she got to point 13.

'Mrs Gower, on this date you sustained a serious, life-threatening injury,' she read. 'Hannah, what do you say to that? … Did Matthew stab you?'

I looked at her, then I looked down at the paper in front of us. I didn't say anything for a couple of seconds. *Speak!*

Say something! Why haven't you said anything? Silence filled the room. I'd taken too long to answer so I knew I couldn't say 'no'. If it wasn't true, I would have said no straight away … A couple more seconds passed. *You've taken too long to answer, just say 'yes'*. And the word came out of my mouth. Just like that.

'Yes.'

Straight away, I regretted it. *What the fuck have I done?*

My solicitor fixed me with a serious look from behind her thick-rimmed glasses: 'What? Yes, he *did* stab you?'

'Yes, he did,' I repeated.

She didn't seem surprised. Why would she be? All the evidence in the court bundle, the documents, the statements from the nursery, all the hospital visits … they all pointed to one thing. It was obvious. All these things weren't accidents. I knew it and she knew it too. I just had to say it out loud – and now, I felt like the weight of the world had been lifted off my shoulders. Yes, he did stab me. That was the truth. And yet, at the same time, I felt instantly guilty. Horribly, horribly guilty.

'Right, so your position has changed,' she said slowly. 'So now we're going to go for you having the children returned to your sole care. Let's look at these other points, shall we?'

She started going through some of the other incidents in the bundle and I was hesitant, ready to admit the truth on some of them, but not all. I couldn't do all of them. I don't know why but it took me a good few months before I was ready to tell the truth about everything. The lies had been drummed into me for so long that I was even afraid to admit the whole truth to myself. It was like looking into sunlight after years of being kept in darkness. I couldn't look straight into the light all at once – it was too much. I don't think that's uncommon in situations like mine. After all, I'd had no idea this was going to happen today. It just came out – and now I was sitting there in immense shock. Stunned, guilty and extremely fucking worried. *What the fuck have I done?* All I could think about was Matt, so after a few minutes I had to stop her and ask her a question of my own.

'When I go home tonight, what shall I tell Matt I said?'

'What do you mean "when you go home"? You're not going home. You can't go back there now.'

I'm not going home tonight?

I'm not going home …

Really?

It seemed extraordinary. Why would I not go home? But my solicitor was adamant. Until now it had never occurred to me that if I admitted this to somebody, they wouldn't put me back in that situation. I was so shocked. Half an hour later, she went out of the room and spoke to her assistant, and asked her to ring round some refuges, to see if they had space for me.

'A refuge, what is that?' I asked.

'Hannah, a refuge is a safe house where women and children go when they are fleeing domestic abuse, when they've got nowhere else to go,' she explained. 'They are secret locations so that their abusers can't track them down and find them. That's where we need to send you.'

I had no idea places like this existed. I had no idea there was somewhere I could go to get away from Matt, where I would be safe. It was all new to me.

The assistant started making calls and one lady from a refuge asked to speak to me on the phone in the solicitor's office. Suddenly everything came into sharp focus. I panicked.

'Oh my God, I can't do this,' I gasped.

'You can, Hannah. You can ...' she reassured me. 'Stay strong. You've already told the truth. You can't go back home now. You know that.' She was right – Matt definitely would have killed me if I had gone back home and told him what had happened.

Gently, she urged me to take the phone and I managed to tell the woman a little bit about my situation. She asked me how long the abuse had been going on, asked me about the first incident, the worst and the last. Then she went over some basic facts: where do we live? What are his details? Are there children involved and where are they now?

I was having serious second thoughts. *This feels like the biggest mistake of my life. At least at home I know what to expect. Right now I have no idea what is happening to me from one minute to the next. And what about Matt? What's he going to do when he finds out?* I'd been conditioned for so long to lie and protect him, the consequences of betraying him were made so blatantly clear to me that I was frightened, very frightened – for my own life as well as for my children. What would he do to us? I couldn't put anything past him.

'Right, we need to go to the police station,' my solicitor said. 'Come on then.'

'What? Now?'

'Yes, now.'

'Okay.' I accepted what she said because I really had no choice and I had no idea what was going on. Nothing felt real. I got my handbag and we walked for ten minutes to the police station. There, my solicitor did all the talking, telling them why we were there and what needed to happen next. The police asked to hear it directly from me.

'What do I say?' I asked her.

'Just tell the truth.'

What the fuck is the truth? There had been so many lies over the years, I didn't even know what the truth was anymore. So I took it slowly, describing the daily beatings, the prostitution, the stabbing and some of the other incidents through the years. Finally, I told them that my children were gone. We waited to hear back but after a few hours we were told that all the local refuges were full and the only one which had a space for me was in Devon. *Devon? That was hours away.* Matt had the car and I had two days of visitation a week with my children. How in the hell was I meant to manage that from Devon?

'No,' I said firmly. 'There's no way I'm going there. Twice a week I have to come up and visit my children. I don't want to risk not seeing them.'

Next, my solicitor marched me up to the magistrates' court where we applied for a non-molestation order (NMO) against Matt, which, if granted, meant he wouldn't be allowed to approach me or use any threatening language or violence against me. We were lucky to be seen but my solicitor explained that this was an emergency safeguarding measure and the court regarded it as urgent business, taking priority over other cases. She wrote out my statement on a scrap of paper – it wasn't a long document, it summed everything up, saying how he'd forced me into prostitution, that he had stabbed me and how I'd suffered verbal, emotional and physical abuse on a daily basis for many years. I read it, signed it, then sat behind my solicitor in the courtroom while she made the application and the judge granted the order. It was all over in a few minutes. Once he was served with the order Matt wouldn't be allowed to contact me directly or indirectly, or instruct or encourage any other persons to do so for the course of a year. If he did he could be arrested. It didn't mean all that much to me at the time, after all I wasn't convinced a bit of paper could stop Matt if he wanted to find me and kill me. I just went along with what my solicitor told me to do. She seemed to know what was happening so I put my trust in her. I felt lost and in a daze.

It was getting late and the solicitor had to leave. She said we would do my statement another day but for now the most important thing was getting me somewhere to stay for the night. She walked me back to the police station before walking back to her car to go home. Tomorrow we would serve Matt with the order and retrieve some of my things from the house but for now I had to be safe.

'Right, stay here, Hannah, and do not move unless you are going with the police somewhere,' she instructed. 'Can you do that? You are not going home to Matthew tonight. Do you understand?'

'Yeah, okay. I understand.'

She left and I stayed in the reception area at the police station for what felt like hours.

By now, Matt was ringing me constantly. He had given me the business phone expecting a call to let him know when to pick me up but of course I hadn't called. I didn't answer the phone. I just stared at it, ringing insistently in my hand, thinking: *What do I do? If I turn it off, he'll know I've turned it off.* So I just let it ring. But the more he rang, the more worried I felt. I asked one of the policemen what I should do.

'Don't answer, Miss Morgan,' the policeman replied. I had asked them to call me by my maiden name as I didn't want to be Mrs Gower anymore. They were so nice to me, the police officers, and even let me use the phone charger behind the desk when my battery ran low, but I felt completely bewildered by what was happening. I sat there in the station, twiddling my thumbs, looking at my feet, reading the notices on the wall, looking at the people behind the counter, listening to the phones ringing, looking at the clock, thinking: *What have I done? What have I done?* I was frightened but at the same time, I knew there was no going back. *Stay strong, Hannah. For years and years you've prayed to get away from that monster and that day is finally here. So stay strong – you're not going to go back. Ever.*

That evening Matt reported me missing to the police. And for a while the local police did actually think I was a missing person until they discovered that I was sat in the police station, with an important note attached to my file: *Husband is not to know.* Our local station were informed of the situation and then rang Matt back to tell him that I was 'safe and well'. That was all he was told. I wondered what he thought ... and that worried me too. The hours dragged and by 11pm it was clear I would not be getting into a refuge that night. The police said I needed to stay in a hotel overnight. Did I have enough money to cover that? There was about £300 in my bank account from my benefit money and the cash I'd earned, enough for a room for the night. The next thing, I was sat in a large police van, being driven to the hotel.

On the way, I realised I wasn't prepared for an overnight stay.

'I have nothing with me,' I told the policeman driving.

'Alright, I'll take you to Tesco.'

'Are you coming in with me?'

'No, I'll sit outside.'

I wandered down the aisles of Tesco as if in a dream. *Is this really the best plan? Perhaps I should do a runner?* I was in so much shock and panic I didn't know what to do for the best. I was so worried about the repercussions of leaving Matt. This all went through my head as I picked up some belVita biscuits. *No, Hannah, just think of all the years you've wanted to get away and now it's finally happening.* I put some shower gel in my basket, a toothbrush, toothpaste, deodorant and a body puff to wash with. At the check-out, I looked at phone chargers but didn't buy one, just in case I wouldn't have enough money left for food. Then, I went back to the police van. The policeman dropped me at the hotel – watching me from the van to make sure I checked in. Up the stairs, I found my room but struggled to open the door. I'd never used a hotel key card before. Now a passing guest helped me to touch it to the keypad until the green light flashed up. It was so simple, I felt foolish. I thanked him, stepped inside the hotel room and, for a fleeting moment, I felt free.

The feeling didn't last long. My mind was in torment. Other than my hospital visits, it was my first night away from Matt in all the years we'd been together and I should have enjoyed a full eight hours of uninterrupted rest. But I couldn't – fear and worry kept me up most of the night. Laying naked under the covers since I had no pyjamas, I went through everything that had happened that day and worried about what would be happening at home. *Where is he now? Does he know what I've done? What will he do when he finds out? Will I be safe? How can I escape if there are no refuge places available? Will I have to move to Devon?* The thought of what might happen next even had me running to the toilet to throw up a couple of times. I was so scared. I must have dozed off for about 20 minutes as the sun began to rise and turned the sky pale blue but I didn't stay unconscious for long. I snapped awake just past 7am. By now my phone battery had died but I had arranged to go back to the solicitor's this morning at 9am where I knew I could charge it again. I was in such a state of shock, I felt like I was walking in slow motion. So I ran myself a bath and tried to let the warm waters soothe me. Then, instead of topping up the hot water, I turned on the cold shower tap by mistake and sprayed myself with freezing water. That woke me up a little!

I walked back to the solicitor's office, and there my solicitor gave me the plan for the day.

'Okay, I've spoken to the police this morning,' she said. 'They are going to take you to the police station near to your house. The police there are going to escort you back to the house so you can collect some of your things and they will serve Matt with the non-molestation order. I'll start ringing round the refuges this morning so hopefully we'll have a place for you by tonight.'

She took me back to the police station and even though I'd eaten a couple of belVita biscuits that morning, my stomach turned over at the thought of returning to the marital home, of seeing Matt again. I knew I would be safe with the police and knew Matt well enough to know he wouldn't kick off, as that would have blown everything. Still, I didn't want to see him.

Then I had more waiting around in reception again. The minutes ticked by so slowly and sitting there, on my own, the fears started to creep in. As much as I tried to keep it together, it all got too much for me and I started to sob. Kindly, a policewoman with a short black bob put her arm around me and led me to a little room, where she brought me tea and tissues. Sat in the reception area, to my amazement, I saw that it had started to snow. I love the snow but I was never allowed to enjoy it when I was with Matt. He didn't let me go out and make snowmen with the kids and if he caught me staring out of the window he would give me a sharp kick up the bum and tell me to get on with my housework. I didn't deserve to see the snow, he said. Now I watched, mesmerised, as the soft flakes fell gently outside, covering everything with a light white dusting. A tingling sensation raced up my spine. *God is speaking to you, Hannah, This snow – this is your reward for leaving Matt.*

This is the beginning of your new life. Hold onto it. Keep strong. You've already done one day away from him – just do the same today. Stay away from him today. Do the same tomorrow. And you'll survive.

At 4pm a police officer approached me.

'Are you ready, Miss Morgan? I'm going to take you back to your local police station.'

I nodded, yes. I was ready.

19

'Goodbye'

The drive to the police station took around 20 minutes, during which time I chatted happily to the policeman about the police car. It was a welcome distraction from my own thoughts as he carefully explained all the different flashing lights and buttons and demonstrated how the siren worked. But the moment we arrived at the station, everything began to feel more real. I got out of the car, thanked the policeman and was taken into the station through the back door by a local police officer where I recognised a few faces, people I'd come into contact with over the years. He showed me to a small room and there a policewoman joined us. They asked if it was okay if they had a read of the NMO before they served Matt with it. They knew about Matt, of course. He'd had many run-ins with the police and he had made his contempt for them clear so I think this was an interesting development from their point of view. I watched as they read through my statement, scanning their faces as they came to the bit about how he had forced me into prostitution. *Christ, I wonder what they think of me right now?* I felt embarrassed and ashamed. But everyone was kind, courteous and professional and nobody seemed to judge me. Two young officers introduced themselves and said they would now accompany me to the house.

Ten minutes later I was stood outside the house, flanked either side by a male and female police officer. At least with them by my side, I felt safe. We knocked and Matt opened it, with Lindsey standing behind him. I took one quick glance at Matt, then quickly looked away. I couldn't face him, couldn't face his lies. His face was a picture of concern, an act put on for the sake of the police officers standing there with me, as if to say: 'Oh my darling wife, you're safe!' It made me sick to my stomach. I bet he wanted to kill me right now.

But there was no time to waste – I had one important thing on my mind right now.

I pushed past him and darted up the stairs. Had he found the secret stash of money I had hidden away for the past few months? I went straight to Katie's room, opened up the top cupboard, rummaged round the back, found my old perfume box and opened it up. Thank God the money was still there! Over £4,000. I squashed the rolled-up notes in my bra and asked the policewoman who had followed me up the stairs to retrieve some bin bags from the kitchen downstairs so I could collect my things. I couldn't face going down there myself. Meanwhile, from down in the hallway, I could hear the policeman serving Matt with the NMO.

As soon as I had the bags, I started packing away all the things I wanted to take with me. First to go in were the girls' cuddly toys and Daisy the Cow, a small hand-sized cuddly toy that I had been sent free in the post when I signed up to a baby club when I was eight weeks pregnant. Daisy was special to me because she was the first cuddly toy that my firstborn child had ever had. The girls had one exactly the same so when I squeezed her it made me feel close to them. Next I packed pictures of the girls, paintings, drawings and cards that they had done for me, religious statues and then my clothes, underwear and toiletries. I also took my antique Rolex watch, which was my 21st birthday present, and my engagement ring. At least I had money now. If there was anything I'd left behind, I could buy it again. Lindsey came up the stairs and into the room while I packed my stuff.

'Hannah, what's happening?' she asked. 'Where are you going?'

Shit, what do I say?

'Hannah doesn't even know where she's going herself yet,' the policewoman cut in. 'She hasn't been told.'

Thank God for that! I had no idea what to say.

Next, I opened my wardrobe and, to save time, hooked handfuls of hangers into the bags. The police officers started taking the bags and boxes to the police car, with at least one of them loitering by the front door to keep an eye on Matt, and after 20 minutes I was done. I went into the girls' bedroom and looked at the beds that my children had once slept in, looked over their things for what might have been the last ever time and let out a big sigh. Everything had happened so quickly – all in the space of one day – and now I had to say goodbye to my children's life at home with me. Despite everything, I felt a tug of grief at my heart for all that I was leaving behind. After all, I had enjoyed many happy, loving times with my children in this house. We'd shared tickles, puzzles, stories, bath-time fun and so many wonderful cuddles. Now, in this moment I had to say goodbye to it all. It was hard. Next, I looked into my own bedroom. The room I'd slept in all these years, the bed where he'd raped me countless times, the window he had nearly pushed me out of, the now-emptied wardrobe and drawers ... And I could feel his presence downstairs. I wanted to leave. I didn't want to be there a moment longer than I had to.

'We can go now,' I told the policewoman.

As I came down the stairs, Matt started to plead with me: 'You don't have to do this, sweetheart. You don't have to leave. I know why you're doing it, it's because you're in shock the girls have gone and you don't want to be here in the house anymore ...'

I didn't hear anything more as I walked past him, out the front door and up the garden path towards the police car, now full to bursting with all my stuff. The officers both got into the front seats and I held open the door handle of the back passenger door for a moment. Then I hesitated.

'Can you just give me a minute but don't go anywhere?' I said to the policewoman. I turned to go back up the path and at that point the male officer said: 'We're not going to let you go on your own,' so they both walked alongside me as I returned to Matt and I stood in the garden, opposite him. I looked him square in the eye, without saying a word, then I gave him a hug.

I wasn't coming back. As much as he was an evil, horrible bastard, this was the end. And I knew it. This part of my life was over. I hated him and loathed everything he had done to me, but Matt had been my husband, this house had been my home, for years, it was where I'd had both children and I had to acknowledge in some way that this was the end of our life together.

I kissed him, I smelled him one last time, looked at him and said: 'Goodbye.' Then I strode back up the garden path and I didn't look back until I was sat safely in the back of the police car.

'Are we ready?' asked the policeman at the wheel, looking at me from the rear-view mirror. I nodded. We started to drive off and I looked out of the back window, one last look at Matt and his mum, standing there looking confused, worried and sad. We turned the corner and that was it. They were gone. I had no idea what would happen to me now. I was venturing into the unknown. All I knew was that this part of my life was over forever and I would never return to this house again.

In the police car, the officers told me that since the refuges were still full, they would take me to another hotel, this one further away. They needed to get me out of the county and as far away from Matt as possible so they had reserved me a room at a hotel 100 miles away. We started the drive along the motorway. At some point I saw a sign welcoming me to a new county. *Fucking hell, I'm miles away from him now.* As every mile slipped behind me and the distance between me and Matt grew and grew, I felt a heavy weight shifting from my heart. Sitting there, in the back of that police car, surrounded by bulging black bin liners, I actually felt happy, like I'd achieved something, even if I didn't quite know what. *I've escaped. I've left the county. I don't know what today or tomorrow is going to bring but it doesn't matter. I'm ready to face the world without him.* I didn't know how but I had faith. Faith that it was all going to work out.

When we arrived at the hotel, the police accompanied me to the check-in desk, to make sure this was the right location. Fortunately, I now had plenty of cash to cover my expenses – in any case, the police assured me that once I was settled I could apply to get my money reimbursed. I unfurled my wad of rolled-up notes, handed over the right money and then the receptionist asked: 'Have you got any ID?'

'No, what do I need ID for?'

'If anyone's paying cash we need to take ID, to check for money laundering,' he explained.

Now the policeman stepped in: 'We can vouch for her, she is who she says she is.'

'No, I'm sorry. It's not enough, we need ID,' the receptionist insisted.

'Are you joking?' the police officer said sceptically and called over the hotel manager who confirmed the policy. As a result I had to pay for that first night with my bank card, which I had been very reluctant to do as, at this stage, my bank statements were still going to the house. As it turned out, I had every reason to be concerned

It took several trips to and from the police car to get all the stuff into my room – luckily, I was on the ground floor so there were no stairs to climb. The police officers said that they would arrange for me to start giving my statement at the nearest police station the next day. That night I finally enjoyed a good night's sleep. The next day, I arranged to receive only paperless bank statements from now on. I also went to my bank on the high street and paid in some of my cash. Then I bought a pay-as-you-go mobile phone with a new number so Matt couldn't contact me and I called my social worker. There were still no refuge spaces available so I had to stay in the hotel for the time being.

The following week I was put in touch with the local domestic abuse services and they told me a room would be available the following week. I spoke to the refuge manager over the phone, giving her a brief description of the kind of things Matt had done to me. I still felt very nervous whenever I talked about the abuse, unsure after so many years of Matt dripping poison into my ear that anyone would actually believe me. And every time someone did, I felt that little bit more certain of myself, that little bit more confident.

Now I settled into a new routine. Every morning I got up, washed, dressed, had breakfast and then walked over to the police station where I spent all day giving my statement. It took days! There was so much to say and even though I couldn't remember all the hundreds of smaller incidents of violence, most of the more serious incidents came back to me in vivid detail. It was strange – just like reliving them all over again. After all these years of being told to shut up, to keep quiet, to keep his evil secrets, it was a huge relief to be able to talk at last. And though each day left me drained and emotional, I felt a huge weight lifting from my heart. For years I'd hidden these terrible truths and, as hard as it was to admit what he had done, I was so grateful for the chance to speak out. To be listened to, to be believed … it meant so much to me and I appreciated the fact that the police had arranged for me to see the same female officer every day. Annie was warm, caring and sympathetic, she didn't judge me and even when I was telling her about some of the worst abuse she didn't appear shocked. This made it so much easier to talk about.

The only day of the week that I didn't go to the police station was Wednesdays, when I had my weekly visit with the girls, and weekends. The council had cancelled our joint Monday visit, which at first was devastating. I was so desperate to see the children I even told the social worker I would do the joint visit with Matt.

'Hannah, you can't do that,' she replied. 'What if he follows you home?'

'Can't one of us leave early?'

'No.'

As crazy as it sounded, I was willing to do anything to see my girls, even if it meant spending time in Matt's company. I couldn't see how dangerous that would be for me as the visits were supervised. But I wasn't always thinking straight during this period. It was a very difficult two weeks: alone in the world for the first time in my life, my moods swung wildly between sadness, elation, confusion, fear and hope – I always had hope.

One day, I found myself wandering around John Lewis, deeply depressed. How had I let things get this far? Sometimes I couldn't quite believe I didn't have my children with me anymore – the girls were everything to me and I thought I had done my best to care for them … now, they were in someone else's care. How much had they been affected by what they'd witnessed? I felt so shit, depressed, confused, alone and out of control of my life. It was then I walked past the Ted Baker concession and my eye landed on a beautiful mint-green coat. Matt hated Ted Baker clothes – he said they were common – and he never let me wear pastel colours as he insisted they were only for young girls – 'immature and childish'. I wasn't allowed to choose my own clothes with Matt. But this coat, this beautiful cashmere, silk-lined coat was gorgeous. I loved it and I couldn't help myself; I tried it on. I pulled the soft lining over my shoulders, did up the belt, looked at myself in the mirror and thought: *Wow! It really suits me!* Then I looked at the price tag – £249! *Jesus, quarter of a grand for a coat! No, I can't spend that much money.* So I hastily returned the coat to the rail and spent the next half an hour walking round the rest of John Lewis, feeling even worse than before.

As I roamed the aisles, Adele's hit song 'Rolling in the Deep' started playing on the overhead PA system. The familiar driving drum beat got hold of me and when I heard her singing about the scars of love I thought about Matt and everything he'd done to me. As Adele sang about her man having her heart inside of his hands I thought: *Yes. You did, Matt. You really did, but now I'm coming out of the dark.* I listened to the whole song, the emotions welling up inside me, and as Adele belted out the last chorus I thought: *Fuck you, Matt.* And I headed back to the Ted Baker concession.

I was so proud that day, striding out of John Lewis, my gorgeous cashmere coat swinging in the black Ted Baker bag over my shoulder. My 'fuck you' coat. Back at the hotel, I put it on and sashayed around reception, showing it off to the lovely staff with whom I'd made friends. It was so beautiful, so pretty, so *me*! I loved it and I didn't regret for a single second spending the money on myself. This wasn't just a coat, after all. It was a symbol of my freedom and my first positive step on the road to finding myself again. I wore that coat every day afterwards and for years it was my most treasured possession – after Daisy, of course. Today, I still have it but it only comes out on special occasions.

It was my last night in the hotel. I'd nearly finished my statements and the next day the police officer was coming to take me to the refuge. I'd packed all my things away in their bags again and was enjoying a few drinks at the bar with a Welshman called Phil who was staying at the hotel on business. We'd had a couple of beers so I was very chatty, telling him all about how I'd left my husband and was waiting to move into a refuge. But I ran out of fags and my purse was in my room so I asked to borrow £20 from him to go to the shop on the corner and would give it back to him on my return. He handed me the cash so I went out and bought a packet of Benson & Hedges before having a quick fag outside. When I got back into the hotel, I headed to my room to get the money to pay Phil back. And as I was coming back down the corridor towards the bar, I saw a woman through the glass panel of the corridor door. *That's funny – that lady looks a bit like Lindsey.* I opened the door to walk back to the main reception and Lindsey was standing right there. FUCK!

I nearly jumped out of my skin. *How the fuck did she find me here?* My heart started to race. I walked fast straight past her, but she had seen me come through the corridor door and it was too late to turn around to go back to my room. I walked into the bar area, gave Phil his £20 and said in a low voice: 'My mother-in-law is here, can you ask the hotel staff to call the police?'

I had no idea how she had found me but at this stage my only thought was to stay safe. I thought that might be back in my room so I strode back past Lindsey as she loitered by the lifts. 'Hannah, will you just talk to me? Just talk to us,' she pleaded.

'No.'

She made a quick call on her mobile and the next thing I saw was Matt walking with haste round the corner, heading straight towards me. I panicked. What do I do? I couldn't go back to my room or he might follow me in there and then we would be alone! I couldn't even escape through my bedroom window as they only opened a fraction. I grabbed hold of a man walking past the lifts and begged him: 'Please ... please help me. My name is Hannah Morgan, can you ask the hotel staff to call the police and tell them my ex-husband is here?'

The staff all knew why I was staying here – they were aware that I was fleeing domestic abuse so they would understand the importance of calling the police. The man nodded and walked off to get help.

Matt came to a standstill in front of me. I didn't know what else to do – I ran out to the front of the hotel. *There's CCTV here, on the outside of the hotel, so I must stay where the cameras can see me ...*

Matt followed me outside.

'Hannah, just talk to me,' he begged. 'Just let me know what's going on.'

But I just shook my head, *no*, unable to speak, and I covered my face with my hands, frozen in that pose for what seemed like an eternity. *The police will be here in a minute, the police will be here in a minute, the police will be here in a minute, it's fine, don't worry ...*

Except the police never showed up and Matt wouldn't take no for an answer so I had no choice – I had to lower my hands and start talking to him. But I made sure I stayed in that entrance all that time, where I knew the CCTV cameras were trained. I didn't know what else to do. My mobile phone was in my room and I didn't know how to get away from them and into my room without alerting them to my room number. I felt like a trapped animal. From the moment Matt turned up, and was standing in front of me, it felt like I was back under his spell. He made me feel so guilty for leaving him. At least I managed to keep them away from my room – they kept asking if they could come and sit in my room but I said *no* over and over again. I wondered how they had found me. Later, I found out that the bank had sent one final paper statement to the house before switching my account to paperless. And of course the final item on the statement was the transaction for my first night in the hotel. Just my bad luck!

The whole encounter was just bizarre. At one point I agreed to sit in the car, but only because Lindsey was getting so cold and she had been ill that winter, and on the condition that I kept the car keys and sat in the driver's seat. For the next few hours they both did their best to find out what I'd been up to. I didn't tell them anything other than to confirm I'd been at the police station. Matt assumed my actions were part of a game plan we had once discussed many months back when he had suggested we pretend to split up in order to get the kids back. He thought that's what I was doing. And then at some point, once social services were out of our lives, we'd get back together and it would be fine. He felt very secure in his control over me, never suspecting for a second I would actually leave him for real.

'If I have to get arrested, that's fine,' he said. 'I get it. If that's the game we're playing to try to get the kids back that'll be okay. But you have to stay in touch.'

I played along, agreeing that this was the best way forward and that at some point I would come back. But it was a lie. I knew I was never going back – once upon a time I would have considered it but not now – I just had to make sure I survived the night. And then by this time tomorrow, I'd be gone. That was one thing he didn't know. He had no idea I was leaving the hotel.

The hours dragged by – it was so late now. Finally, at 5am, I said I was too tired to talk anymore and wanted to go to bed.

'Can you make sure you call me?' he said before I went inside.

'Sure.'

'Can we have your new number?'

'No. I can't, or it won't look real.'

'Well, can you make sure you keep in contact with us at least? Make sure you text us.'

'Yeah, okay then …' I agreed, with no intention of doing so. Then I said goodbye, walked back into reception and watched as they got back in the car and drove off. *Thank God for that!*

I staggered back to my room, stunned, confused and so very relieved that they were gone. But why did that happen? Had Matt just breached his NMO? And why did I just spend five hours chatting to him? I had hoped all that time that at some point I would see a flashing blue light, a roar of sirens and the police would appear to take him away. But it never happened. *Keep him talking* … that was my plan. It was the only one I could think of that wouldn't get me killed. After all, if I'd told him I had made a full statement to the police, I might not have survived the night. I fought with all my might not to get sucked under his spell. At times, I almost found myself relenting, feeling like I owed him the time to talk …

Not this time, Hannah … I had to stay strong.

I was woken by Annie banging on my door at 9am the next morning.

'Good morning. How are you?' she asked cheerily as I opened the door. 'Overslept, did you?'

'Yeah, I did,' I replied, groggy and tired. 'Matt turned up here last night.'

I briefly told her what happened as I was getting all my stuff together. She was shocked and went back to the front desk to discuss it with them and ask for the CCTV footage. The staff confirmed they had received the requests by Phil and the lift guy but they had declined to call the police. I couldn't believe it! Their excuse was that Matt wasn't kicking off so they had no reason to call the police on him. I was stunned at their stupidity. Just like when the taxi drove off and left me in the middle of the street, they could have had my death on their consciences that night.

'It's okay, you're leaving now,' Annie reassured me. 'He won't find you again. It's going to be fine.'

Just before we left the hotel, we confirmed my arrival over the phone with the refuge and the manager texted us the address. It wasn't too far, but I won't reveal the location because this could put other women at risk. What I can say is that the moment we pulled up at the large Victorian house, I started to shake with nerves. Here I was, taking another giant leap into the unknown, and I was petrified. For the last two weeks I'd settled into hotel life, getting used to my own company again, adapting to the new environment and new routine, and now it was all change again. This would be the fourth place where I'd laid my head in a fortnight and now I would be living with other women too. *What were their backgrounds? What would they be like? How would we all get on?* My mind raced with questions.

The manager for the refuge met us at the front door with a welcoming smile.

'You must be Hannah,' she said warmly. 'Why don't we get your things in first and then we'll do the paperwork?' The three of us dragged my boxes and bin bags into the office and then it was time for Annie to leave. This was harder than I'd imagined. After all, she had been there for me most days as I'd unburdened myself, listening with care, compassion and sympathy as I told her everything about my life with Matt. She was the only person who knew the whole truth and the one constant in my life right now. Saying goodbye to her made me feel nervous, sick and alone.

'You're going to be alright, Hannah,' she whispered as we hugged a tearful goodbye. 'Don't worry, they're going to look after you here. You're stronger than you think. Trust me.'

I thanked her, gave her one last hug and then she left. The door closed behind her and now I turned back to the refuge manager – I had no choice, I had to put my trust and my faith into her and the other people at the refuge. My life was in their hands.

I did the paperwork, she read me the rules and regulations, then it was time to see my new room. Slowly, I followed her up the staircase of the old building, breathing in the dank smell, listening to the echoes of my own footsteps on the floor and thinking about the long road ahead.

A new life, Hannah. A fresh start.

He won't find you here.

He's gone.

20

'Keep Them Together' – A Decision Never Questioned

I felt nervous and unsettled during my first few days at the refuge. It was such a dramatic change to my life and at first, apart from the odd 'good morning', I mainly stayed in my small room on the first floor of the three-storey household, sorting out my belongings and getting used to the new sounds around me – women talking, footsteps on the staircase, doors opening and closing, and children playing, fighting and crying. I didn't sleep much the first couple of nights, too worried about how I was going to fit in. There were eight of us in total and of the eight, there were only two – myself and another – who didn't have children staying with them. It felt strange at first to live with so many small families, their presence a constant and sometimes painful reminder of my own children. I'd wander into the kitchen in the morning, watch the breakfast chaos unfolding with all the little ones and think: *If I had left sooner, I could have been in here with my girls.*

Gradually, over the next couple of weeks, I introduced myself to all the other residents and I was pleased to find the women were friendly and welcoming. We were all in the same boat, after all, and though we had different stories and backgrounds, we were supportive of one another. Some nights, when the kids were in bed, we'd gather in the large kitchen with a few drinks and share our stories or the events of the day. It was a tough time for all of us – we were all in transition, in one way or other. This was not how any of us had seen our lives turning out but it was definitely a positive step on the road and there were moments when we all had to remind each other that we were doing the right thing. There was something about being with other women that felt reassuring and comforting. It had been a long time since I had been allowed to have friends, a long time since I had spoken to anyone openly and honestly about my life. For so many years I had to hide the truth and it felt like I was finally being myself again, reconnecting to the outside world as myself, as Hannah.

Practically, the refuge was a very safe place too. There were CCTV cameras everywhere, and our post was directed to a PO Box address where it was collected by a staff member at the local sorting office and brought to us. We had rules about who was allowed to know our whereabouts and there were strictly no male visitors allowed on the premises. In the kitchen, there was a whiteboard with a marker pen and if you were in you would tick the box with your name next to it and when you went out you had to rub your tick off. There were cleaning rotas for the communal areas and we helped each other out by babysitting or walking each other to and from the train station so nobody had to come home alone in the dark. There were also good facilities to cope with the large number of residents – four fridge-freezers, two cookers, two toasters, two microwaves, four washing machines, two tumble dryers, an ironing board, a shower room, a bathroom and a downstairs toilet. On occasion, I got myself very drunk and once or twice I fell asleep on the toilet. Then the other women had to pick the toilet door lock with a dinner knife to get me out. I wasn't the only one, though; we were all coping with our various traumas in whatever way we could.

A couple of weeks after I moved in, I got back in touch with my mum. I'd actually called her from the hotel I'd stayed in. We hadn't spoken since summer the previous year but it didn't go well.

'Mum, it's me,' I said when she answered the phone.

'Okay ...' she replied, warily.

'Can you talk at the moment?'

'I'm not sure I want to talk to you, Hannah,' she said, then she hung up.

I was devastated by her reaction but I understood. She didn't know I'd left Matt. At the refuge, I tried to make contact again, choosing this time not to ring her but to text. At least I knew she would read it. I explained in the text that I'd broken free from Matt and now I was living in a refuge. I also said that all of the violence that everyone had suspected for so long was true. She called me straight away and it was so good to hear her voice after such a long time. She was tearful and upset, devastated to find out that the abuse was real all along and all of my 'accidents' had in fact been inflicted by Matt. I did my best to reassure her that I was safe now.

'I'm so sorry, Hannah,' she whispered.

'What are you sorry for, Mum?'

'For not knowing. I should have known! For not being there for you.'

'Oh, Mum, you couldn't have done anything. Honestly, you don't have anything to be sorry about.'

'What about the girls?'

'They're still in care. I'm going to try and get them back on my own. I've been thinking about you, Mum. All over Christmas and your birthday too … I've missed you.'

'Oh, I've missed you too.' And then we both broke down in tears. It was wonderful to get close to my mum again. I'd been feeling very alone in the world and needed her badly. I was grateful she was there for me. As soon as we were back in touch, I made sure she also got access to see the girls during my visits. Over time, I reconnected with my brother, and my sister too – for the first time in years, I had my family back. We all went to see my girls, sometimes on the allotted days, and sometimes we swapped the days over randomly so Matt wouldn't know when it was happening, just in case he turned up. I had to take a lot of long train journeys to get to the contact centre but it was worth it.

Shortly after arriving at the refuge, I got a call from the police. The woman introduced herself as the detective constable working on my case against Matt and said the police were going through my statement now. She was very reassuring, telling me that my statement seemed very strong as I had a good recollection for dates, times and descriptions. She also praised me for leaving.

'What about Matt?' I asked. 'Have you spoken to him yet?'

'We've made contact, Hannah, but he's proving hard to nail down, refusing to answer the door or call us back,' she explained. 'But don't worry. We are aware that he will be at the family court and we will be waiting for him there. If needs be we'll just wait outside the court and nick him from there.'

By the time the final placement hearing began it had been nearly three months since I left Matt. My secret stash of money had run out completely but the refuge helped me to claim benefits – income support and housing benefit – so I had very little money and relied on public transport. On the first morning of the hearing I had to get up by 5am in order to get to court for the 9.30am start and though I was still very worried about the outcome of the final hearing I was more hopeful than before. I had established a good relationship with my social worker, I'd finished my police statement and I was seeing through on my commitment to bring Matt to justice. In my room at the refuge, we had set up bunkbeds in anticipation of the girls coming home with me and the manager had submitted a glowing report to the judge in support of my case.

Nevertheless, that first day in court was pretty hard – Matt was there, of course, but I managed to avoid him, sticking closely to my barrister. First we heard from the local authority's representative about how the girls were doing and what they wanted for the children. He said Poppie was still very affected by everything that she had seen at home and, despite my leaving Matt, he was convinced it would be better for the children, and help them to settle, if they had permanent placement orders. I knew this was coming but it was still a tough and very long day in court. That night, after I got back to the refuge, I downed a lot of vodka at the kitchen table. I felt horrendous afterwards but it was enough to let me sleep soundly until 5am when I got up the next day and did it all again. This went on for three long weeks – with a week off in between – as we heard evidence from Matt, the social workers, the guardian, the paediatrician and the psychologist as well as two members of staff from the nursery.

And I too gave evidence against Matt. I spoke about our whole relationship and what he had done to me in the time we were together. That was hard, especially since Matt went into the witness box straight afterwards to deny it all. But my barrister said I was the more credible witness. She said no one believed Matt at this stage. After all, the evidence for the abuse had been overwhelming even before I spoke out. So what was the point of Matt contradicting me? He claimed he wanted the children returned to his and his mother's care but he knew that was never going to happen. Truthfully, he was just there to ensure the girls didn't come back to me – that was the level of nastiness I was up against. I just clung to the hope that the judge would pay attention to the report by the independent social worker who had recommended that I be given the chance to parent on my own if I left Matt.

But now we also had the psychologist's report back and it indicated that I had a long journey of recovery ahead of me, and the girls couldn't afford to wait. They would need me to focus on them and give them my total attention and this might be difficult while I was struggling to recover myself. The report concluded that the girls needed a permanent placement to feel settled. It was a devastating blow to my case.

'It's not looking good,' said my solicitor. 'The judge is more likely to go with the psychologist's recommendation rather than the independent social worker's. It's unlikely you'll get the children back.'

That was really hard to hear but I appreciated her honesty and support, as it helped me to prepare for the worst, which I needed to do. Nonetheless I fought with every ounce of strength in my body. I felt that I deserved a chance to prove myself.

'If I can leave Matt, I can do anything,' I insisted. 'I can recover and look after my girls at the same time. The children will be my strength, we will all heal together. Trust me. I'll prove it. I won't need a second chance.'

My solicitor understood – she knew how far I would go to ensure the girls were well cared for. So I remained hopeful, said my prayers every night and reminded myself that even if I didn't get them back, at least my children were safe and happy – and that was all that mattered.

Throughout most of the case I did my best to ignore Matt. Occasionally, he tried to talk to me but I wouldn't even look at him. Once he scribbled on a Post-it note and passed it to me – a request for the name of a nursery staff member. I wrote the name down on the note and passed it back along the desks. Then he sent *another* note, which I screwed up and ignored. How dare he try to make conversation with me!

When Matt gave his evidence in the witness box, he brought up something I'd confided in him about my teenage years that I found really upsetting. I couldn't listen to him using my past against me like this and I ran out of the court in tears – it was then I spotted Lindsey sitting in a side room, patiently waiting for Matt. Matt – the man she knew very well had tried to kill me. She, of all people, knew what he was like. I couldn't believe that after everything he had done she was still standing by him. I approached her.

'Why are you doing this, Lindsey?' I asked. 'Why are you supporting Matt? You know what he's done. You know it. He's only here to stop me having the kids again and if he does, you won't see them either. Can't you see how stupid this is, Lindsey? Why stand by him?'

She didn't have much to say for herself, *umming* and *ahhing* nervously before finally admitting quietly that she knew what he'd done. I just stared at her. *She's scared*, I realised. *She's too scared to betray him in case he kills her.*

The hearing lasted six weeks and towards the end, the judge addressed the court: 'This application is for *both* children. The local authority wishes to have the children placed permanently. Obviously the mother has broken free and she should be commended for this.

'So how do we all feel about the mother possibly having the youngest child back? There are no behavioural issues with the younger child. Because if we don't look into the possibility of the mother having one of the children back, then it's almost as though she is being punished for being a victim of domestic abuse. I would be grateful if all parties gave this some consideration and returned on Thursday with their position.'

The court rose, we all stood up and the judge left. The court wasn't due to sit again until Thursday so we had all of Wednesday to consider the judge's proposal.

My barrister took me into a side room.

'Hannah, have a think about what the judge has proposed and let me know on Thursday when we're back as to whether you'd like to put yourself forward to have just Katie back.'

'I don't need time to think about it,' I replied. There was a moment's silence between us. 'Keep them together.'

'Really?'

'Yes, absolutely. The girls shouldn't be split up.'

She looked at me for a moment. She knew how much my children meant to me. She knew how much I desperately wanted them back with me.

'Hannah, I think that's very brave of you,' she said quietly.

But it wasn't a choice in my mind. They had lost so much already, they didn't deserve to lose each other. For Katie, her big sister had been there her whole life. How could I take her away? And Poppie had lost everything – her parents, grandma, home, friends, neighbours – she couldn't lose her little sister as well. They needed each other so much right now and I couldn't imagine for a moment breaking that important bond between them.

On Thursday we were back in court and the judge asked each party in turn what their view would be on Katie coming to live with me. It seemed we were all in agreement about one thing – the children should stay together.

The trial came to an end and the night before the judge's verdict, I felt sick with worry. Downstairs, in the kitchen, I paced up and down, unable to sit still for a moment. The other women in the refuge understood – many of them had faced similar situations – and were supportive and encouraging. I even got a couple of good-luck cards. One read: 'Good luck for tomorrow – I hope your babies come home.' But I just couldn't sleep that night. I didn't know how I was going to cope if the judge found in the local authority's favour. *Just stay positive*, I told myself over and over. *Whatever happens, the girls are staying together.* I tried to tell myself it was a win–win situation. And ultimately Matt wasn't getting them back so at least I had nothing to worry about there.

For the judge's verdict, I travelled to court alone, accompanied only by Daisy the Cow, curled up neatly in the palm of my hand. Since she had been Poppie's first ever toy I felt a strong connection to the girls when I held her little black-and-white body. Daisy gave me comfort and reassurance. An hour later I found myself staring around the court as we waited for the judge to appear. I had spent so long here over the past few weeks, it was a familiar space to me now but one that came with deep emotion and uncertainty.

'Court rise!' the usher shouted.

Now we all stood up as the judge took his seat at the front of the court in his dark emerald-green leather chair with the crease in the top right-hand corner. I had looked at this chair for so long now it was forever imprinted on my mind. I squeezed Daisy tightly as the judge started to read his judgment and crossed my fingers in my other hand.

Then he outlined the case and all the evidence he had heard. I couldn't tell where he was going at first – he congratulated me on having the courage to leave Matt and to pursue justice. It felt like it was going well until he got to the last bit of the judgment. And that was when my last hopes were crushed. The judge felt that in the circumstances adoption was the only option and he granted placement to the local authority.

I knew it was coming – I knew because my barrister had prepared me; she had said it was unlikely the judge would go against the psychologist's report. And yet, and yet … I hoped, I prayed every night. I had faith. It was so hard to hear those words from the judge.

I felt like a glass, shattering into a million pieces, and I must have looked devastated because the judge actually apologised to me. How had it come to this? My beautiful girls. My babies.

At least they are staying together, I told myself, desperately clinging to the positives. *At least I've done all I can and now they can be told what's happening in their life. They will have certainty. Even though they're not coming home to Mummy, they will know which direction their life is going and they can settle down.* The children couldn't be told anything until the council had that final placement order but now at least the social worker would visit the girls and tell them that they would be going to a new home. I cried all the way back on the train and when I arrived at the refuge I poured myself a large drink in the kitchen. I could hardly face going upstairs to my room and seeing the empty bunkbeds there. Everything felt like it was happening to someone else. Was this really my life? The shock of losing my children left me numb so that I could hardly process what had happened.

I continued to see the girls once a week, bringing them gifts and showering them with love and affection. But over time, the visits were phased down and eventually we were due to have our final visits. Matt ended up losing his visitation rights completely after assaulting the social worker, while his mum said goodbye to the girls a week later. And the following Friday it was time for my family to say goodbye. My sister, brother and mum all came and brought with them giant-sized gift bags for the girls. I had begged them not to cry during the visit: 'If you need to cry, wait till you're out the door, please. For their sakes. I want this to be a positive and happy experience for them.' So even though it was really sad, and Mandy did get a little tearful, she managed to keep it under control until they'd left the room, for which I was very grateful. Later that day, Mandy wept in my arms. She'd only seen Poppie a couple of times and had never had a chance to meet or bond with Katie. Then it was my turn – my last visit with the girls took place a week later.

It was going to be a special day so I made a special effort for my girls and my sister helped me. Since I was surviving on benefits – which mostly went on travel and food – Mandy lent me £200 to buy a new outfit and some presents for the children. I tried to make myself look as nice as I could for them – in a new white dress, with make-up, jewellery and my new blonde hair washed and dried. (I had gone back to being a blonde after leaving Matt.) I even went into town that morning to have my eyebrows waxed and tinted. I just wanted to look my very best for them. I bought them each a silver necklace that said 'Good luck' and also a heart cushion, with their names on the front and the words 'Together forever' on the back. They knew this would be our last visit together and when we met at the contact centre, I sensed their sadness, but I tried to be as positive as possible, and I think that helped. They were both very cuddly and playful and they gave me a goodbye gift too – a canvas bag which they had drawn on, some chocolates, a photo frame and canvas prints of their hands and feet.

Towards the end, when it was time for me to leave, I said to Katie: 'Katie, it's time for Mummy to go now. Do I get a big cuddle?'

'Yes!' she said with a grin, and putting down her toy she came over to give me a massive cuddle. I held her tight and said: 'Goodbye, I love you. I will always love you.'

'And I will always love you too,' she said.

I smiled: 'Good. And make sure you love your new mummy and daddy as well.'

'I will.'

'Be good, I love you. Bye bye.' I kissed her soft little hands that I held in my own.

Then I spoke to Poppie: 'Poppie, it's time for Mummy to go now.'

Katie piped up behind me: 'Mummy's going now, Poppie.'

At first Poppie was reluctant to come over. I sensed her hesitation; she didn't want this to be the end.

'Pickle …?' I called out gently. It was my pet name for her.

'Pickle?' I said again.

She turned and ran at me, jumping into my arms. I caught her, sat her on my lap and said: 'That was a lovely jump, wasn't it?'

She nodded and I gave her a big squeeze. Then I couldn't help it, I started to get emotional. *Don't let the girls see you cry!* Quickly, I blinked the tears away as we were cuddling and thankfully Poppie didn't see.

'Be good, be happy,' I said. 'And remember, you're Katie's big sister so you've got a really important job to do, haven't you?'

'To look after Katie,' she said solemnly.

'Yes. And Katie will look after you too.'

Then she stood up and I held both her hands as we looked at one another.

'Pickle, you know you're not going to see me for a while now, don't you?' I said quietly.

She nodded her head slowly, a very sad look on her face.

'But you're going to have a new mummy and daddy. They're going to look after you and they're going to love you so much.'

She smiled, I kissed her hands and she ran off to play.

Now I stood up to leave, moving slowly as I felt so very fragile at that moment. Inside, my heart splintered. *Don't make this hard for them*, I reminded myself. After all, they were still so little – just three and five. So the smile stayed on and my voice remained cheerful as I called out: 'Okay, girls, I'm going now. Be good. Goodbye. I love you.'

The last thing I heard as I stepped out of the door was Katie's little voice: 'Goodbye, Mammy.'

And Poppie calling after me: 'I love you, Mammy.'

That was the last time I saw my children. I'm not allowed to have any physical contact with them now and though I have been assured I will have 'postal contact' once a year, so far the local authority has failed to fulfil this. But not a single minute has passed when I haven't thought about them. They are always in my heart and Daisy the Cow goes with me everywhere – she sleeps in my bed every night and when I kiss her goodnight I imagine those kisses are for my lost girls. In my darkest moments, when I am struck by the grief of losing them, I tell myself that one day we will be reunited. And whenever I think about them, talk about them or look at their photos, I can't help but smile. I still feel so close to them both – my girls, my children, Poppie and Katie. Wherever they are now, and whatever they are doing, I just hope they know their mother loves them. And always will.

21

Another Empty Chance

Matt was arrested during the trial. The police managed to get hold of him and asked him to attend the police station, which he did. There, they nicked him on 24 counts against me. It could have been more – many more – but these 24 incidents were the only ones for which I could remember the dates, places and times. The counts were for grievous bodily harm (GBH), actual bodily harm (ABH), common assault, and causing or inciting prostitution for gain. Matt was interviewed under caution and gave 'no comment' answers to every question, then he was bailed and I had to wait to find out if he was going to be charged. I was warned that it may take some time to charge him as my statement was so long and each allegation had to be thoroughly investigated to see whether there was corroborating evidence from either a witness, medical records or any other institution. But I had no idea how long I would end up waiting – or what it would cost me.

Once the court case was over, I was keen to find my own place and start work. The refuge had worked wonders in reconnecting me with the world and giving me the secure base I needed to restart my life but I couldn't stay there forever. For one thing, as long as I was there I couldn't work as they deemed this a security risk so I had to wait till I moved out to get a job. First, I had to decide which borough to be rehoused in and once I had chosen I went to the council offices and told them all about my circumstances and why I wanted to live in the area, and then I was allowed to start bidding on properties. Amazingly, I was offered the very first property I bid on, which was a one-bedroom flat. The day I moved out of the refuge and into the council flat was very special. It felt so good to have my own space, to finally stand on my own feet and to have a home of my own. I decorated it pink throughout – the hallway, bedroom, living room and even the kitchen – only painting the bathroom blue for contrast. It was mine, after all, and I was determined to do things my way from now on.

I landed a part-time job as a general assistant in a nearby stately home and even passed my driving test and got my own car. In all the time I'd been with Matt I had driven without a licence, something I had to tell the police during my statements. It wasn't my only confession – Matt had embroiled me in so many of his schemes, including the fraud on his mother, so I had to tell them all about those too. Of course I worried that at some point they might decide to arrest me too for fraud but I didn't care anymore. After so many years of lies, I just had to tell the whole truth and, fortunately, the police understood that in all these schemes I had no real choice in the matter.

Returning to the working world was nerve-wracking at first. It had been well over a year since my last job ended, and in my first few weeks I spent a lot of time asking for permission to do certain tasks. But it didn't take long until I got into the swing of things and I really began to enjoy it. The place was busy and exciting. Then, after a while, if I was about to ask someone a petty question, I'd stop myself and think: *If you ask them, what answer do you think they will give you?* Then I'd do what I thought their answer would be. At first I was just working part-time, two days a week – 16 hours – but I loved it so much I soon went up to full-time and was promoted from general assistant to supervisor. I was very happy there – my manager, the staff and the chefs in the kitchen were all lovely and I was soon working weekends and bank holidays too. The pay wasn't spectacular but it was all my own, for a change, and I enjoyed the fast-paced environment.

Frankly, being busy suited me. I couldn't bear having nothing to do and going home to an empty flat each night was depressing. Alone with my thoughts, I'd worry about Matt being out on bail, finding me and killing me. I always had a feeling I was being watched and this made me insecure. Or I would brood about the girls, wondering where they were now, what they were doing and if they were happy. Listening to music helped – I could sit down and have a good cry to 'Run' by Leona Lewis, 'Happy Ending' by Mika and 'Everywhere' by Fleetwood Mac, as well as Wilson Phillips's 'Hold On' and Kirsty MacColl's 'Days', which was special to me and the girls. My nightly conversations with Mum and Mandy helped too. Ever since we had re-established contact in the refuge, Mum had been there for me every single day and life would have been much harder without her support.

Mentally, I was now taking up the reins of my own life again and that meant making decisions – big and small – about everything! But I'd been Matt's prisoner for so long, I struggled to make the most basic choices. What do I want to eat? What should I do at night? What clothes do I buy? Sometimes, I'd find myself in the middle of a shop, staring at rows and rows of shoes on a shelf, thinking: *How do I find out what pair I want to buy?* Gripped by indecision, I felt like stopping a stranger to ask them what they thought, just to get the selection over and done with. It was the same for everything – food, drink, clothes, pyjamas – Matt had made every decision for so long, I didn't even know my own tastes anymore.

Sometimes it was the really small decisions on how to fill my time. What should I do this morning? Do I go out for a walk? Do I stay in? Wash my hair? Have a bath or shower instead? Do I use the blow dryer or leave my hair down to dry by itself? For all these tiny choices that most people take for granted, I had to pause and think about what I wanted to do. Sometimes it was too much for me and I felt overwhelmed, but then I'd take a deep breath, remind myself how lucky I was to be alive, to be free and have the luxury of making these decisions at all. And I'd move on.

I had been advised by the social workers to take the Freedom Programme, which is a free 12-week course designed to help victims of domestic violence make sense of what has happened to them. This was actually a really useful course and certainly very eye-opening. For so long, I thought Matt's behaviour to me was unusual, that we were different somehow. Nobody would believe me, that's what he told me over and over again ... it contributed to my feeling that I was alone in the world. So it was a shock to learn just how widespread domestic violence is in this country. On average two women are killed each week in England and Wales by their partner or ex-partner. I was lucky to escape with my life. If I hadn't left when I did he would almost certainly have killed me. And I know this because Matt's behaviour, far from being unusual, is frighteningly common.

Abusers up and down the country, in all different communities and from different walks of life, use the same tactics to control their partner – from bullying, to shouting, controlling the money, making all the decisions, undermining their confidence, isolating them from friends and family, raping them in private, humiliating them in public and telling them what to wear, eat and say. These are all common ways of controlling a partner, much of the time backed up with the threat of violence or actual violence. Control – that was the crucial word. It was all about controlling me and I found it instructive to see the patterns of behaviour outlined so clearly. I recognised each and every one. The Freedom Programme named the controlling partner in the relationship the 'Dominator' and Matt was the ultimate 'Dominator', using every trick in the book to manipulate and keep me under his control.

Generally, I tried to move forward as best I could with my life. I even found a boyfriend – a nice guy, someone who was supportive and loving towards me and made me feel good about myself for the first time in ages. But it wasn't all plain sailing – my body image was all screwed up. At first I put on loads of weight just because I could eat what I wanted and after being on crazy crash diets for so long, starved and made to take diet pills, I rebelled. Every time I tucked into something that I knew Matt wouldn't approve of, I felt good. *Fuck you, Matt – I can eat this now, so I will.* Even if I wasn't hungry I'd put away giant choc-chip cookies, large Chinese takeaways, pizza, chocolate and crisps. I could easily eat nine bags of crisps in one sitting, and I did it just because I could! Naturally, my weight crept up till I was 14 stone but I tried not to let it bother me. It was all part of the process of pushing Matt out of my head and reclaiming my life. I even stopped wearing make-up because he had forced me to wear make-up every day for the punters. I wasn't going to do things for other people anymore. I decided I had to start pleasing myself instead. I also started divorce proceedings – while Matt set about a campaign to win me back.

On Valentine's Day I was at my mum's place as we were due to go out for a meal for her birthday when there was a knock on the front door. I opened it up to see a flower-delivery guy, holding a huge bouquet. I thought they must be for my mum, but the guy said: 'I've got a delivery for Hannah.'

'That's me,' I replied, bewildered. Then I realised it must be from my new boyfriend. But 30 seconds later my boyfriend turned the corner and walked up to the house. He was joining us for Mum's meal.

'Are these from you?' I asked, pointing at the huge flower arrangement with the balloons bobbing alongside.

'No,' he laughed. And that's when my blood ran cold. They must be from Matt. I popped one of the balloons with the cigarette I was holding, then I told the delivery driver:

'I refuse to accept these. Please send them back.'

Then we all went out for a family meal. I was always nervous whenever I went to my mum's place. Of course I loved being part of her life again but whenever I drove into the area my palms started to sweat. It put me on edge, driving up the same roads I'd driven with him, retracing the journeys I'd taken with him in the past. When we returned five hours later the floral arrangement was sitting on the doorstep, alongside a note from Matt declaring his undying love for me. So I emailed the officer in charge of my case and told her all about the delivery.

She emailed back the following Monday: 'Hi, Hannah – thanks for this. I assume you want something done about it so I'm drafting up a statement to send to you; you need to sign it, send it back, and we'll nick him for it.'

Matt was arrested for witness intimidation, a charge later increased to the more serious crime of perverting the course of justice. What a fool he was!

That same month I met the girls' adoptive parents. I don't know what I was expecting when I stood waiting in the small room of the local authority building but I can honestly say I was pleasantly surprised and relieved when the parents came into the room. I won't describe them at all, for their own protection, but what I can say is that I got a really good vibe and they both seemed very warm and genuine. The way they spoke about Poppie and Katie to me was kind and loving and they told me a little bit about their journey to adoption while I filled them in on my life with Matt. It wasn't an easy encounter, and I was glad that my mum was there too. We chatted for a while and then the social worker took pictures of the four of us together. When it was time to leave, I gave them each a big hug. The whole encounter had been lovely, very natural and positive, and I was so pleased they had agreed to meet me and my mum, which they had no obligation to do. I could finally picture who my girls were with, which helped me greatly, even to this day.

A whole year after Matt was arrested, the detective constable, or DC, in charge of my case rang me to tell me that the Crown Prosecution Service (CPS) had charged Matt with eight offences. At first I was disappointed that the charges had been reduced so drastically from 24 to eight but she explained that it was a case of 'quality over quantity'. She said they didn't want to go to trial for 24 charges only for him to be found guilty of five. The CPS wanted a strong case, and one that resulted in guilty charges on all counts. That meant using only the cases for which we had corroborating evidence so that it wasn't just a case of my word against his. And for each count there was third-party evidence that backed up my version of events, making our case against Matt really tight. The DC explained that someone at the nursery had vouched for the fact they had seen me with a black eye, while two members of the nursery had also confirmed they had seen me with a fat lip and a black eye and agreed to give evidence, and the rest were confirmed by medical records. For the prostitution, even though there were loads of 'Lydia' websites, this didn't necessarily prove he had personally set them up, so for this one count it would be my word against his. But the DC felt confident about putting it to the court.

'We'll see what the judge says but I think we're looking at a trial towards the end of the year ...' she concluded. I went out that night and celebrated with my boyfriend. At last, Matt was going to get what he deserved!

By now my sister was five months pregnant with her first child. She felt guilty about telling me at first but when she did, I was so excited for her. She had nothing to feel guilty about, I reassured her. I was just thrilled that she had the chance to be a mother, and that I would get the chance to be an auntie. Then, when she found out she was having a girl, I was over the moon. Blessed with another little girl in our family! It was meant to be. Later that year baby Demi was born to my sister and her partner Graham. It was so wonderful to meet her, hold her, kiss her and shower her with love and affection. My sister has been very open and generous with her daughter, including me as much as possible in Demi's life. To be honest, spending time with Demi has meant the world to me. She has kept me going through some of the darkest times of the past few years.

As the trial date approached I started to think more and more about what lay ahead, mentally preparing myself for the ordeal to come. I knew it wouldn't be easy but I was ready to face Matt and to fight for justice. So it came as a huge blow when the CPS requested a postponement.

'A YEAR?' I gasped in disbelief when the DC told me the news. 'They want to put it off for a whole year?'

I was shocked. All this time I had been psyching myself up and now I felt utterly deflated.

'I know it's disappointing, Hannah, but CPS has got to make sure our case is water-tight,' she said. 'We don't want to bring the case to court underprepared.'

'But they've had my statement all this time. It took a year to charge him and now they want another year. What more do they need?'

'Please, trust us on this, Hannah. I feel your frustration, I really do, but it will be worth it in the long term. We want to go to trial in the best shape possible so that we get the best outcome.'

I had no choice. I had to trust to her.

Meanwhile, the adoption order was brought to court and I decided to make one last attempt to get the girls back. The adoptive parents were lovely, and I had absolutely no concerns about their parenting, but I felt I deserved a chance to be the mother I knew I could be to my children. It had been two whole years since I'd left Matt, I had a full-time job, a home and a car, I had done the Freedom Programme, completed all the parenting courses, taken counselling, issued divorce proceedings and was in the midst of prosecuting Matt. I felt my girls deserved one last chance to live with their mother and I deserved the chance to get them back. After all, I had done everything the local authority had asked of me. The big problem was that since I was now working, I no longer qualified for legal aid and I couldn't afford thousands of pounds in legal fees so I had to represent myself.

Every night for weeks I studied the case law, trying to understand the complex legal language and requirements in order to oppose the order on my own. It was a two-stage process and the first part was to apply for permission to oppose the adoption order. In the spring I stood up in the family court and presented my case to the judge – quite coincidentally, the same judge as before – and he decided that on the merits of the case I put to the court, I met the criteria and he granted me permission to appeal the order.

That gave me some hope. The second part of the trial was heard the following month and it was then I went into the witness box and outlined my case against adoption. I told the judge I had done everything possible to establish a good life for myself and my children. I had maintained the separation from Matt, we were awaiting trial, I now had a stable working life, I had reconnected with my family, who gave me their full support in this application, and I was prepared to move heaven and earth to have my children returned to my sole care.

'I recognise that the girls are now settled in schools,' I said. 'But I will move close to them so that they can stay in their present schools. I'll do whatever is necessary to make the transition as smooth as possible for them. I will do whatever is asked of me. I've left one life before and I can certainly do it again. And I'm ready to do it tomorrow.'

After my evidence, I sat down, not just hopeful this time, but confident. What more could they ask of me? I felt I had met every challenge, every requirement that they had set. The council outlined their case and then it was a matter for the judge to consider his verdict. The following morning, I found myself staring at the same green leather chair with the crease I had stared at two years earlier. Here I was, ready to be judged once more as a mother: fit or unfit?

At first the judge commended me for moving forward positively with my life, for establishing myself in the world and completing all the requirements set by the council. But then he reminded the court that the girls were settled in their potential adoptive placement and it would unsettle them too much to move. By now, he said, they hadn't seen me in such a long time and would need to be reintroduced into my life gradually. The judge felt this would be too much for them at their young ages and even passed comment as to why the trial with Matt hadn't happened yet. He concluded that the adoption order should be allowed to go ahead and my application for residency was denied. That was it. Over. The girls were gone for good.

At each turn I try to look for the positives in every situation. That is just my personality. It's how I cope with the difficulties in life but, on this one occasion, I felt the judge's decision was very unfair. Being 'disruptive' was not a good enough reason to deny my children their mother who loved them so desperately. I wasn't given a chance to prove myself. I had left Matt, I had done everything asked of me – was I being punished now for being a victim of domestic violence?

I felt that from the word go the whole system had been weighted against me. By making my final 'goodbye visits' two years earlier, the local authority was actively breaking that precious bond between me and my children, making it all the harder for me to prove that I should be allowed back into their lives. And why give me a visit with the potential adoptive parents if they were then going to allow me a chance to challenge the adoption? In the end, I don't think I ever stood a chance; the whole thing was for show. Once they had got me out of the children's lives and the kids had gone to live with their 'forever family' I had virtually no chance of getting them back. Our bond was broken, they were placed, end of story.

In my quieter moments, when I allow the 'what ifs' to surface, I do wonder if the delay with the trial also made a difference to the outcome with the adoption. After all, with Matt still out in the world, the judge might have wondered if he really wanted to give the children back to me. Perhaps he felt this was an unnecessary risk to their welfare, though he never said as much.

And what if it had been a different judge? Perhaps this judge was unwilling to go back on his original decision and another judge may have seen the case from a fresh perspective. But I can't dwell too long in that negative thought space. It's unhealthy and it doesn't get me anywhere. Life has dealt me this hand so I put my faith in God and trust He knows what He is doing. I remind myself that the girls' new parents are a beautiful couple. They are genuine, warm and loving and I know that all four of them – and their two cats! – will enjoy a lovely life together. And that one day, one day, when the time is right, I will see my daughters again.

Seven months later we finally went to trial.

22

In the Dock

Oh God, not again!

I felt another wave of nausea hit me and I ran to the toilet, my stomach heaving. Today was the day when I was finally due to give evidence against Matt. It had been nearly three years since I'd said that little word that set me free – 'Yes', the answer I had given to the solicitor who asked me if Matt had stabbed me. Yes. Such a small word and yet it had meant everything to me. It had marked the start of my new life and triggered the fight for justice that had led me to this moment. Now I was finally going to have my say, I was going to share the truth with the world. Not a cowed, silent wife anymore, I was ready to face my tormentor. Yes!

But the whole morning, I'd been on and off the toilet like a jack in the box and my insides were so churned up I couldn't eat or drink a thing, not even a cup of tea. Now I pulled on the black suit jacket I'd bought especially for this day, did up my smart black trousers, slipped into my black patent heels and applied my make-up as best I could with shaky hands. Then Mandy helped straighten my hair; hers was a calm reassuring presence on a nerve-filled morning. Thankfully, I was staying at my sister's house this week since it was nearer to court than my place and together we got in the car at 7.45am to pick up Mum on the way to the Crown Court.

It almost hadn't happened. A week before the trial Matt had sacked his legal team and applied to the court for a delay to allow his new representatives to read through the paperwork. But the police were adamant we should push ahead and the DC herself went before the judge to argue against any further delays. She told the judge that Matt had had plenty of time to prepare his case and that I had already waited too long for justice. Thankfully, the judge agreed and the trial began with opening statements by the barristers. Now I was due to give my evidence. I clasped Daisy the Cow to my chest all the way to court, taking comfort and strength from her little woollen body.

When we arrived, Mum and Mandy took their seats in the public gallery while I waited in a little side room until I was called. I didn't have to wait long before the court usher came to get me. Thankfully, I knew what to expect as the police had gone through the process with me a few weeks earlier and I'd met the barrister leading the CPS case the day before. He seemed like a very nice, patient man and was pleased to be on the case. He had actually advised my mum and sister not to sit in the public gallery, thinking it would put me off during my evidence, but I disagreed. I wanted them there – so they were the first people I saw when I went into court, smiling at me, giving me encouraging nods. I also saw Matt. The court officers had offered to put a screen up between us but I rejected this idea. I knew I'd be a better witness if I was facing him. Now I glanced very briefly at him for the first time in two and a half years – *Wow, he looks so small and ugly! How did I ever love that man?*

I took my place in the witness box, said a polite 'good morning' to the judge, nodded at the jury and then the usher approached with the Bible. I put my hand on it – still shaking vigorously – and clutched Daisy tightly with my other hand. Then I repeated in a loud, clear voice: 'I swear by Lord Almighty God that the evidence I give shall be the truth, the whole truth and nothing but the truth.' Pausing in between lines to look at every single jury member as I did so. I wanted them to know this was the truth.

'You can sit down if you want to, Miss Morgan,' the judge offered.

'No, it's all right. Thank you, Your Honour. I'll stand.'

First it was my QC's turn and he took me through my evidence. He got me to confirm my name, then he asked me for the background to the relationship – how I had met Matt and what things were like between us at first. There were signs before the wedding, of course, but I described how Matt had changed very quickly after we married, becoming violent and controlling. It took me about ten minutes to relax but once we got going, I felt confident and strong giving my evidence. My QC took me through each incident in chronological order and I told him exactly what had happened on each occasion. When we got to the stabbing, an exhibit book was given to me by the usher and my QC asked me to turn to look at a certain page number in the book. I turned to the page and there was a photo there, but I couldn't work out what the photo was of. *What is that? It looks like the body of a pig with mud on it.* Then I swivelled the picture 90 degrees and suddenly the penny dropped. It was the picture of *me* taken after I'd been stabbed.

'Oh my fucking God,' I exclaimed. 'I have never seen this photo before!'

It was such a shock I almost started crying. I was panicking now, my eyes darting around the court, to the judge, the jury and the usher, and back to my QC. *What do I do? What do I do?* I felt desperate.

'Can we remove the exhibits from Miss Morgan promptly, please?' my barrister said, and the usher took the book away. I never knew he was going to show me a photo of the injury but I think that was probably one of his tactics, to see what my reaction would be.

That part really shook me up but it was reassuring knowing my mum and my sister were sat in the back and after a few deep breaths I regained my composure. I faced the jury the whole time, careful to give my answers directly to them, knowing that it was they who would be deciding Matt's guilt, nobody else. There were eight men and four women and I made sure I looked all of them in the eye as I gave my evidence. Meanwhile, Matt watched me intently from the defendant's dock. He was wearing a tan fine-dogtooth jacket, and I was surprised to see him leaning on a walking stick. *What a con! There's nothing physically wrong with him. It's just an act to make him look old and decrepit and not like a man who beats his wife. Well, I'm here to expose every lie that evil man has told.* And after that first glance, I didn't look in his direction at all.

My barrister took me through my evidence during the morning session and we talked about the reasons I spent so long denying the violence. I tried my best to explain the control Matt had over me, his threats to kill me, to take the kids away, to have me thrown in jail for fraud and the way he isolated me from my friends and family. We got through all my evidence just before lunch, then we had a break, but I wasn't allowed to speak to my mum or sister in case they influenced my evidence. So I went back to sit in the small side room alone while my sister brought me a meal deal from Boots, accompanied by one of the court admin staff. 'You're doing great,' Mandy said as she handed it to me. 'Keep it up.'

I couldn't wait until the day was over, when I would finally be able to hug my mum and sister. Then I ate my BLT sandwich and Walkers Max paprika crisps and drank my bottle of Coke alone in that room, while taking a moment to be still and silent. It had gone okay so far, I thought, but I knew the afternoon was going to be much, much tougher. *You're halfway through, Hannah. Just breathe. And remember you're doing this for your girls.* I had to be prepared for the worst since I was about to be cross-examined by Matt's barrister.

I returned to the witness box for the afternoon session and it took all of five minutes of questioning by Matt's barrister for me to want to crawl into a corner and die. It was horrible. I knew he was only doing his job but it is truly awful to spend so long being forced to lie and then, the moment you tell the truth, to be accused of lying. I hated it. I felt like I wanted to cry, I had a big lump in my throat and I wanted to run away and hide. Then, as if from nowhere, I heard a small voice inside my head: *Do not let him see this getting to you. Carry on, Hannah. You're a trouper. You're a strong woman, look at everything you've overcome. JUST KEEP*

GOING. I heard that voice and I breathed in hard. Yes, I would carry on. I wasn't going to be bullied into backing down, not now that I'd come this far. Not ever. I lifted my head up, cleared my throat and looked the barrister square in the eyes.

'No, I'm not lying,' I said in a clear voice. 'Matt did hit me just as I said and he knows it.'

It wasn't long before I had my emotions back under control and I was answering all the questions in a firm and steady voice, disputing every 'suggestion' of his that I was lying.

'Miss Morgan,' the barrister started in his plummy voice, 'I'm going to suggest that this *so-called* assault didn't actually happen on this day …'

'Well, you can suggest that all you like but it did,' I said firmly. I wasn't angry, just clear, calm and polite. But he tested me to my limit. He asked me questions and then, if he didn't like my answer, he came back at me a few minutes later with an almost identical question, trying to catch me out. In the end, I confronted this tactic head-on.

'I'm not sure if you think I'm going to make up an answer and tell you something different but I do believe you've already asked me this,' I said pointedly. 'This is my answer and I'll tell you the same thing again.'

Towards the end of the day, Matt's barrister accused me of taking money from Matt since our divorce. *Well now, this was an interesting turn of events.* I was only too happy to fill the jury in on what was going on here. I explained that Matt had started putting money into my account every week for the past year, claiming he wanted to support me. I had told him that I didn't want his money and would rather be poor than accept any money off him. Then, I spoke to him about all of the allegations against him, about the stabbing and the assaults, and he didn't deny any of it, occasionally offering a pathetic apology 'for everything that's happened'. The best part was that I had actually recorded that telephone conversation and at that point I offered to play it to the court.

Matt's barrister looked dumbfounded – he hadn't expected this – but then I had learned a few things from Matt over the years. *Get your defence in before the battle commences*, he'd said. And I had paid attention.

'And by the way,' I went on. 'I don't keep his money. Every week I split it in two and put a tenner into each of my girl's bank accounts. I haven't kept a single penny of that money and I can prove it.'

After that Matt's barrister had no more questions.

Then we were done. I was released from the witness stand and court was over for the day. Out in the corridor I found the DC waiting for me – she wasn't allowed to listen to my evidence in court so she was anxious to find out how I'd got on.

'How did it go?' she asked.

'Yeah, okay, I think.'

At that moment my barrister emerged and came straight over to us both.

'Hannah, you were one of the best witnesses I have had or even seen in 30 years,' he declared proudly. 'Congratulations. You did a great job.'

That made me feel so good. Then my mum and sister came out of court, both a bit emotional, my sister looking a little excited. It must have been really hard for them to hear about what had happened to me but they were so supportive.

Both threw their arms around me and said: 'Well done! You did amazingly, you were brilliant.' It was such a relief to get it over with but also I felt like it had gone well. I went back to my sister's house that night and I was so happy to forget it all for a few hours as I played with my adorable niece.

The next morning I received an unexpected phone call from the officer in charge of the case.

'Hannah, that recording of the phone call with Matthew that you say you have, do you still have it?'

'Yeah, but it's at home.'

'Is there any chance you can get it down to us at court today?'

'Yes,' I replied without hesitation. If there was anything I could do to strengthen our case I was going to do it. So I drove three hours back home and then to the court to deliver the recording I had of that conversation with Matt. Another one of Matt's plans that had backfired! I grinned broadly as I handed the Dictaphone over to the two police officers at court, all the while thinking how much Matt's barrister must be regretting asking me about the money.

After I gave my evidence in court, there were several more witnesses to be heard. The head teacher and a colleague of the nursery where I'd worked gave evidence for our case, as did one of the nursery workers and another colleague at nursery who confirmed seeing me with a black eye. Then the prosecution case was closed and the defence called their witnesses. There weren't many. First up was Lindsey. She made a bit of a hash of her evidence, to be honest, and I can't believe it helped Matt's case at all. The day I was stabbed, Lindsey was questioned by the police and she signed a statement. My barrister had a printout of that statement and she was asked to confirm that it was her signature on it. Amazingly, she denied it. Why? Was she scared of what Matt might do to her if she admitted signing her own statement, just like he had blown up at me?

Then my barrister called the policeman who had taken her statement on the day to confirm in the witness box that she did actually sign it and after that Lindsey's evidence was completely discredited. Nobody believed a word she said. Matt was the last witness and did his usual performance of bluster and denials. I was pleased not to have to listen to it – instead I went back to work and waited for the trial to end.

By now I had moved jobs and was managing a restaurant. The approach to Christmas meant we were rushed off our feet – a very welcome distraction from what was going on in court and all the doubts that kept popping into my head. Far from being pleased with my evidence, I became more uncertain with every day that passed. Had I done enough? Would the jury believe me? I kept thinking about all the things I could have said or should have said but didn't. Then, at 12.10pm, a week after I'd given my evidence, I got a text from the DC:

'Trial's concluded, jury have gone out. I'll let you know as soon as I know anything. Have a good day.'

There was nothing more anybody could do. It was now up to the jury to decide.

For the rest of the afternoon, I was a bundle of nerves, checking my phone every 10 minutes, hardly able to keep still for a second. I worked like a demon, flying around the restaurant with even more energy than usual. Even so, the hours dragged painfully by. At 5.20pm my mobile phone rang. Everyone at work knew what it was about – I had been very honest with my staff and colleagues about what I was going through and they watched me race up the stairs to take the call in the office.

'Hello …?' I said anxiously.

'Hello, Hannah.' It was the DC.

'Hi.'

'Right, we're all done for the day. Are you sitting down, Hannah?'

'No, but it's fine,' I replied, pacing nervously up and down.

'Right, Hannah, it's good news: guilty on all charges.'

Agghghh! My heart felt like it might burst with joy. *Guilty on all charges. Oh my God. Oh my God. Oh my God.* I could have screamed. Instead, I started to cry. Big bloody tears of relief and joy. It had been such a long journey and I had overcome so much to get here. I couldn't believe I'd done it. *Fucking hell, I've done it! I've actually done it.*

I ran out of the fire-exit door, into the cold dark winter night, and screamed from the fire-escape staircase: 'Guilty on all charges!"

Below me, a couple of the chefs peeped out of the fire-exit door below and looked up at me on the stairs. Pat, one of our chefs, laughed: 'I think the whole town has heard you, Hannah!'

He was smiling – he knew how much this meant to me.

The DC was still on the phone and she now filled me in on the details: 'It was a unanimous decision of the jury so all 12 members said guilty, Hannah. But it gets better than that … he has been remanded in custody and he is on his way to prison as we speak. He is in the back of a van going to prison right now!'

'Oh my God, that's amazing. Thank God he's going to prison! I can't believe it ...'

Victory. It was such a long time coming but it was worth the wait. I had been patient, I'd done everything right and I'd been rewarded. Now it was over. It was finally over. I didn't need to do anymore, it was enough. I'd done enough. Guilty on all charges.

'The sentencing isn't going to be for a couple of months,' she said. 'But you can be sure we're looking at double figures.'

I cried, I thanked her for everything she'd done and for all the support she'd given me, then I asked her what would happen next.

'Next, Hannah, you enjoy your Christmas! Come on ... ring Mum up, ring Mandy up, tell them the good news. If you're at work, try not to exert yourself and don't drink too much after the restaurant closes. Happy Christmas, Hannah. You deserve it.'

And you know what? It really was a happy Christmas. Even though my girls weren't with me, I enjoyed one of the best Christmases of my life that year. It certainly made up for all those terrible Christmases in the past that Matt had ruined and made me suffer through. I laughed, I ate, I drank, I was with my family and loved ones, and inside I felt that God was truly shining on me. Matt was in prison and I had won. After everything I had endured, I had finally won.

23

Sweet 17

The final chapter of my life with Matt was written on the day of sentencing. It took six months from the day he was found guilty until I was to discover Matt's punishment for his crimes. Six long months of waiting for probation reports to be written and various other delays, but finally the day arrived and it was a beautiful sunny morning when I pulled up to court in my smart emerald-green dress with my boyfriend at my side and my family waiting for me. I was nervous that day, almost as much as when I had to give evidence against Matt. My heart pounded in my chest, my mouth was dry, there were butterflies in my stomach and I felt sick. But it wasn't caused by fear this time, it was the excitement and anticipation of knowing that this was it, this was the end of a very long and painful journey. This would be the last time I would have to go to court for Matt. Once today was over I could put it all behind me and focus on the road ahead.

I was pleased my family had come to support me on this important day – my mum, sister and brother accompanied me, as well as my auntie Jane, uncle Simon and cousin Emma. There was also Mina, a woman from a domestic violence charity who had come along to give support and to help me manage the media. Ever since I had found out about the charity that helps women and families fleeing domestic violence I had vowed to do everything in my power to help them get their message out there. After all, if I had known that refuges existed earlier, I would have tried to leave a lot sooner if my life had enabled me to do that. I wanted others to know there was a lifeline out there for them too, that they had a way out of their situation. So I had done a 10km walk to raise funds for them the previous year and now I had volunteered to be involved in their promotional campaigns. I felt my heart thudding in my chest as we all greeted one another outside the court – I knew to expect a sentence of at least ten years as the officer in charge of my case had said it would be 'double figures' but dare I hope for more? Even ten years would be good. That would be at least as long as he had made me suffer.

At 9.50am we went through security to take our seats in the public gallery of the court. Matt's mum Lindsey arrived in a wheelchair, being pushed by her brother, but I didn't say anything to her. By now we hadn't spoken in more than two years. I could hardly look at her, knowing that she had stood up for Matt all this time. It was disgusting. I had my eyes fixed on the defendant's dock below us but there didn't appear to be any sign of Matt. Where was he? There was still no Matt by the time the usher called out for us all to 'rise' and the judge took his seat at the front of the court. I was pleased it was the same judge that we'd had for the original trial as he had witnessed me giving evidence. We all took our seats and within minutes we were all dismissed for a discussion among the lawyers. Frustrating! But ten minutes later we were called back in and now it was explained that Matt would appear via video link as he was recovering in the prison infirmary from a suspected minor heart attack. At least, that was what he claimed – actually a nurse who had checked him over said all his observations were normal. *Oh, another one of those chest-clutching moments like the one he faked when he was going to push me out of the window? Or maybe he just didn't want to face us all today and knew he was getting a long stretch.*

I held my boyfriend's hand as the judge explained we were here for the sentencing of Matthew Gower. He outlined in detail the charges for which Matt had been found guilty and gave a brief summary of Matt's brutal campaign against me during the course of our relationship. I could see it was very upsetting for the extended members of my family to hear the details of what Matt had done to me and how he had prostituted me out. It's one thing giving them the quick overview of his crimes, it's quite another hearing them read out in forensic detail in court, and I saw my cousin Emma wiping away shocked tears.

The judge said that Matt had demonstrated no remorse and he would be imposing the maximum sentence of 17 years.

Oh my God. I watched my mum's mouth drop open and her eyes widen in amazement.

Seventeen years? Oh my God, it was more than I could have ever dreamed of. Seventeen years was double the length of time he had kept me prisoner. I was so happy I felt the tears welling up behind my eyes. My aunt and uncle turned round to look at me and I smiled: it was a tearful smile, but one of joy. This was one of the best feelings I'd ever had in my whole life. Mum looked at me, her eyes dancing with joy, and my sister looked at me and mouthed 'Seventeen years!' and I grinned back. This was the moment I had dreamed of for so long.

By this point Matt's video link up had actually been cut off by the judge so unfortunately he wasn't there to hear his sentence. He'd become quite argumentative earlier in the hearing so the judge decided to throw him out – digitally speaking. That was a shame – I would have loved to have seen his face when the judge gave him his sentence. But there was even more good news to come; the judge ordered Matt serve a minimum of three-quarters of his sentence before he could be considered for release for good behaviour. And I nearly laughed at that – well, the chances of Matt behaving well were practically zero so I had every confidence he would serve at least 12 years, if not a lot longer! This exceeded all my wildest hopes and expectations.

I have to say that even though Matt had dragged me through the hell of a trial by jury, and I had waited years for the slow wheels of justice to turn, the process had worked. It had worked! I had done all the right things and now I was being rewarded for my patience and perseverance. Matt was going to prison for a very, very long time. The judge knew just how much courage it had taken for me to see this through to the end and, more than that, he knew what a real threat Matt posed to the wider public.

Outside the court, Mum retrieved the bottle of champagne she'd had to surrender at security upon arrival at court, and handed out some plastic flutes. I gave my mum the honour of popping the cork and she poured out the champagne – making sure I got the first glass – as the traffic sped past us up on the high street. We drank the bubbly, shook our heads in wonder, and grinned broadly at one another. When my barrister emerged from court, I introduced him to the family, who all thanked him warmly and shook his hand. I gave him a massive hug and said: 'Thank you, I will never forget you.' He left and my family and I all went out for lunch. It was still only 11.30am when we took our seats at the pizza restaurant and I requested the most expensive bottle of champagne on the menu!

The waitress seemed a bit bemused.

'What are we celebrating?' she asked. 'It's quite an unusual time to be out drinking.'

'I'm a survivor of domestic violence,' I told her proudly. 'And my ex-husband has been sentenced to 17 years in prison today.'

'Well, that definitely sounds like something worth celebrating. Have a wonderful lunch.'

We did. It was one of the best days of my life.

24

We Will Remember Them … Poppie and Katie

A lot of things changed after that day. The sentencing had been the release I needed to put the past behind me and move on with my life. Yes, I had won. Against all the odds and in the face of huge challenges, I had beaten Matt. But there was more to it than that. I could feel my own worth a bit more. I felt I had contributed something to society – there was one less abuser on our streets, thanks to me. I had to recognise that it had taken a huge amount of emotional strength not just to leave Matt, but to go through with the trial. It was hard, it was traumatic and I felt at times as if I was every bit as much in the dock as him. But I had done it and now I was free. However many times Matt had told me about how worthless I was, I had proved him wrong and it was time for me to start valuing myself a bit more.

After the trial, I lost a lot of weight. It just happened naturally – I didn't put myself on any special diet, I just didn't comfort eat anymore. I didn't feel like stuffing my face with rubbish as a 'fuck you' to Matt for starving me. He had got his punishment, he was gone from my life and now

I could start to look after myself. I took more pride in my appearance – putting on make-up, having my nails done, doing my hair every day and choosing some nice new clothes. I know I still have problems with self-esteem and body image but I hope to address these issues soon. These aren't things that simply disappear overnight. When I first left Matt and was staying at the refuge, I had a few counselling sessions from the mental health charity Mind, which helped, but so much has changed since then. I recognise the need for some therapy to help me process everything that has happened since, like the children being adopted and Matt going to prison.

I also split up with my boyfriend. For a few years he was there for me when I needed a shoulder to cry on. But things didn't work out between us and we have gone our separate ways. The thing is that I'm not ready for a relationship yet. I know I have a lot of issues to deal with before I can meet the right person and enjoy a healthy relationship. That's all I want – a healthy, happy, supportive and loving relationship, just like everybody else. But while I'm still dealing with the emotional fallout from Matt, I know it's not the right time. It is hardly surprising but I have issues around sex and intimacy and, even though Matt is out of my life, he is still very present in my head. And those are big things I need to address. I also need to address my relationship with alcohol. I recognise that this is not always a healthy one and this probably goes way back to my past when Dad bought me booze as a teenager. But I have leant on it far too much in recent years and I am more than aware that the answer to my problems does not lie in a bottle of red wine. I have been to a couple of AA meetings recently and I can feel there may be a time coming when alcohol and I have to part ways completely.

I have my ups and downs still and in my darkest moments I don't think that I will ever truly be loved. Yes, I know that everybody deserves love – even me! – but it is going to take some time and a lot of healing before I allow that to happen. You can take the chains off the prisoner and you can set them free but it is the invisible chains that are hardest to break, the ones inside your mind. I struggle with those daily. And though I have massive regrets about not being able to leave sooner, I am slowly coming to terms with the past. The thing is that I didn't know that if I left Matt and took the children with me there would be somewhere for us to go where we would be safe. I felt there was a real risk of him killing all three of us. Nobody told me that refuges existed. I just didn't know and that's why I'm so determined to spread the word and increase awareness for other women in similar situations. Since the trial ended I have worked with domestic abuse charities to raise much-needed funds and awareness and have also been campaigning for the Domestic Abuse Bill. If I can save one life, help one person escape abuse or allow one mother to keep her children then whatever I've been through will have had some meaning, and done some good for others.

The sentencing released me from my past and every day since I've grown in confidence and self-esteem. For the first time last year I took myself on a holiday abroad on my own, visiting Barcelona. It was amazing and I loved every minute. Now I've caught the travelling bug and I want to visit loads more countries and experience different languages, cultures, food and see everything that life has to offer. For so long all

I did was survive, now I want to live! I'm so lucky to be alive in this beautiful world and I would dearly like to experience some of it. My list of 'dream countries' to visit grows daily: Australia, South Africa, New Zealand, the United States, Thailand, India, Dubai, Ibiza and loads more. I want to swim with dolphins, stroke kangaroos, climb on top of elephants, walk along Lake Garda, swim in a crystal blue sea, watch an African sunset ... and so much more. And I want to do it all alone. Yes, I'm ready to face my future, whatever it holds for me, good or bad, in my own company. I think travelling will be the only way I will truly find myself.

Will I have more children one day? I have no idea. The guilt would be enormous, even though I know Poppie and Katie would want me to be happy. I hope that one day, when they're old enough to understand, they'll read this book and see that all I ever wanted was to be a good mum to them both. I hope so. There is enough on my plate right now, just trying to be the best version of myself, exploring the world around me, enjoying my independence, doing a little good and helping as much as I can to save and change lives.

I won't deny that it is still very hard to live without my girls. Still now, after all this time, I don't think I've come to terms with having my children taken away. Every day I live in shock – I've just learned how to cope with it better, to manage it. I've learnt how to get up out of bed and get on with the day, then put myself to bed at night and do the same thing the next day. Looking back, I see that my whole life with Matt was geared towards surviving, to keeping us all alive, and at the time, in the situation I was trapped in, I couldn't have done more. But they deserved better and now I'm glad they have it. I'm just sad they couldn't have it with me. At least if they read this then they will know how hard I fought for them and I hope one day we will all be reunited. Their birthdays are hard, of course, but my family rallies round and we always do something nice together like have a meal or bake a cake, sing 'Happy Birthday' and record it on the phone. One day I hope we can show the girls all these videos. To show them I never forgot. When that time comes, I want them to find a mother they can be proud of, to show them that I haven't wasted a moment after leaving Matt. *Look*, I want to say, *I've written a book, I've travelled the world, I've helped other people.* I want to be the mum they always deserved.

I work with the elderly right now but that might not be forever – I am considering doing a law degree and becoming a family lawyer, because I think that is something I would be good at. After all, I know I represented myself well in the family court and I'm not afraid to speak up in difficult situations. If this whole experience has shown me anything, it is just how capable I really am. I've always been a grafter, and under Matt's supervision I gained a whole raft of qualifications in childcare and child psychology, not that I think I will be using them anytime soon. I don't think I could bear to work with children – it would just be too painful. But I'm hugely qualified and I know I could do an Open University law degree if I put my mind to it. I can do *anything* if I put my mind to it. I look back at how far I've come and I say to myself – *Well now, Hannah, that really is something!*

So, yes, I'm excited about the future and I have to say that my faith helps me every day to accept the past and to live in the moment. I have always had unconditional faith in

God as far back as I can remember, and as the years have passed it has just grown stronger. After all, when I was living with Matt, there were times when I had nothing but hope; that was the one thing he couldn't take away from me. I hoped that something would change eventually. *If God can bring me to these circumstances*, I told myself, *He'll bring me through them*. I prayed every night then and I still do now, and if there is anything I'm particularly grateful for, I'll give thanks to Him for that blessing. When I was at my lowest point in life, He was there for me. I believe He guided me and gave me strength when I most needed it. And He is still with me today.

When I think back to that young girl, sitting on the bench at the train station all those years ago, wondering what to do, I weep for the choice she made that day. But it was not the end for her and it's not the end for anyone else either. I've been through my own personal hell to deliver an important message to all the other young girls, women and wives who are sitting on their own benches in pain, confused and uncertain. That message is: *Get help*. Reach out to somebody today. You are not alone, there is help out there and there are many caring people who can help you change your circumstances. The police will believe you, they will protect you using the law and they will find safe accommodation. You are strong enough to get through this and you are worth so much more. Because they, the 'Dominators', they don't change. They never will. This is not a one-off, an exception, and there is no justification for violence or abuse. You are not responsible for their actions and if you stay it will only get worse and worse from here. Trust me. I've journeyed a long way to bring this message, to reach you all, and I very nearly didn't make it. So reach out your hand today and we'll find a path to safety together.

Take a deep breath, take my hand and, together, let's walk away … to the life that you deserve. To the life of happiness you always dreamed of.

Take my hand … Come with me …

Help and Advice

You've read my story so you can see how Matt's behaviour towards me changed and became controlling and abusive in many different ways – emotionally, physically, financially and psychologically. Abuse isn't always physical. Some behaviour is 'controlling and coercive' without ever becoming violent and this too is a crime. I've listed here some advice from the experts on how to recognise these behaviours and where you can go for help and advice. *Remember – you are not alone!* Domestic abuse is much more common than you think and one in three women will experience some form of it at some point in their lifetime. There is a lot of help out there for anyone experiencing these kind of issues and *you will be believed.* The first step for anyone – victim or a friend or relative – is recognising the signs of abuse.

COERCIVE CONTROL

What is it? Coercive control is a form of abuse. It is an act or pattern of acts of assault, threats, humiliation and intimidation or other abuse that is used to harm, punish or frighten the other person. It makes that person dependent on their abuser by isolating them from support, exploiting them, depriving them of independence and regulating their everyday behaviour.

Coercive control is a criminal offence. Just like in my case with Matt, coercive control creates invisible chains and a sense of fear that affects every single second of your life and every decision that you make. It is like being taken prisoner in another person's world – everything you do is wrong so you become trapped in this world of confusion, contradiction and fear.

Aspects of coercive control include:

Isolating you from friends and family
Depriving you of basic needs, such as food
Monitoring your time
Taking your phone away
Monitoring you via online communication tools or spyware
Taking control over aspects of your everyday life, such as where you can go, who you can see, what you can wear and when you can sleep
Depriving you of access to support services, such as medical services
Repeatedly putting you down, such as saying you're worthless

Humiliating, degrading or dehumanising you
Unreasonable demands, including sexual ones
Controlling your finances
Making threats or intimidating you
Making jealous accusations
Destruction of your possessions
Gaslighting – this means lying and manipulating you to think you are wrong and your memory is playing tricks on you
Reinforcing traditional gender roles
Turning your kids against you

If you recognise these elements in your own relationship, or that of a friend or family member, seek help. If you feel that you are walking on eggshells all the time and you alter your own behaviour because you are frightened of how your partner will react, you are being abused. There are many ways of reaching out for help and those you contact will believe you.

WOMEN'S AID

Women's Aid is a grassroots organisation offering help, advice, support and life-saving services to victims of domestic abuse.

This includes 'The Survivor's Handbook' (https://www.womensaid.org.uk/the-survivors-handbook), which provides a range of information including legal and housing advice, tips on how to create a safety plan and advice for people with specialist housing needs. It's available in 11 languages and in audio.

They also run a website to support children and teenagers who may be living in a home affected by domestic violence, or who may be in a violent relationship themselves, called 'The Hideout': http://www.thehideout.org.uk.

If you are worried about your web-browsing history there is also advice on how to cover your tracks online.

Website: www.womensaid.org.uk
Email: helpline@womensaid.org.uk

REFUGE

Refuge runs specialist services for survivors and victims of domestic abuse. They run the National Domestic Abuse Helpline and provide refuges through a network of emergency temporary accommodation, including culturally specific services for women from minority ethnic communities and cultures. They support women in the community and help with legal issues.

National Domestic Abuse Helpline: 0808 2000 247

Contact their free 24/7 National Domestic Abuse Helpline for immediate support. Their expert advisers offer confidential, non-judgemental support and information as well as access to specialist domestic violence services across the country.

Their website contains a lot of help and information for victims as well as for those who want to help someone they care about.

Website: www.refuge.org.uk

Supporting Someone You Know

Deciding what to do can take time. If you are supporting a friend or relative you suspect is a victim of domestic violence, they may be overwhelmed by fear, shame, guilt and embarrassment. They may be dependent on their partner, emotionally and financially, and they may have worries about the safety of their children if they leave.

What can you do?

Be patient, offer them a safe space to speak, don't judge them and above all don't criticise them for staying. Reaching out to access support is a courageous first step for any victim of abuse. Here's some advice from Refuge on how you can help:

Give them time to open up. You may have to try several times before they will confide in you.

Try to be direct. Start by saying something like, 'I'm worried about you because ...' or 'I'm concerned about your safety ...'

Do not judge them or their partner – this may alienate them or make them feel ashamed.

Believe them – too often people do not believe someone when they first disclose abuse.

Reassure them that the abuse is not their fault and that you are there for them – no one is responsible for another person's behaviour.

Don't tell them to leave or criticise them for staying. Although you may want them to leave, they have to make that decision in their own time.

Focus on supporting them and building up their confidence – acknowledge their strengths and remind them that they are coping well in a challenging and stressful situation.

Abusers often isolate people from friends and family – help them to develop or keep up their outside contacts. This will help boost their self-esteem.

Encourage them to contact a local domestic violence organisation like Refuge or call the Freephone 24-hour National Domestic Violence Helpline to discuss their support options.

Be patient. Leaving an abusive partner is a process. It can take time for someone to recognise they are being abused and even longer to make decisions about what to do. On average, a woman will leave seven times before she makes the final break. Let them know that you are there for them, no matter what they decide to do.

RIGHTS OF WOMEN

Rights of Women offers confidential legal advice on domestic and sexual violence. They produce free information sheets, which can be downloaded from their website.

Family law advice line: 020 7251 6577 (Monday, Tuesday, Wednesday and Thursday 7pm–9pm; Friday 12 noon–2pm)

Criminal law advice line: 020 7251 8887 (Tuesday 11am–1pm)

Immigration and asylum law advice line: 020 7490 7689 (Monday 12 noon–3pm; Thursday 10am–1pm)
Textphone advice line: 020 7490 2562 (on the days and times above)
Administration: 020 7251 6575
Fax: 020 7490 5377
Email: info@row.org.uk
Website: www.rightsofwomen.org.uk

THE FREEDOM PROGRAMME

The Freedom Programme is a domestic violence information programme primarily designed for women as victims of domestic violence. It examines the roles played by attitudes and beliefs on the actions of abusive men and the responses of victims and survivors. The aim is to help them to make sense of and understand what has happened to them. The programme also describes in detail how children are affected by being exposed to this kind of abuse and how their lives are improved when the abuse is removed. It is a free 12-week programme provided by hundreds of agencies across the UK.

You can search their online database for a programme in your area or contact the Freedom Programme helpline on 01942 262 270 or email their helpdesk: chris@fpcharity.co.uk.

Website: https://www.freedomprogramme.co.uk

MORE HELP AND SUPPORT

The Men's Advice Line, for male domestic abuse survivors – 0808 801 0327

The Mix, free information and support for under-25s in the UK – 0808 808 4994

National LGBT+ Domestic Abuse Helpline – 0800 999 5428

Samaritans – a 24/7 service providing free, one-to-one, confidential, non-judgemental support to those in crisis: call 116 123, visit the website www.samaritans.org or email jo@samaritans.org

IN AN EMERGENCY

Do not delay – if you or your children are in any danger, call 999 immediately.

Acknowledgements

I'd like to thank so many people for everything they've contributed to helping me get through. I wouldn't be where I am today without any of you. To everyone who has ever shown me kindness, understanding and unconditional support after so many years of no contact. To everyone who was willing to support my fight for justice. To the people who were part of mine and my children's lives: I'm sorry for all that was and I'm eternally grateful for everything you did for my girls and I.

To all the new friends I've made! You've all played a big part in my new life and my recovery, and I really am nothing without you. You've never failed me. Thank you for tireless reassurance.

To my BFF, thank you for the hours (and days) of talking, laughing and crying! Forever my best man, untouchable we stand!

My special friend, you know why I'm thanking you.

To my fellow survivors I'm proud of you and your journeys. Thanks for always checking in on me.

To my old neighbours, you'll always be my family, thank you for everything you did for us, and continue to do.

To the person who gave me the final push I needed to get rid of a toxic person in my life, thank you for crossing paths with me. You've enabled me to learn so much about myself, so thank you for that. Always here for you! God bless your family.

All of my family – near and far – after all the years that have passed, it's like I've never been away. Thank you for accepting me back into your lives and for everything you've had to put up with! Love you xxx

To my friends in the past … I'm sorry … I coped as best as I could and did what I needed to do to get through … XX

I'd like to thank all the authorities/services who helped me. To the policewoman who looked after me, I'll never forget you and to my social worker who I would love to hear from – you'll never be forgotten either! I still cry for you sometimes and I really hope I've made you proud …

Lord God, unconditional everlasting love and faith in you. Music has been a huge help, motivator, inspiration and given priceless reassurance. Thank you for the music, thank you God.

Hope. I'd like to thank Hope, for once upon a time, it was all I had … Hope conquers all …

I'd especially like to thank my mum, my sister and my partner for all their unconditional love and support.

Matt, I wouldn't be the beautiful strong woman and brave mother that I am today, if it wasn't for you. This book is going to help save and change many lives. It's going to raise awareness, of which there will never be enough. This book helps to weaken the likes of you. An inspiration to all womankind, and help, information and advice point to the world, it wouldn't have been possible without you …